Lectures on Calvinism

LECTURES ON

CALVINISM

BY

DR. ABRAHAM KUYPER

*Former Prime Minister
of the Netherlands*

**Six Lectures Delivered at Princeton University
Under Auspices of the L. P. Stone Foundation**

WM. B. EERDMANS PUBLISHING COMPANY

Grand Rapids   **Michigan**

CALVINISM
by Dr. Abraham Kuyper

Copyright, 1931, by
Wm. B. Eerdmans Publishing Company
All rights in this book are reserved. No part may be reproduced
in any manner without permission in writing from the publisher,
except brief quotations used in connection with a review in a
magazine or newspaper.

Library of Congress Number 3-15183

Reprinted, November 1983

ISBN 0-8028-1607-X

*These lectures were first delivered
at Princeton University in 1898
under auspices of the
L. P. Stone Foundation.*

Photolithoprinted by Eerdmans Printing Company
GRAND RAPIDS, MICHIGAN, UNITED STATES OF AMERICA

CONTENTS

Biographical Note

ABRAHAM KUYPER 1837-1920

Dr. Abraham Kuyper was born in Maassluis, The Netherlands, October 29, 1837. His parents were the Reverend Jan
Hendrik and Henriette Huber Kuyper. At Maassluis, and at
Middelburg, where his father was called in 1849, he attended
school. His teachers, we are told, took him at first to be a dull
boy. They must have changed their opinion when at the early
age of twelve he was able to enter the Gymnasium at Middelburg.
In due time he was matriculated at the Leyden University, from
which he was graduated with highest honors. It was here also
that he took his Doctorate in Sacred Theology in 1863, when
he was about twenty-six years of age.

A year later he began his ministry in Beesd; was then called to
Utrecht, and from there, in 1870, to Amsterdam. In 1872 he
became Editor-in-chief of *De Standaard* (*The Standard*), a daily
paper, and the official organ of the Anti-Revolutionary party,
which in politics represents the Protestant contingent of the Dutch
nation. Shortly after, he assumed the editorship of *De Heraut*
(*The Herald*), a distinctively Christian weekly paper, published
on Fridays. For more than forty-five years he filled both these
exacting positions with extra-ordinary vigor and power.

In 1874 he was elected a member of the lower house of Parliament, which office he served until 1877. In 1880 he founded the
Free University of Amsterdam, which takes the Bible as the unconditional basis on which to rear the whole structure of human
knowledge in every department of life.

Then followed twenty years of strenuous labor, in the University and out of it, when some of his greatest treatises were
written covering a period that may well be regarded as having
exerted a most important influence on the ecclesiastical and political history of his country. It was by his almost superhuman

i

labors, no less than by his strength and nobility of character, that he left "footprints on the sands of time" with such indelible clearness, that in 1907, when his seventieth birthday was made the occasion of a national celebration, it was said: "The history of The Netherlands, in Church, in State, in Society, in Press, in School, and in the Sciences of the last forty years, cannot be written without the mention of his name on almost every page, for during this period the biography of Dr. Kuyper is to a considerable extent the history of The Netherlands."

In 1898 he visited the United States of America, where he delivered the "Stone Lectures" at Princeton Theological Seminary. It was then that Princeton University conferred the Doctorate of Laws upon him. (It is these lectures that are contained in the pages of this present volume.)

Upon his return to The Netherlands, he resumed his labors as leader of the Anti-Revolutionary party, until in 1901 he was summoned by Queen Wilhelmina to form a Cabinet. He served as Prime Minister until 1905. Then a year or more was spent in travel, a graphic account of which appeared in a two-volume work, *Om de Oude Wereld-Zee* (Around the Old World-Sea), the entire edition of which was sold before it was printed.

After that, Dr. Kuyper resided in the Hague as Minister of State, in the public eye the foremost figure in the land, and in some respects without a peer in the world. At seventy-five years of age he began in the columns of *De Heraut* the series of weekly articles: "Van de Voleinding" (Of the End of the World), three hundred and six articles in all, which took six years to complete. *De Maasbode*, a Roman Catholic publication in The Netherlands, refers to this work as, "most unique and without a rival in all the literature on the subject." References to the end of the world are traced throughout all the books of the Bible, and carefully exposited, while the Revelation of St. John is dealt with section by section. When he was eighty-two years old Dr. Kuyper was laying out plans for another great work on *The Messiah*. But the end came on November 8, 1920.

During all these years his work was many-sided to an astounding degree. As has been said: "No department of human knowledge was foreign to him." And whether we take him as student, pastor or preacher; as linguist, theologian or university professor; as party leader, organizer or statesman; as philosopher, scientist, publicist, critic or philanthropist — there is always "something incomprehensible in the mighty labors of this indefatigable wrestler; always something as incomprehensible as genius always is." Even they who differed with him, and they were many, honored him as "an opponent of ten heads and a hundred hands." They who shared his vision and his ideals prized and loved him "as a gift of God to our age."

What was the secret of this almost superhuman power?

In 1897, at the twenty-fifth anniversary of his editorship of *De Standaard*, Dr. Kuyper said: "One desire has been the ruling passion of my life. One high motive has acted like a spur upon my mind and soul. And sooner than that I should seek escape from the sacred necessity that is laid upon me, let the breath of life fail me. It is this: That in spite of all worldly opposition, God's holy ordinances shall be established again in the home, in the school and in the State for the good of the people; to carve as it were into the conscience of the nation the ordinances of the Lord, to which Bible and Creation bear witness, until the nation pays homage again to God."

Few men have had an ideal before them like this. Few men have been as obedient to the demands of such a purpose in life as he. He gave himself literally body, soul and spirit to this high calling. He lived with watch in hand. Every hour of day and night had its own appointed task. His writings number more than two hundred works, many of them of three and four volumes each, and cover an extraordinary range of subjects.

As a man he was singularly appreciative of a word or act of kindness on the part of others. The writer of this note here speaks from personal experience. Dr. Kuyper knew something of the holy art of love. He prided himself on being a man of the people. It is remembered by many with admiration and gratitude, that however pressed by his multifarious labors, he never refused audience to any that came to him for counsel and help.

Dr. Kuyper never claimed originality. His life and labors cannot be explained from himself alone. We confine ourselves here to the more deeply spiritual undercurrent of his life, as the secret of his phenomenal power.

In his early years the religious life in his country was at a low ebb. "Church life was cold and formal. Religion was almost dead. There was no Bible in the schools. There was no life in the nation."

But intimations of better things to come were not wanting. As far back as 1830, Groen van Prinsterer, a member of Parliament, began to protest against the spirit of the times. "This brought about a revival of Gospel preaching — that by nature all men are sinners in need of the atoning blood of Christ. Great offense was taken at this. It was not long before Evangelicals could not be tolerated. It was not irreligion that was wanted, but religion such as would please every one, Jews included."

Hence when the subject of this sketch was a university student, it was not strange that he felt no inclination toward the gospel ministry. He had no sympathy, he said, with a church which trampled her own honor under foot; nor with a religion which was represented by such a church. He drifted along with the modern stream, and warmly took part in applauding Professor Rauwenhoff, who openly denied the bodily resurrection of Jesus.

A series of experiences, however, made deep impression upon the young scholar.

The University of Groningen offered a prize for the best essay on John a Lasco, the great Polish Reformer. By the advice of his teachers, Kuyper resolved to become one of the competitors. Imagine the disappointment when an earnest search in all the great libraries of his country and in those of all Europe failed to produce the necessary material for the work. As a last resort, Dr. de Vries, one of the professors at Leyden, who had taken a deep interest in the promising young scholar, advised him to visit his (Dr. de Vries') father at Haarlem, as he was a fine student of history and had an extensive library. He went, but only to hear the venerable preacher tell him that he would look for these books, but that he had no remembrance of ever having seen one of a Lasco's works in his collection. A week later Kuyper returned, by appointment. Let him tell himself the experience of that hour:

"How can I make you share my feelings when, being admitted to the venerable preacher, I heard him say to me in the most matter-of-fact way, while pointing to a rich collection of duodecimos heaped on a side table: 'This is what I have found.' I could scarcely believe my eyes. Having searched in vain all the libraries in The Netherlands; having carefully examined the catalogues of the greatest libraries in all Europe; having read again and again in anthologies, and in records of rare books, that the titles of a Lasco's works are simply copied, without the works themselves ever having been seen; that his works, if any are still in existence, are extremely rare; that most of them are as good as lost; that with a possible exception of two or three, no one has had them in hand for as much as two hundred years — and then as by a miracle to be brought face to face with a richer collection of Lasciana than could be found in any library in Europe; to find this treasure, which was the 'to be or not to be' of my prize essay, with a man to whom I had been referred by a faithful friend, but who did not even know that he had it in his possession and who but a week ago scarcely so much as remembered the name of a Lasco — in all seriousness one must, in his own experience, have been surprised like this, to know what it means to see a divine miracle confront him in his path."

It need scarcely be said that he won the prize. But the experience did more — "it reminded him of God." It threw a doubt upon his rationalism. He could no longer deny that there was such a thing as "the finger of God."

Another experience came to him about this time in the reading of the famous English novel, *The Heir of Redclyffe,* by Charlotte Yonge. He devoured the book. It gave him an impression of church life in England such as was almost altogether lacking at the time in the church in The Netherlands. It brought him in touch with the deep significance of the sacraments, with the impressive character of liturgical worship, and with what he afterward used to speak of as "The Anointed Prayer Book." But over and above this, he felt in his own soul an irresistible acknowledgment of the reality of every spiritual experience through which the book's hero, Philip de Norville, passed. The utter self condemnation of the broken-hearted man, indeed, his complete self abhorrence, the brilliant young student applied to himself; it became to him a power of God unto salvation.

Looking back upon this experience he writes: "What my soul went through in that moment, I have only later fully understood; but yet in that hour, nay, from that very moment, I learned to despise what formerly I admired, and to seek what formerly I spurned. But enough. You know the lasting character of the impression of such an experience; what the soul encounters in such a conflict belongs to that eternal something, which presents itself to the soul years afterward, strongly and sharply defined, as though it happened but yesterday."

But, under God, it was the simple country folk of his first parish that were instrumental in leading him into that fullness of spiritual life toward which his former experiences had pointed. As he ministered to them, they admired his talents; and soon they learned to love him for what he was; but they set themselves earnestly to united and individual prayer for his entire conversion to Christ. "And," as Kuyper writes afterward, "their faithful loyalty became a blessing to my heart, the rise of the morning star of my life. I had been apprehended, but I had not yet found the Word of reconciliation. In their simple language they brought me this in the absolute form in which alone my soul can rest. I discovered that the Holy Scripture does not only cause us to find justification by faith, but also discloses the foundation of all human life, the holy ordinances which must govern all human existence in Society and State."

Thus began his Christian life. At the Cross he made the great surrender of himself to his Savior and to His service. "To bear witness for Christ" became the passion of his life. That Christ is King in every department of human life and activity was the keynote which he kept ringing in all his writings, addresses and labors, whether as theologian or as statesman, as a leader in politics, as president of the Christian labor union, as promoter of Christian education, it was all done from the burning conviction, that: "Christ rules not merely by the tradition of what He *once* was, spake, did and endured; but by a living power which even now, seated as He is at the right hand of God, He exercises over lands and nations, generations, families and individuals."

Thus the finding of some lost books, the reading of a novel, the teaching of uncultured folk, were experiences which explain in part Dr. Kuyper's great work.

The more one acquaints himself with the vast scope of the varied labors of this great man, the more deeply one becomes impressed with the striking significance of the devotional, mystical output of his pen. Profound theological learning, great statesmanship, extraordinary intellectual acumen along any line is not thought as a rule to be compatible with childlike simplicity of faith, mystical insight and sweetness of soul. But in the words of a reviewer of his devotional masterpiece, *To be Near Unto God,* "This book of meditations disproves the idea, that a profound theologian cannot be a warmhearted Christian." The author himself tells the story: "The fellowship of being near unto God must become reality, in the full and vigorous prosecution of our life. It must permeate and give color to our feeling, our perceptions, our sensations, our thinking, our imagining, our willing, our acting, our speaking. It must not stand as a foreign factor in our life, but it must be the passion that breathes throughout our whole existence."

In pursuit of this ideal, Dr. Kuyper took time to add to his gigantic labors the writing of a devotional meditation every week. He wrote more than two thousand of them. They are entirely unique in character. They are well said to form a literature by themselves, and are in line with the best works by Dutch mystics, such as Johannes Ruysbroek, Cornelius Jansinius, and Thomas a Kempis.

With almost unabated vigor, Dr. Kuyper kept up his labors until shortly before the end. Standing by his deathbed, a friend and colleague asked him: "Shall I tell the people that God has been your Refuge and Strength to the end?" Though weak, the reply came at once in a distinct whisper: "Yes, altogether."

— Adapted from Dr. John Hendrik de Vries' Introduction to his translation of Dr. Kuyper's devotional classic, *To Be Near Unto God.*

Lectures on Calvinism

FIRST LECTURE

CALVINISM A LIFE-SYSTEM*

A TRAVELER from the old European Continent, disembark-
ing on the shore of this New World, feels as the Psalmist
says, that "His thoughts crowd upon him like a multitude." Compared with the eddying waters of your new stream of life, the old
stream in which he was moving seems almost frostbound and
dull; and here, on American ground, for the first time, he realizes
how so many divine potencies, which were hidden away in the
bosom of mankind from our very creation, but which our old
world was incapable of developing, are now beginning to disclose
their inward splendor, thus promising a still richer store of sur-
prises for the future.

You would not, however, ask me to forget the superiority which,
in many respects, the Old World may still claim, in your eyes, as
well as in mine. Old Europe remains even now the bearer of a
longer historical past, and therefore stands before us as a tree
rooted more deeply, hiding between its leaves some more matured
fruits of life. You are yet in your Springtide,—we are passing
through our Fall;—and has not the harvest of Autumn an enchantment of its own?

But, though, on the other hand, I fully acknowledge the advantage you possess in the fact that (to use another simile) the train
of life travels with you so immeasurably faster than with us,—leaving us miles and miles behind,—still we both feel that the life in
Old Europe is not something separate from life here; it is one and

---

* Notes with a * prefixed have been appended by the editor.

the same current of human existence that flows through both Continents.

By virtue of our common origin, *you* may call us bone of your bone,—*we* feel that you are flesh of our flesh, and although you are outstripping us in the most discouraging way, you will never forget that the historic cradle of your wondrous youth stood in our old Europe, and was most gently rocked in my once mighty Fatherland.

Moreover, besides this common parentage, there is another factor which, in the face of even a wider difference, would continue to unite your interests and ours. Far more precious to us than even the development of human life, is the crown which ennobles it, and this noble crown of life for you and for me rests in the Christian name. That crown is our common heritage. It was not from Greece or Rome that the regeneration of human life came forth;— that mighty metamorphosis dates from Bethlehem and Golgotha; and if the Reformation, in a still more special sense, claims the love of our hearts, it is because it has dispelled the clouds of sacerdotalism, and has unveiled again to fullest view the glories of the Cross. But, in deadly opposition to this Christian element, against the very Christian name, and against its salutiferous influence in every sphere of life, the storm of Modernism has now arisen with violent intensity.

In 1789 the turning point was reached.

Voltaire's mad cry, "Down with the scoundrel," was aimed at Christ himself, but this cry was merely the expression of the most hidden thought from which the French Revolution sprang. The fanatic outcry of another philosopher, "We no more need a God," and the odious shibboleth, "No God, no Master," of the Convention;—these were the sacrilegious watchwords which at that time heralded the liberation of man as an emancipation from all Divine Authority. And if, in His impenetrable wisdom, God employed the Revolution as a means by which to overthrow the tyranny of the Bourbons, and to bring a judgment on the princes who abused *His* nations as *their* footstool, nevertheless the principle of that

Revolution remains thoroughly *anti-Christian,* and has since spread like a cancer, dissolving and undermining all that stood firm and consistent before our Christian faith.

There is no doubt then that Christianity is imperilled by great and serious dangers. Two *life systems*[1) are wrestling with one another, in mortal combat. Modernism is bound to build a world of its own from the data of the natural man, and to construct man himself from the data of nature; while, on the other hand, all those who reverently bend the knee to Christ and worship Him as the Son of the living God, and God himself, are bent upon saving the "Christian Heritage." This is *the* struggle in Europe, this is *the* struggle in America, and this also, is the struggle for principles in which my own country is engaged, and in which I myself have been spending all my energy for nearly forty years.

In this struggle Apologetics have advanced us not one single step. Apologists have invariably begun by abandoning the assailed breastwork, in order to entrench themselves cowardly in a ravelin behind it.

From the first, therefore, I have always said to myself,—"If the battle is to be fought with honor and with a hope of victory, then *principle* must be arrayed against *principle;* then it must be felt that in Modernism the vast energy of an all-embracing *life-system* assails us, then also it must be understood that we have to take our stand in a life-system of equally comprehensive and far-reaching power. And this powerful life-system is not to be invented nor formulated by ourselves, but is to be taken and applied as it pre-

---

1) As Dr. James Orr (in his valuable lectures on *the Christian view of God and the world,* Edinb., 1897, p. 3) observes, the German technical term *Weltanschauung* has no precise equivalent in English. He therefore used the literal translation *view of the world,* notwithstanding this phrase in English is limited by associations, which connect it predominatingly with *physical* nature. For this reason the more explicit phrase: *life and world view* seems to be more preferable. My American friends, however, told me that the shorter phrase: *life system,* on the other side of the ocean, is often used in the same sense. So lecturing before an American public, I took the shorter phrase, at least in the *title* of my first lecture, the shortest expression always having some preference for what is to be the general indication of your subject matter. *In* my lectures, on the contrary, I interchanged alternately both phrases, of *life-system* and *life and world view* in accordance with the special meaning predominating in my argumentation. See also Dr. Orr's note on page 365.

sents itself in history. When thus taken, I found and confessed,
and I still hold, that this manifestation of the Christian principle is
given us in *Calvinism*. In Calvinism my heart has found rest.
From Calvinism have I drawn the inspiration firmly and resolute-
ly to take my stand in the thick of this great conflict of principles.
And therefore, when I was invited most honorably by your Faculty
to give the *Stone*-Lectures here this year, I could not hesitate a
moment as to my choice of subject. Calvinism, as the only decisive, lawful, and consistent defence for Protestant nations against
encroaching, and overwhelming Modernism,—this of itself was
bound to be my theme.

Allow me, therefore, in six lectures, to speak to you on Calvinism.

> 1. On Calvinism as a Life-system;
> 2. On Calvinism and Religion;
> 3. On Calvinism and Politics;
> 4. On Calvinism and Science;
> 5. On Calvinism and Art;
> and 6. On Calvinism and the Future.

Clearness of presentation demands that in this first lecture I begin by fixing the *conception* of Calvinism *historically*. To prevent
misunderstanding we must first know what we should not, and
what we should, understand by it. Starting therefore from the
current use of the term, I find that this is by no means the same
in different countries and in different spheres of life. The name
Calvinist is used in our times first as a *sectarian* name. This is not
the case in Protestant, but in Roman Catholic countries, especially in Hungary and France. In Hungary the Reformed Churches
have a membership of some two and a half millions, and in both
the Romish and Jewish press of that country her members are constantly stigmatized by the non-official name of "Calvinists," a de-
risive name applied even to those who have divested themselves of
all traces of sympathy with the faith of their fathers. The same

phenomenon presents itself in France, especially in the Southern parts, where "Calviniste" is equally, and even more emphatically, a sectarian stigma, which does not refer to the faith or confession of the stigmatized person, but is simply put upon every member of the Reformed Churches, even though he be an atheist. George Thiébaud, known for his anti-Semitic propaganda, has at the same time revived the anti-Calvinistic spirit in France, and even in the Dreyfus-case, "Jews and Calvinists" were arraigned by him as the two anti-national forces, prejudicial to the "esprit gaulois." Directly opposed to this is the *second* use of the word Calvinism, and this I call the *confessional* one. In this sense, a Calvinist is represented exclusively as the out-spoken subscriber to the dogma of fore-ordination. They who disapprove of this strong attachment to the doctrine of predestination cooperate with the Romish polemists, in that by calling you "Calvinist," they represent you as a victim of dogmatic narrowness; and what is worse still, as being dangerous to the real seriousness of moral life. This is a stigma so conspicuously offensive that theologians like Hodge, who from fulness of conviction were open defenders of Predestination, and counted it an honor to be Calvinists, were nevertheless so deeply impressed with the disfavor attached to the "Calvinistic name," that for the sake of commending their conviction, they preferred to speak rather of Augustinianism than of Calvinism. The *denominational* title of some Baptists and Methodists indicates a *third* use of the name Calvinist. No less a man than Spurgeon belonged to a class of Baptists who in England call themselves "Calvinistic Baptists," and the Whitefield* Methodists in Wales to this day bear the name of "Calvinistic Methodists." Thus here also it indicates in some way a confessional difference, but is applied as the name for special church denominations. Without doubt this practice would have been most severely criticized by Calvin himself. During his life-time, no Reformed Church ever dreamed of naming the Church of Christ after any man. The Lutherans have done this, the Reformed Churches never. But beyond this sectarian, confessional, and denominational use of the name "Calvinist," it serves

---

* George Whitefield, born in 1714, in Gloucester, England; died in 1770, in America. Preacher of unusual eloquence.

moreover, in the *fourth* place, as a *scientific* name, either in a historical, philosophical or political sense. Historically, the name of Calvinism indicates the channel in which the Reformation moved, so far as it was neither Lutheran, nor Anabaptist nor Socinian. In the philosophical sense, we understand by it that system of conceptions which, under the influence of the master-mind of Calvin, raised itself to dominance in the several spheres of life. And as a political name, Calvinism indicates that political movement which has guaranteed the liberty of nations in constitutional statesmanship; first in Holland, then in England, and since the close of the last century in the United States. In this *scientific* sense, the name of Calvinism is especially current among German scholars. And the fact that this not only is the opinion of those who are themselves of Calvinistic sympathies, but that also scholars who have abandoned every confessional standard of Christianity, nevertheless assign this profound significance to Calvinism. This appears from the testimony borne by three of our best men of science, the first of whom, Dr. Robert Fruin, declares that: "Calvinism came into the Netherlands consisting of a logical system of divinity, of a democratic Church-order of its own, impelled by a severely moral sense, and as enthusiastic for the moral as for the religious reformation of mankind."[1] Another historian, who was even more outspoken in his rationalistic sympathies, writes: "Calvinism is the highest form of development reached by the religious and political principle in the 16th century."[2] And a third authority acknowledges that Calvinism has liberated Switzerland, the Netherlands, and England, and in the Pilgrim Fathers has provided the impulse

---

1) R. Fruin, *Tien Jaren uit den Tachtig-jarigen Oorlog,* p. 151.

2) R. C. Bakhuizen Van den Brink, *Het Huwelijk van Willem van Oranje met Anna van Saxen;* 1853, p. 123: "Zoo al de laatste in tijdsorde, zoo was het Calvinisme de hoogste ontwikkelingsvorm van het Godsdienstig-staatkundig beginsel der zestiende eeuw. Zelfs de rechtzinnige staatkundigen dier eeuw, zagen met niet minder verachting en afschuw neder op den Geneefschen regeeringsvorm — als men het in onze dagen zou kunnen doen, wanneer een Staat het socialisme tot beginsel mocht aannemen. Een hervormingskamp, die zoo laat na het ontstaan der Hervorming kwam als dat bij ons, in Frankrijk en in Schotland plaats had, kon niet anders dan Calvinistisch en ten voordeele van het Calvinisme zijn."

to the prosperity of the United States.[1] Similarly Bancroft, among you, acknowledged that Calvinism "has a theory of ontology, of ethics, of social happiness, and of human liberty, all derived from God."[2] Only in this last-named, strictly scientific sense do I desire to speak to you on Calvinism as an independent general tendency, which from a mother-principle of its own, has developed an independent form both for our *life* and for our *thought* among the nations of Western Europe and North America, and at present even in South Africa.

The domain of Calvinism is indeed far broader than the narrow confessional interpretation would lead us to suppose. The aver-

---

1) CD. BUSKEN HUET, *Het Land van Rembrandt;* 2de druk, II, p. 223.

P. 159: "Was uit den aard der zaak de religie eene der hoofdzenuwen van den Kalvinistischen Staat," enz. (om andere redenen de negotie):

en p. 10, Noot 3: "De geschiedenis van onze vrijwording is voor een groot gedeelte geschiedenis van onze hervorming, en de geschiedenis van onze hervorming is grootendeels geschiedenis van de uitbreiding van het Kalvinisme." Bakhuizen Van den Brink, *Studiën en Schetsen,* IV, 68, v. g.

2) *History of the United States of America,* Ed. New York, II, p. 405. Cf. VON POLENZ, *Geschichte des Französischen Protestantismus,* 1857, I, p. viii: "Eine Geschichte . . . in welcher der *Geist,* den Luther in Frankreich geweckt, dieses mit Eigenem und Fremden genährt und gefördert, Calvin aber gereinigt, geregelt, gehütet, gestärkt, fixirt und als en bewegendes Ferment über die Schranken des Raums und der Verhältnisse weiter getrieben hat, der in seinen mannigfachen Strahlen alle geschichtlichen Moment mehr oder weniger beruhrenden *Brenn- und Lichtpunkt* bildet. Nennen wir diesen Geist, uneigentlich und anachronistisch zwar, aber, da er ohne Calvin sich verflüchtigt haben wurde, nicht unwahr, *Calvinismus:* so ist meine Geschichte, ausser der des französischen Calvinismus im engeren und eigentlichen Sinne, die seiner einwirkung auf Religion, Kirche, Sitte, Gesellschaft und sonstige Verhältnissen Frankreichs."

C. G. McCRIE, *The Public Worship of Presbyterian Scotland;* 1892, p. 95: It may lead some to attach value to these sentiments of Calvin if they know in what light the system which bears his stamp and his name is regarded by an Anglican Churchman of learning and insight, which give him a right to be heard in such a matter. "The Protestant movement," wrote Mark Pattison, "was saved from being sunk in the quicksands of doctrinal dispute chiefly by the new moral direction given to it in Geneva. 'Calvinism saved Europe.' "

P. HUME BROWN, *John Knox;* 1895, p. 252: Of all the developments of Christianity, Calvinism and the Church of Rome alone bear the stamp of an absolute religion.

P. 257: The difference between Calvin and Castalio, and between Knox and the Anabaptist, was not merely one of doctrine and dogma: their essential difference lay in the spirit with which they respectively regarded human society itself.

R. WILLIS, *Servetus and Calvin;* 1877, p. 514, 5: There can be little question, in fact, that Calvinism, or some modification of its essential principles, is the form of religious faith that has been professed in the modern world by the most intelligent, moral, industrious, and freest of mankind.

CHAMBERS, *Encyclopedia;* Philadelphia; 1888, in voce Calvinism: "With the revival of the evangelical party in the end of the century Calvinism revived, and it still maintains, if not an absolute sway, yet a powerful influence over many minds in the Anglican establishment. It is one of the most living and powerful among the creeds of the Reformation."

DR. C. SYLVESTER HORNE, *Evangelical Magazine,* August, 1898. *New Calvinism,* p. 375 ff., and DR. W. HASTIE, *Theology as Science;* Glasgow, 1899, pp. 100-106: My apology and plea for the Reformed Theology, in presence of the other theological tendencies of the time, have been founded upon the two most general and fundamental points of creed that can be taken: the universality of its basis in human nature, as the condition of its method, and the universality of God, as the ground of its absolute truth.

sion to naming the Church after a man gave rise to the fact that
though in France the Protestants were called "Huguenots," in the
Netherlands "Beggars," in Great Britain "Puritans" and "Presbyterians," and in North America "Pilgrim Fathers," yet all these
products of the Reformation which on your Continent and ours
bore the special Reformed type, were of Calvinistic origin. But
the extent of the Calvinistic domain should not be limited to these
purer revelations. Nobody applies such an exclusive rule to Christianity. Within its boundaries we embrace not only Western Europe, but also Russia, the Balkan States, the Armenians, and even
Menelik's empire in Abyssinia. Therefore it is but just that in the
same way we should include in the Calvinistic fold those Churches
also which have diverged more or less from its purer forms. In
her XXXIX Articles, the Church of England is strictly Calvinistic, even though in her Hierarchy and Liturgy she has abandoned
the straight paths, and has met with the serious results of this departure in Puseyism and Ritualism. The Confession of the Independents was equally Calvinistic, even though in their conception
of the Church the organic structure was broken by individualism.
And if under the leadership of Wesley most Methodists became
opposed to the theological interpretation of Calvinism, it is nevertheless the Calvinistic spirit itself that created this spiritual reaction against the petrifying church-life of the times. In a given
sense, therefore, it may be said that the entire field which in the
end was covered by the Reformation, so far as it was not Lutheran
and not Socinian, was dominated in principle by Calvinism. Even
the Baptists applied for shelter at the tents of the Calvinists. It
is the free character of Calvinism that accounts for the rise of these
several shades and differences, and of the reactions against their
excesses. By its hierarchy, Romanism is and remains uniform.
Lutheranism owes its similar unity and uniformity to the ascendancy of the prince, whose relation to the Church is that of "summus episcopus" and to its "ecclesia docens." Calvinism on the
other hand, which sanctions no ecclesiastical hierarchy, and no
magisterial interference, could not develop itself except in many
and varied forms and deviations, thereby of course incurring the
danger of degeneration, provoking in its turn all kinds of one-sided
reactions. With the free development of life, such as was intended

by Calvinism, the distinction could not fail to appear between a *centre,* with its fulness and purity of vitality and strength, and the broad *circumference* with its threatening declensions. But in that very conflict between a purer *centre* and a less pure *circumference* the steady working of its spirit was guaranteed to Calvinism.

Thus understood, Calvinism is rooted in a form of religion which was peculiarly its own, and from this specific religious conscious-ness there was developed first a peculiar theology, then a special church-order, and then a given form for political and social life, for the interpretation of the moral world-order, for the relation be-tween nature and grace, between Christianity and the world, be-tween church and state, and finally for art and science; and amid all these life-utterances it remained always the self-same Calvinism, in so far as simultaneously and spontaneously all these develop-ments sprang from its deepest life-principle. Hence to this extent it stands in line with those other great *complexes* of human life, known as Paganism, Islamism and Romanism, by which we dis-tinguish four entirely different worlds in the one collective world of human life. And if, speaking precisely, you should co-ordinate Christianity and not Calvinism with Paganism and Islamism, it is nevertheless better to place Calvinism in line with them, because Calvinism claims to embody the Christian idea more purely and accurately than could Romanism and Lutheranism. In the Greek world of Russia and the Balkan States, the national element is still dominant, and therefore the Christian faith in these countries has not yet been able to produce a form of life of its own from the root of its mystical orthodoxy. In Lutheran countries, the interfer-ence of the magistrate has prevented the free working of the spirit-ual principle. Hence of Romanism only can it be said that it has embodied its life-thought in a world of conceptions and utterances entirely its own. But by the side of Romanism, and in opposition to it, Calvinism made its appearance, not merely to create a differ-ent Church-form, but an entirely different form for human life, to furnish human society with a different method of existence, and to populate the world of the human heart with different ideals and conceptions.

That this had not been realized until our time, and is now ac-knowledged by friend and enemy in consequence of a better study of history, should not surprise us. This would not have been the case, if Calvinism had entered life as a well-constructed system, and had presented itself as an outcome of study. But its origin came about in an entirely different way. In the order of existence, life is first. And to Calvinism life itself was ever the first object of its endeavors. There was too much to do and to suffer to devote much time to study. What was dominant was Calvinistic practice at the stake and in the field of battle. Moreover the nations among whom Calvinism gained the day—such as the Swiss, the Dutch, the English and the Scotch—were by nature not very philosophically predisposed. Especially at that time, life among those nations was spontaneous and void of calculation; and only later on has Calvinism in its parts become a subject of that special study by which historians and theologians have traced the relation between Calvinistic phenomena and the all-embracing unity of its principle. It can even be said that the need of a theoretical and systematical study of so incisive and comprehensive a phenomenon of life only arises when its first vitality has been exhausted, and when for the sake of maintaining itself in the future, it is compelled to greater accuracy in the drawing of its boundary lines. And if to this you add the fact that the stress of reflecting our existence as a unity in the mirror of our consciousness is far stronger in our philosophical age than it ever was before, it is readily seen that both the needs of the present, and the care for the future, compel us to a deeper study of Calvinism. In the Roman Catholic Church everybody knows what he lives for, because with clear consciousness he enjoys the fruits of Rome's unity of life-system. Even in Islam you find the same power of a conviction of life dominated by one principle. Protestantism alone wanders about in the wilderness without aim or direction, moving hither and thither, without making any progress. This accounts for the fact that among Protestant nations Pantheism, born from the new German Philosophy and owing its concrete evolution-form to Darwin, claims for itself more and more the supremacy in every sphere of human life, even in that of theology, and under all sorts of names tries to overthrow our Christian traditions, and is bent even upon exchanging the heritage of our fathers for a hopeless modern Buddhism. The leading thoughts that had their rise in the

French Revolution at the close of the last, and in German philosophy in the course of the present century, form together a life-system which is diametrically opposed to that of our fathers. Their struggles were for the sake of the glory of God and a purified Christianity; the present movement wages war for the sake of the glory of man, being inspired not by the humble mind of Golgotha but by the pride of Hero-worship. And why did we, Christians, stand so weak, in the face of this Modernism? Why did we constantly lose ground? Simply because we were devoid of an equal unity of life-conception, such as alone could enable us with irresistible energy to repel the enemy at the frontier. This unity of life-conception, however, is never to be found in a vague conception of Protestantism winding itself as it does in all kind of tortuosities, but you do find it in that mighty historic process, which as Calvinism dug a channel of its own for the powerful stream of its life. By this unity of conception alone as given in Calvinism, you in America and we in Europe might be enabled once more to take our stand, by the side of Romanism, in opposition to modern Pantheism. Without this unity of starting point and life-system we must lose the power to maintain our independent position, and our strength for resistance must ebb away.

The supreme interest here at stake, however, forbids our accepting without more positive proof the fact that Calvinism really provides us with such an unity of life-system and we demand proofs of the assertion that Calvinism is not a partial, nor was a merely temporary phenomenon, but is such an all-embracing system of principles, as, rooted in the past, is able to strengthen us in the present and to fill us with confidence for the future. Hence we must first ask what are the required *conditions* for such general systems of life, as Paganism, Islamism, Romanism and Modernism, and then show that Calvinism really fulfills these conditions.

These conditions demand in the first place, that from a special principle a peculiar insight be obtained into the three fundamental relations of all human life: viz., (1) our relation *to God,* (2) our relation *to man,* and (3) our relation to *the world.*

Hence the first claim demands that such a life system shall find its starting-point in a special interpretation of our relation to God. This is not accidental, but imperative. If such an action is to put its stamp upon our entire life, it must start from that point in our consciousness in which our life is still undivided and lies comprehended in its unity,—not in the spreading vines but in the root from which the vines spring. This point, of course, lies in the antithesis between all that is finite in our human life and the infinite that lies beyond it. Here alone we find the common source from which the different streams of our human life spring and separate themselves. Personally it is our repeated experience that in the depths of our hearts, at the point where we disclose ourselves to the Eternal One, all the rays of our life converge as in one focus, and there alone regain that harmony which we so often and so painfully lose in the stress of daily duty. In prayer lies not only our unity with God, but also the unity of our personal life. Movements in history, therefore, which do not spring from this deepest source are always partial and transient, and only those historical acts which arose from these lowest depths of man's personal existence embrace the whole of life and possess the required permanence.

This was the case with *Paganism*, which in its most general form is known by the fact that it surmises, assumes and worships God *in the creature*. This applies to the lowest Animism, as well as to the highest Buddhism. Paganism does not rise to the conception of the independent existence of a God beyond and above the creature. But even in this imperfect form it has for its starting-point a definite interpretation of the relation of the infinite to the finite, and to this it owed its power to produce a finished form for human society. Simply because it possessed this significant starting-point was it able to produce a form of its own for the whole of human life. It is the same with *Islamism*, which is characterized by its purely anti-pagan ideal, cutting off all contact between the creature and God. Mohammed and the Koran are the historic names, but in its nature the Crescent is the only absolute antithesis to Paganism. Islam *isolates God from the creature*, in order to avoid all commingling with the creature. As *antipode*, Islam was possessed of an equally far-reaching tendency, and was also able to originate an entirely peculiar world of human life. The same is the case with *Romanism*. Here also the papal tiara,* the hierarchy, the mass, etc., are but the outcome of one fundamental thought: viz., that God enters into fellowship with the creature *by means of a mystic middle-link,* which is the Church;—not taken as a mystic organism, but as a visible, palpable and tangible institution. Here the Church stands *between* God and the world, and so far as it was able to adopt the world and to inspire it, Romanism also created a form of its own for human society. And now, by the side of and opposite to these three, Calvinism takes its stand with a fundamental thought which is equally profound. It does not seek God *in* the creature, as Paganism; it does not *isolate* God *from* the creature, as Islamism; it posits no *mediate communion* between God and the creature, as does Romanism; but proclaims the exalted thought that, although standing in high majesty above the creature, God enters *into immediate fellowship with the creature,* as God the Holy Spirit. This is even the heart and kernel of the Calvinistic confession of predestination. There is communion with God, but only in entire accord with his counsel of peace from all eternity. Thus there is no grace but such as comes to us immediately from God. At every moment of our existence, our entire spiritual life rests in God Himself. The "Deo Soli Gloria" was not the starting-point but the result, and predestination was inexorably maintained, not for the sake of separating man from man, nor in the interest of personal pride, but in order to guarantee from eternity to eternity, to our inner self, a direct and immediate communion with the Living God. The opposition against Rome aimed therefore with the Calvinist first of all at the dismissal of a Church which placed itself between the soul and God. The Church consisted not in an office, nor in an independent institute, the believers themselves were the Church, inasmuch as by faith they stood in touch with the Almighty. Thus, as in Paganism, Islamism and Romanism, so also in Calvinism is found that proper, definite interpretation of the fun-

---

* Originally a Persian headdress. The tiara of papacy denotes its triple power: temporal, spiritual, purgatorial.

damental relation of man to God, which is required as the first condition of a real life-system.

———

Meanwhile I anticipate two objections. In the first place, it may be asked whether I do not claim honors for Calvinism which belong to Protestantism in general. To this I reply in the negative. When I claim for Calvinism the honor of having re-established the direct fellowship with God, I do not undervalue the general significance of Protestantism. In the Protestant domain, taken in the historic sense, Lutheranism alone stands by the side of Calvinism. Now I wish to be second to none in my praises of Luther's heroic initiative. In his heart, rather than in the heart of Calvin, was the bitter conflict fought which led to the world-historic breach. Luther can be interpreted without Calvin, but not Calvin without Luther. To a great extent Calvin entered upon the harvest of what the hero of Wittenberg had sown in and outside Germany. But when the question is put, Who had the clearest insight into the reformatory principle, worked it out most fully, and applied it most broadly, history points to the Thinker of Geneva and not to the Hero of Wittenberg. Luther as well as Calvin contended for a direct fellowship with God, but Luther took it up from its subjective, anthropological side, and not from its objective, cosmological side as Calvin did. Luther's starting-point was the special-soteriological principle of a justifying faith; while Calvin's extending far wider, lay in the general cosmological principle of the sovereignty of God. As a natural result of this, Luther also continued to consider the Church as the representative and authoritative "teacher," standing between God and the believer, while Calvin was the first to seek the Church *in the believers themselves.* As far as he was able, Luther still leaned upon the Romish view of the sacraments, and upon the Romish cultus, while Calvin was the first in both to draw the line which extended immediately from God to man and from man to God. Moreover, in all Lutheran countries the Reformation originated from the princes rather than from the people, and thereby passed under the power of the magistrate, who took his stand in the Church officially as her highest Bishop, and therefore was unable to change either the social or the political life in accordance with its principle. Lutheranism restricted itself to an exclusively ecclesiastical and theological character, while Calvinism put its impress in and outside the Church upon every department of human life. Hence Lutheranism is nowhere spoken of as the creator of a peculiar life-form; even the name of "Lutheranism" is hardly ever mentioned; while the students of history with increasing unanimity recognize Calvinism as the creator of a world of human life entirely its own.

The second objection we have to meet is this: If it is true that every general development form of life must find its starting-point in a peculiar interpretation of our relation to God,—how then do you explain the fact that *Modernism* also has led to such a general conception, notwithstanding it sprang from the French Revolution, which on principle broke with all religion. The question answers itself. If you exclude from your conceptions all reckoning with the Living God just as is implied in the cry, "no God no master," you certainly bring to the front a sharply defined interpretation of your own for our relation to God. A government, as you yourselves experienced of late in the case of Spain, that recalls its ambassador and breaks every regular intercourse with another power, declares thereby that its relation to the government of that country is a strained relation which generally ends in war. This is the case here. The leaders of the French Revolution, not being acquainted with any relation to God except that which existed through the mediation of the Romish Church, annihilated all relation to God, because they wished to annihilate the power of the Church; and as a result of this they declared war against every religious confession. But this of course very really implied a fundamental and special interpretation of our relation to God. It was the declaration that henceforth God was to be considered as a *hostile power,* yea even as dead, if not yet to the heart, at least to the state, to society and to science. To be sure, in passing from French into German hands, Modernism could not rest content with such a bare negation; but the result shows how from that moment it clothed itself in either pantheism or agnosticism, and under each disguise it maintained the expulsion of God from practical and theoretical life, and the enmity against the Triune God had its full course.

Thus I maintain that it is the interpretation of our relation to God which dominates every general life system, and that for us this conception is given in Calvinism, thanks to its fundamental interpretation of an immediate fellowship of God with man and of man with God. To this I add that Calvinism has neither invented nor conceived this fundamental interpretation, but that God Himself implanted it in the hearts of its heroes and its heralds. We face here no product of a clever intellectualism, but the fruit of a work of God in the heart, or, if you like, an inspiration of history. This point should be emphasized! Calvinism has never burned its incense upon the altar of genius, it has erected no monument for its heroes, it scarcely calls them by name. One stone only in a wall at Geneva remains to remind one of Calvin. His very grave has been forgotten. Was this ingratitude? By no means. But if Calvin was appreciated, even in the 16th and 17th centuries the impression was vivid that it was One greater than Calvin, even God Himself, who had wrought here *His work*. Hence, no general movement in life is so devoid of deliberate compact, none so unconventional in which it spread as this. Simultaneously, Calvinism had its rise in all the countries of Western Europe, and it did not appear, among those nations, because the University was in its van, or because scholars led the people, or because a magistrate placed himself at their head; but it sprang from the hearts of the people themselves, with weavers and farmers, with tradesmen and servants, with women and young maidens; and in every instance it exhibited the same characteristic: viz., strong *Assurance of eternal Salvation*, not only without the intervention of the Church, but even in opposition to the Church. The human heart had attained unto eternal peace with its God: strengthened by this Divine fellowship, it discovered its high and holy calling to consecrate every department of life and every energy at its disposal to the glory of God: and therefore, when those men or women, who had become partakers of this Divine life, were forced to abandon their faith, it proved impossible, that they *could* deny their Lord; and thousands and tens of thousands burned at the stake, not complaining but exulting, with thanksgiving in their hearts and psalms upon their lips. Calvin was not the author of this, but God who through His Holy Spirit had wrought in Calvin that which He had wrought in them. Calvin stood not above them, but as a brother by their side, a sharer with them of God's blessing. In this way, Calvinism came to its fundamental interpretation of an immediate fellowship with God, not because Calvin invented it, but because in this immediate fellowship God Himself had granted to our fathers a privilege of which Calvin was only the first to become clearly conscious. This is the great work of the Holy Spirit in history, by which Calvinism has been consecrated, and which interprets to us its wondrous energy.

There are times in history when the pulse of religious life beats faintly; but there are times when its beat is pounding, and the latter was the case in the 16th century among the nations of Western Europe. The question of faith at that time dominated every activity in public life. New history starts out from this *faith,* even as the history of our times starts from the *unbelief* of the French Revolution. What law this pulse-like movement of religious life obeys, we cannot tell, but it is evident that there is such a law, and that in times of high religious tension the inworking of the Holy Spirit upon the heart is irresistible; and this mighty inworking of God was the experience of our Calvinists, Puritans and Pilgrim Fathers. It was not in all individuals to the same degree, for this never happens in any great movement; but they who formed the centre of life in those times, who were the promoters of that mighty change, they experienced this higher power to the fullest: and they were the men and women of every class of society and nationality who by God Himself were admitted into communion with the majesty of His eternal Being. Thanks to this work of God in the heart, the persuasion that the whole of a man's life is to be lived as *in the Divine Presence* has become the fundamental thought of Calvinism. By this decisive idea, or rather by this mighty fact, it has allowed itself to be controlled in every department of its entire domain. It is from this mother-thought that the all-embracing life system of Calvinism sprang.

This brings us of itself to the second condition, with which, for the sake of creating a life system every profound movement has to comply: viz., a fundamental interpretation of its own touching *the relation of man to man.* How we stand toward God is the first, and how we stand toward man is the second principal question which decides the tendency and the construction of our life. There is no uniformity among men, but endless multiformity. In creation itself the difference has been established between woman and man. Physical and spiritual gifts and talents cause one person to differ from the other. Past generations and our own personal life create distinctions. The social position of the rich and poor differs widely. Now, these differences are in a special way *weakened* or *accentuated* by every consistent life system, and Paganism and Islamism, Romanism as well as Modernism, and so also Calvinism have all taken their stand in this question in accordance with their primordial principle. If, as Paganism contends, God dwells *in* the creature, a divine superiority is exhibited in whatever is high among men. In this way it obtained its demigods, hero-worship, and finally its sacrifices upon the altar of Divus Augustus. On the other hand, whatever is lower is considered as godless, and therefore gives rise to the systems of caste in India and in Egypt, and to slavery everywhere else, thereby placing one man under a base subjection to his fellowman. Under Islamism, which dreams of its paradise of *houries,** sensuality usurps public authority, and the woman is the slave of man, even as the kafir** is the slave of the Moslim. Romanism, taking root in Christian soil, overcomes the absolute character of distinction, and renders it relative, in order to interpret every relation of man to man *hierarchically.* There is a hierarchy among the angels of God, a hierarchy in God's Church, and so also a hierarchy among men, leading to an entirely aristocratic interpretation of life as the

---

* From a Persian word signifying "black-eyed."
** Kafir is an Arabic word denoting "unbeliever."

embodiment of the ideal. Finally Modernism, which denies and abolishes every difference, cannot rest until it has made woman man and man woman, and, putting every distinction on a common level, kills life by placing it under the ban of uniformity. One type must answer for all, one uniform, one position and one and the same development of life; and whatever goes beyond and above it, is looked upon as an insult to the common consciousness. In the same way Calvinism has derived from *its* fundamental relation to God a peculiar interpretation of man's relation to man, and it is this only true relation which since the 16th century has ennobled social life. If Calvinism places our entire human life immediately before God, then it follows that all men or women, rich or poor, weak or strong, dull or talented, as creatures of God, and as lost sinners, have no claim whatsoever to lord over one another, and that we stand as equals before God, and consequently equal as man to man. Hence we cannot recognize any distinction among men, save such as has been imposed by God Himself, in that He gave one authority over the other, or enriched one with more talents than the other, in order that the man of more talents should serve the man with less, and in him serve his God. Hence Calvinism condemns not merely all open slavery and systems of caste, but also all covert slavery of woman and of the poor; it is opposed to all hierarchy among men; it tolerates no aristocracy save such as is able, either in person or in family, by the grace of God, to exhibit superiority of character or talent, and to show that it does not claim this superiority for self-aggrandizement or ambitious pride, but for the sake of spending it in the service of God. So Calvinism was bound to find its utterance in the democratic interpretation of life; to proclaim the liberty of nations; and not to rest until both politically and socially every man, simply because he is man, should be recognized, respected and dealt with as a creature created after the Divine likeness.

This was no outcome of envy. It was not the man of lower estate who reduced his superior to his level in order to usurp the higher place, but it was all men kneeling in concert at the feet of the Holy One of Israel. This accounts for the fact that Calvinism made no sudden break with the past. Even as in its early

stage Christianity did not abolish slavery, but undermined it by a
moral judgment, so Calvinism allowed the provisional continuance
of the conditions of hierarchy and aristocracy as traditions belong-
ing to the Middle Ages. It was not charged against William of
Orange that he was a prince of royal lineage; he was the more
honored for it. But inwardly Calvinism has modified the structure of society, not by the envying of classes, nor by an undue esteem for the possessions of the rich, but by a more serious interpretation of life. By better labor and a higher development of
character the middle and working classes have provoked the nobility and the wealthier citizens to jealousy. First looking to God,
and then to one's neighbor was the impulse, the mind and the
spiritual custom to which Calvinism gave entrance. And from this
holy fear of God and this united stand before the face of God a
holier democratic idea has developed itself, and has continually
gained ground. This result has been brought about by nothing
so much as by fellowship in suffering. When, though loyal to the
Romish faith, the dukes of Egmont and Hoorn ascended the
same scaffold on which, for the sake of a nobler faith, the work-
ing-man and the weaver had been executed, the reconciliation between the classes received its sanction in that bitter death. By
his bloody persecutions, Alva the Aristocrat advanced the prosperous development of the spirit of Democracy. To have placed
man on a footing of equality with man, so far as the purely human
interests are concerned, is the immortal glory which incontestably belongs to Calvinism. The difference between it and the
wild dream of equality of the French Revolution is that while in
Paris it was one action in concert *against* God, here all, rich and
poor, were on their knees *before* God, consumed with a common
zeal for the glory of His Name.

————————

The third fundamental relation which decides the interpretation
of life is the relation which you bear *to the world*. As previously
stated, there are three principal elements with which you come
into touch: viz., God, man and the world. The relation to God
and to man into which Calvinism places you being thus reviewed,
the third and last fundamental relation is in order: viz., your attitude *toward the world*. Of Paganism it can be said in general,

that it places *too high* an estimate upon the world, and therefore to some extent it both stands in fear of, and loses itself in it. On the other hand Islamism places *too low* an estimate upon the world, makes sport of it and triumphs over it in reaching after the visionary world of a sensual paradise. For the purpose in view however we need say no more of either, since both for Christian Europe and America the antithesis between man and the world has assumed the narrower form of the antithesis between the world and the Christian circles. The traditions of the Middle Ages gave rise to this. Under the hierarchy of Rome the Church and the World were placed over against each other, the one as being sanctified and the other as being still under the curse. Everything outside the Church was under the influence of demons, and exorcism banished this demoniacal power from everything that came under the protection, influence and inspiration of the Church. Hence in a Christian country the entire social life was to be covered by the wings of the Church. The magistrate had to be anointed and confessionally bound; art and science had to be placed under ecclesiastical encouragement and censure; trade and commerce had to be bound to the Church by the tie of guilds; and from the cradle to the grave, family life was to be placed under ecclesiastical guardianship. This was a gigantic effort to claim the entire world for Christ, but one which of necessity brought with it the severest judgment upon every life-tendency which either as heretical or as demoniacal withdrew itself from the blessing of the Church. Hence the stake was fit alike for witch and heretic, for in principle both lay under the same ban. And this deadening theory was carried out with iron logic, not from cruelty, nor from any low ambition, but from the lofty purpose of saving the christianized world, i.e., the world as overshadowed by the Church. Escape from the world was the counterpoise in monastic and partly even in clerical orders, which emphasized holiness in the centre of the Church in order to wink the more lightly at worldly excesses without. As a natural result the world corrupted the Church, and by its dominion over the world the Church proved an obstacle to every free development of its life.

Thus making its appearance in a dualistic social state, Calvinism has wrought an entire change in the world of thoughts and conceptions. In this also, placing itself before the face of God, it has not only honored *man* for the sake of his likeness to the Divine image, but also *the world* as a Divine creation, and has at once placed to the front the great principle that there is a *particular grace* which works Salvation, and also a *common grace* by which God, maintaining the life of the world, relaxes the curse which rests upon it, arrests its process of corruption, and thus allows the untrammelled development of our life in which to glorify Himself as Creator.* Thus the Church receded in order to be neither more nor less than the congregation of believers, and in every department the life of the world was not emancipated from God, but from the dominion of the Church. Thus domestic life regained its independence, trade and commerce realized their strength in liberty, art and science were set free from every ecclesiastical bond and restored to their own inspirations, and man began to understand the subjection of all nature with its hidden forces and treasures to himself as a holy duty, imposed upon him by the original ordinances of Paradise: "Have dominion over them." Henceforth the curse should no longer rest upon the *world* itself, but upon that which is *sinful* in it, and instead of monastic flight *from* the world the duty is now emphasized of serving God *in* the world, in every position in life. To praise God in the Church and serve Him in the world became the inspiring impulse, and, in the Church, strength was to be gathered by which to resist temptation and sin in the world. Thus puritanic sobriety went hand in hand with the reconquest of the entire life of the world, and Calvinism gave the impulse to that new development which dared to face the world with the Roman thought: *nil humanum a me alienum puto,* although never allowing itself to be intoxicated by its poisonous cup.

Especially in its antithesis to Anabaptism Calvinism exhibits itself in bold relief. For Anabaptism adopted the opposite method, and in its effort to evade the world it confirmed the monastic starting-point, generalizing and making it a rule for *all* believers. It was not from Calvinism, but from this anabaptistic principle, that Akosmism had its rise among so many Protes-

* Cf. p. 159 ff.

tants in Western Europe. In fact, Anabaptism adopted the Romish theory, with this difference: that it placed the kingdom of God in the room of the Church, and abandoned the distinction between the two moral standards, one for the clergy and the other for the laity. For the rest the Anabaptist's standpoint was: (1) that the unbaptized world was under the curse, for which reason he withdrew from all civil institutions; and (2) that the circle of baptized believers—with Rome the Church, but with him the kingdom of God—was in duty bound to take all civil life under its guardianship and to remodel it; and so John of Leyden violently established his shameless power at Munster as King of the *New Zion,* and his devotees ran naked through the streets of Amsterdam.* Hence, on the same grounds on which Calvinism rejected Rome's theory concerning the world, it rejected the theory of the Anabaptist, and proclaimed that the Church must withdraw again within its spiritual domain, and that in the world we should realize the potencies of God's common grace.

Thus it is shown that Calvinism has a sharply-defined starting-point of its own for the three fundamental relations of all human existence: viz., our relation to *God,* to *man* and to the *world.* For our relation *to God*: an immediate fellowship of man with the Eternal, independently of priest or church. For the relation of man *to man*: the recognition in each person of human worth, which is his by virtue of his creation after the Divine likeness, and therefore of the equality of all men before God and his magistrate. And for our relation *to the world*: the recognition that in the whole world the curse is restrained by grace, that the life of the world is to be honored in its independence, and that we must, in every domain, discover the treasures and develop the potencies hidden by God in nature and in human life. This justifies us fully in our statement that Calvinism duly answers the three above-named conditions, and

---

* John Beuckelszoon, named John of Leyden after the city of his birth, 1510, Dutch fanatical leader of the Anabaptists in the capture of Munster. Died 1536. The devotees named above, 7 men and 3 women, were holding a nocturnal meeting, in February, 1535, in Amsterdam, when their leader, Hendrick Hendrickz Snyder, cast his clothes into the fire, and commanded his followers to do likewise. At his behest they followed him, running through the streets and crying, "Woe, woe, woe; the vengeance of God, the vengeance of God." They were soon captured. The men were beheaded, the women drowned, except one who escaped. Snyder claimed he had seen heaven, hell, and God, and that the judgment day was at hand.

thus is incontestably entitled to take its stand by the side of Paganism, Islamism, Romanism and Modernism, and to claim for itself the glory of possessing a well-defined principle and an all-embracing life-system.

But even this is not all. The fact that in a given circle Calvinism has formed an interpretation of life quite its own, from which both in the spiritual and secular domain a special system arose for domestic and social life, justifies its claim to assert itself as an independent formation. But it does not yet credit it with the honor of having led humanity, as such, up to a higher stage in its development, and therefore this life-system has not, so far as we have yet considered it, attained that position which alone could give it the right to claim for itself the energy and devotion of our hearts. In China it can be asserted with equal right that Confucianism has produced a form of its own for life in a given circle, and with the Mongolian race that form of life rests upon a theory of its own. But what has China done for humanity in general, and for the steady development of our race? Even so far as the waters of its life were clear, they formed nothing but an isolated lake. Almost the same remark applies to the high development which was once the boast of India and to the state of things in Mexico and Peru in the days of Montezuma and the Incas. In all these regions the people attained a high degree of development, but stopped there, and, remaining isolated, in no way proved a benefit to humanity at large. This applies more strongly still to the life of the colored races on the coast and in the interior of Africa—a far lower form of existence, reminding us not even of a lake but rather of pools and marshes. There is but one world-stream, broad and fresh, which from the beginning bore the promise of the future. This stream had its rise in Middle Asia and the Levant, and has steadily continued its course from East to West. From Western Europe it has passed on to your Eastern States, and from thence to California. The sources of this stream of development are found in Babylon and in the valley of the Nile. From thence it flowed on to Greece. From Greece it passed on to the Roman Empire. From the Romanic nations it continued its way to the Northwestern parts of Europe, and from Holland and England it reached at length your continent. At present that stream is at a standstill. Its Western course through China and Japan is impeded; meanwhile no one can tell what forces for the future may yet lie slumbering in the Slavic races which have thus far failed of progress. But while this secret of the future is still veiled in mystery, the course of this world-stream from East to West can be denied by none. And therefore I am justified in saying that Paganism, Islamism and Romanism are the three successive formations which this development had reached, when its further direction passed over into the hands of Calvinism; and that Calvinism in turn is now denied this leading influence by Modernism, the daughter of the French Revolution.

The succession of these four phases of development did not take place mechanically, with sharply outlined divisions and parts. This development of life is organic, and therefore each new period roots in the past. In its deepest logic Calvinism had already been apprehended by Augustine; had, long before Augustine, been proclaimed to the City of the seven hills by the Apostle in his Epistle to the Romans; and from Paul goes back to Israel and its prophets, yea to the tents of the patriarchs. Romanism likewise does not make its appearance suddenly, but is the joint product of the three potencies of Israel's priesthood, the cross of Calvary, and the world-organization of the Roman Empire. Islam in the same way joins itself to Israel's Monism, to the Prophet of Nazareth, and to the tradition of the Koraishites. And even the Paganism of Babylon and Egypt on the one hand, and of Greece and Rome upon the other, stand organically related to what lay behind these nations, preceding the prosperity of their lives. But even so, it is as clear as day that the supreme force in the central development of the human race moved along successively from Babylon and Egypt to Greece and Rome, then to the chief regions of the Papal dominion, and finally to the Calvinistic nations of Western Europe. If Israel flourished in the days of Babylon and Egypt, however high its standard, the direction and the development of our human race was not in the hands of the sons of Abraham but in those of the Belshassars and the Pharaohs. Again, this leader-

ship does not pass from Babylon and Egypt on to Israel but to
Greece and Rome. However high the stream of Christianity had
risen when Islam made its appearance, in the 8th and 9th centuries the followers of Mahomet were our teachers and with
them rested the issue of the world. And though the hegemony
of Romanism still maintained itself for a short time after the
peace of Munster, no one questions the fact that the higher development, which we are now enjoying, we owe neither to Spain
nor to Austria, nor even to the Germany of that time, but to the
Calvinistic countries of the Netherlands and to England of the
16th century. Under Louis XIV, Romanism arrested this higher
development in France, but only that in the French Revolution
it might exhibit a ghastly caricature of Calvinism, which in its
sad consequences broke the inner strength of France as a nation, and weakened its international significance. The fundamental idea of Calvin has been transplanted from Holland and
England to America, thus driving our higher development ever
more Westward, until on the shores of the Pacific it now reverently awaits whatsoever God has ordained. But no matter what
mysteries the future may yet have to disclose, the fact remains
that the broad stream of the development of our race runs from
Babylon to San Francisco, through the five stadia of Babylonian-
Egyptian, Greek-Roman, Islamitic, Romanistic and Calvinistic civilization, and the present conflict in Europe as well as in America
finds its main cause in the fundamental antithesis between the energy of Calvinism which proceeded from the throne of God, found
the source of its power in the Word of God, and in every sphere of
human life exalted the glory of God,—and its caricature in the
French Revolution, which proclaimed its unbelief in the cry of,
"No God no master"; and which presently in the form of German
Pantheism is reducing itself more and more to a modern Paganism.

Thus notice I was not too bold when I claimed for Calvinism
the honor of being neither an ecclesiastical, nor a theological, nor
a sectarian conception, but one of the principal phases in the general development of our human race; and among these the young-
est, whose high calling still is to influence the further course of
human life. Just now, however, allow me to indicate another cir-

cumstance, which strengthens my principal statement, viz., *the commingling of blood* as, thus far, the physical basis of all higher human development. From the high-lands of Asia our human race came down in groups, and these in turn have been divided into races and nations; and in entire conformity to the prophetic blessing of Noah the children of Shem and of Japheth have been the sole bearers of the development of the race. No impulse for any higher life has ever gone forth from the third group. With the two other groups a twofold phenomenon presents itself. There are tribal nations which have *isolated* themselves and others which have *intermingled*. Thus on the one hand there are groups which have dominated exclusively their own inherent forces, and on the other hand groups which by commingling have crossed their traits with those of other tribes, and thus have attained a higher perfection. It is noteworthy that the process of human development steadily proceeds with those groups whose historic characteristic is not isolation but the commingling of blood. On the whole the Mongolian race has held itself apart, and in its isolation has bestowed no benefits upon our race at large. Behind the Himalayas a similar life secluded itself, and hence failed to impart any permanent impulse to the outside world. Even in Europe we find that with the Scandinavians and Slavs there was hardly any intermingling of blood, and, consequently having failed to develop a richer type, they have taken little part in the general development of human life. On the other hand, the tablets from Babylon in our great Museums by the two languages of their inscriptions still show that in Mesopotamia the Aryan* element of the Accadians** mingled itself at an early period with the Semitic-Babylonian; and Egyptology leads us to conclude that in the land of the Pharaohs we deal from the beginning with a population produced by the mingling of two very different tribes. No one believes any longer the pretended race-unity of the Greeks. In Greece as well as in Italy we deal with races of a later date who have intermingled with the earlier Pelasgians, Etruscians and others. Islam seems to be exclusively Arabic, but a study of the spread of Islamism among

---

* Aryan, from the Sanskrit word Arya, meaning noble — a term formerly used synonymously with Indo-European or Indo-German. The term is sometimes used loosely in the sense of Japhetic.

** From *Accad,* perhaps the southern of the two ancient division of Babylon: Sumer and Accad. Held by some to be non-Semitic. Cf. Gen. 10:10.

the Moors, Persians, Turks and other series of subjected tribes, with whom intermarriage was common, at once reveals the fact that especially with Mahometans the commingling of blood was even greater than with their predecessors. When the leadership of the world passed into the hands of the Romanic nations, the same phenomenon presented itself in Italy, Spain, Portugal and France. In these cases the Aborigines were generally Basques or Celts,* the Celts in turn being overcome by the Germanic tribes, and even as in Italy the East Goths and Lombards, so in Spain the West Goths, in Portugal the Swabians, and in France the Franks instilled new blood into debilitated veins, and to this wonderful rejuvenescence the Roman nations owed their vigor until far into the 16th century. Thus in the life of nations the same phenomenon repeats itself which so often strikes the historian as a result of international marriages among princely families, as we see how the Hapsburgs and the Bourbons, the Oranges and the Hohenzollern, for instance, have been, century after century, productive of a host of most remarkable statesmen and heroes. The raiser of stock has aimed at the same effect in the crossing of different breeds, and botanists harvest large profits by obeying the same law of life with plants; and by itself it is not difficult to perceive that the union of natural powers, divided among different tribes, must be productive of a higher development. To this it should be added that the history of our race does not aim at the improvement of any single tribe, but at the development of *mankind* taken as a whole, and therefore needs this commingling of blood in order to attain its end. Now in fact history shows that the nations among whom Calvinism flourished most widely exhibit in every way this same mingling of races. In Switzerland, the Germans, united with Italians and French; in France, the Gauls, with Franks and Burgundians; in the Lowlands, Celts and Welsh** with Germans; also in England the old Celts and Anglosaxons were afterwards raised to a still higher standard of na-

---

* Celt or Kelt: a member of that western European branch of the Aryan family that includes the Ghadelic peoples, the Scotch Gaelics, the Irish, Erse and Manx, and the Cymric (the Welsh, Cornish and Low Bretons). The Romans knew them as Gauls. They evidently were related to the Teutons. The indiscriminate use of the term Celt has led to much confusion.

** Inhabitants of Wales, part of Great Britain. The word Welsh (Dutch, Waalsch) signifies foreigner. The Welsh language is the Cymric as spoken by the Welsh. Cf. preceding note.

tional life by the invasion of the Normans. Indeed it may be said that the three principal tribes of Western Europe, the Celtic, Romanic and Germanic elements under the leadership of the Germanic, give us the genealogy of the Calvinistic nations. In America, where Calvinism has come to unfold itself in a still higher liberty, this commingling of blood is assuming a larger proportion than has ever yet been known. Here the blood flows together from all the tribes of the ancient world, and again we have the Celts from Ireland, the Germans from Germany and Scandinavia, united to the Slavs from Russia and Poland, who promote still further this already vigorous intermingling of the races. This latter process takes place under the higher exponent that it is not merely the union of tribe with tribe, but that the old historic nations are dissolving themselves in order to allow the re-union of their members in one higher unity, hitherto constantly assimilated by the American type. In this respect also Calvinism fully meets the conditions imposed on every new phase of development in the life of humanity. It spread itself in a domain where it found the commingling of blood stronger than under Romanism, and in America raised this to its highest conceivable realization.

Thus it is shown that Calvinism meets not only the necessary condition of the mingling of blood, but that in the process of human development it also represents, with respect to this, a further stadium. In Babylon this commingling of blood was of small significance; it gains in importance with the Greeks and Romans; it goes further under Islamism; is dominant under Romanism; but only among Calvinistic nations does it reach its highest perfection. Here in America it is achieving the intermingling of *all* the nations of the old world. A similar climax of this process of human development is also exhibited by Calvinism in the fact that only under the influence of Calvinism does the impulse of public activity proceed from the people themselves. In the life of the nations also there is development from the underage period to that of maturity. As in the family-life, during the years of childhood, the direction of affairs is in the hands of the parents, so also in the life of the nations it is but natural that during their under-age period first the Asiatic despot, then some eminent ruler, afterwards the priesthood, and finally both priest and magistrate together should stand at the head of every movement. The history of the nations in Babylon and under the Pharaohs, in Greece and Rome, under Islamism and under the papal system, fully confirms this course of development. But it is self-evident that this could not be a permanent state of things. Just because in their progressive development the nations finally came of age, they must at length reach that stadium in which the people itself awoke, stood up for their rights, and originated the movement that was to direct the course of future events; and in the rise of Calvinism *this* stadium appears to have been reached. Thus far every forward movement had gone forth from the authorities in State, Church or Science, and from thence had descended to the people. In Calvinism, on the other hand, the peoples themselves stand out in their broad ranks and form a spontaneity of their own, press forward to a higher form of social life and conditions. Calvinism had its rise *with the people*. In Lutheran countries the magistrate was still the leader in public advances, but in Switzerland, among the Huguenots, in Belgium, in the Netherlands, in Scotland and also in America the peoples themselves created the impetus. They seemed to have matured; to have reached the period in which they were of age. Even when in some cases, as in the Netherlands, the nobility for a moment took a heroic stand for the oppressed, their activity ended in nothing, and the people alone, by undaunted energy, broke the barrier, and among these it was the "common folk" to whose heroic initiative William the Silent, as he himself acknowledges, owed the success of his undertaking.

Hence, as a central phenomenon in the development of humanity, Calvinism is not only entitled to an honorable position by the side of Paganistic, Islamistic and Romanistic forms, since like these it represents a peculiar principle dominating the whole of life, but it also meets every required condition for the advancement of human development *to a higher stage*. And yet this would remain a bare possibility without any corresponding reality, if history did not testify that Calvinism has *actually* caused the stream of human life to flow in another channel, and has ennobled the social life of the nations. And therefore in closing I assert that Calvinism not only held out these possibilities but has also understood how to realize them. To prove this, just ask yourselves what would have become of Europe and America, if in the 16th century the star of Calvinism had not suddenly arisen on the horizon of Western Europe. In that case Spain would have crushed the Netherlands. In England and Scotland the Stuarts would have carried out their fatal plans. In Switzerland the spirit of half-heartedness would have gained the day. The beginnings of life in this new world would have been of an entirely different character. And as an unavoidable sequence, the balance of power in Europe would have returned to its former position. Protestantism would not have been able to maintain itself in politics. No further resistance could have been offered to the Romish-conservative power of the Hapsburgs, the Bourbons and the Stuarts; and the free development of the nations, as seen in Europe and America, would simply have been prevented. The whole American continent would have remained subject to Spain. The history of both continents would have become a most mournful one, and it ever remains a question whether the spirit of the Leipzig Interim* would not have succeeded, by way of a Romanized Protestantism, in reducing Northern Europe again to the sway of the old Hierarchy. The enthusiastic devotion of the best historians of the second half of this century to the struggle of the Netherlands against Spain, as one of the finest subjects of investigation, only explains itself by the conviction that if the power of Spain at that time had not been broken by the heroism of the Calvinistic spirit, the history of the Netherlands, of Europe and of the world would have been as painfully sad and dark as now, thanks to Calvinism, it is bright and inspiriting. Professor Fruin justly remarks that: "In Switzerland, in France, in the Netherlands, in Scotland and in England, and wherever Protestantism has had to establish itself at the point of the sword, it was Calvinism that gained the day."

Call to mind that this turn in the history of the world could not have been brought about except by the implanting of another prin-

---

* This interim was made in 1548 by Melanchthon and others at the command of Maurice of Saxony. The R. C. ceremonies were declared adiaphoron, and Luther's "Sola" was shunned. It was a very much mediating modification of the Augsburg interim held the same year. Interim denotes "provisional arrangement," in this case between the German Roman Catholics and German Protestants.

ciple in the human heart, and by the disclosing of another world of thought to the human mind; that only by Calvinism the psalm of liberty found its way from the troubled conscience to the lips; that Calvinism has captured and guaranteed to us our constitutional civil rights; and that simultaneously with this there went out from Western Europe that mighty movement which promoted the revival of science and art, opened new avenues to commerce and trade, beautified domestic and social life, exalted the middle classes to positions of honor, caused philanthropy to abound, and more than all this, elevated, purified, and ennobled moral life by puritanic seriousness; and then judge for yourselves whether it will do to banish any longer this God-given Calvinism to the archives of history, and whether it is so much of a dream to conceive that Calvinism has yet a blessing to bring and a bright hope to unveil for the future.

The struggle of the Boers in the Transvaal against one of the mightiest powers must often have reminded you of your own past. In what has been achieved at Majuba, and recently at the occasion of Jameson's raid, the heroism of old Calvinism was again brilliantly evident. If Calvinism had not been passed on from our fathers to their African descendants, no free republic would have arisen in the South of the Dark Continent. This proves that Calvinism is not dead—that it still carries in its germ the vital energy of the days of its former glory. Yea, even as a grain of wheat from the sarcophagi of the Pharaohs, when again commited to the soil, bears fruit a hundredfold, so Calvinism still carries in itself a wondrous power for the future of the nations. And if we, Christians of both Continents, in our still holier struggle, are still expected to achieve heroic deeds, marching under the banner of the Cross against the spirit of the times, Calvinism alone arms us with an inflexible principle, by the strength of that principle guaranteeing us a sure, though far from easy victory.

SECOND LECTURE

CALVINISM AND RELIGION

THE conclusion arrived at in my previous Lecture was first, that, scientifically speaking, Calvinism means the completed evolution of Protestantism, resulting in a both higher and richer stage of human development. Further, that the world-view of Modernism, with its starting-point in the French Revolution, can claim no higher privilege than that of presenting an atheistic imitation of the brilliant ideal proclaimed by Calvinism, therefore being unqualified for the honor of leading us higher on. And, lastly, that whosoever rejects atheism as his fundamental thought, is bound to go back to Calvinism, not to restore its worn-out form, but once more to catch hold of the Calvinistic principles, in order to embody them in such a form as, suiting the requirements of our own century, may restore the needed unity of Protestant thought and the lacking energy to Protestant practical life.

In my present Lecture, therefore, treating of *Calvinism and Religion,* first of all I will try to illustrate the dominant position occupied by Calvinism in the central domain of our worship of the Most High. The fact that, in the religious domain, Calvinism *has* occupied from the first a peculiar and impressive position, nobody will deny. As if by one magical stroke, it created its own Confession, its own Theology, its own Church Organization, its own Church Discipline, its own Cultus, and its own Moral Praxis. And continued historical investigation proves with increasing certainty that all these new Calvinistic forms for our religious life were the logical product of its own fundamental thought and the embodiment of one and the same principle. Measure the energy which

41

Calvinism here displayed by the utter incapability Modernism
evinced in the same domain by the absolute fruitlessness of its endeavors. Ever since it entered its "mystical" period, Modernism
also, both in Europe and in America, has acknowledged the necessity of carving out a new form for the religious life of our time.
Hardly a century after the once glittering tinsel of Rationalism,
now that Materialism is sounding its retreat in the ranks of science, a kind of hollow piety is again exercising its enticing charms
and every day it is becoming more fashionable to take a plunge
into the warm stream of mysticism. With an almost sensual delight this modern mysticism quaffs its intoxicating draught from
the nectar-cup of some intangible infinite. It was even purposed
that, on the ruins of the once so stately Puritanic building, a new
religion, with a new ritual, should be inaugurated as a higher evolution of religious life. Already, for more than a quarter of a century, the dedication and solemn opening of this new sanctuary has
been promised us. And yet it has all led to nothing. No tangible
effect has been produced. No formative principle has emerged
from the imbroglio of hypotheses. Not even the beginning of an
associative movement is as yet perceptible, and the long looked
for plant has not even lifted its head above the barren soil.—Now,
in contraposition to this, look at the giant spirit of Calvin, who,
in the sixteenth century, with one master-stroke, placed before the
gaze of the astonished world an entire religious edifice, erected in
the purest Scriptural style. So rapidly was the whole building
completed that most of the spectators forgot to pay attention to
the wonderful structure of the foundations. In all that the religious modern thought has, I will not say created, as with a
master hand, but heaped together, like an unsuccessful amateur,—
not one nation, not one family, hardly one solitary soul has (to
use Augustine's words) ever found the *requiescat* for his "broken heart," while the Reformer of Geneva, by his mighty spiritual
energy, unto five nations at once, both then, and after the lapse
of three centuries, has afforded guidance in life, the uplifting of
the heart unto the Father of Spirits, and holy peace, forever.
This naturally leads to the question—what was the secret of this
wonderful energy? Allow me to present the answer to this ques-

tion,—first in *Religion as such,* next in religion as manifested in the *Life of the Church,* and lastly in the fruit of Religion for *Practical Life.*

First, then, we must consider *Religion as such.* Here four mutually dependent fundamental questions arise:—1. Does Religion exist for the sake of *God,* or for *Man?* 2. Must it operate *directly* or *mediately?* 3. Can it remain *partial* in its operations or has it to embrace the *whole* of our personal being and existence? and, 4. can it bear a normal, or must it reveal an *abnormal,* i.e., a soteriological character? To these four questions Calvinism answers: 1. Man's religion ought to be not egotistical, and for *man,* but ideal, for the sake of *God.* 2. It has to operate not *mediately,* by human interposition, but *directly* from the heart. 3. It may not remain *partial,* as running alongside of life, but must lay hold upon our *whole* existence. And, 4. Its character should be soteriological, *i.e.,* it should spring, not from our *fallen* nature, but from the *new man,* restored by palingenesis to his original standard.

Allow me, then, successively to elucidate each of these four points.

Modern religious philosophy ascribes the origin of religion to a potency, from which it could not originate, but which acted merely as its supporter and preserver. It has mistaken the dead prop of the living shoot for the living shoot itself. Attention is called, and very properly, to the contrast between man, and the overwhelming power of the cosmos which surrounds him; and now religion is introduced as a mystical energy, trying to strengthen him against this immense power of the cosmos which inspires him with such deadly fear. Being conscious of the dominion which his unseen soul exercises over his own tangible body, he infers, quite naturally, that Nature, also, must be moved by the impulse of some hidden spiritual power. Animistically, therefore, he first explains the movements of nature as the result of an indwelling army of spirits, and tries to catch them, to conjure them, to bend them to his advantage. Then, rising from this atomistic idea to a more comprehensive conception, he begins to believe in the existence of personal gods, expecting from these divine beings, who stand above nature, effectual assistance against the fiendish power of Nature. And finally, grasping the contrast between the spiritual and the material, he pays homage to the Supreme Spirit, as standing over against all that is visible, till, in the end, having abandoned his faith in such an extramundane Spirit, as a personal being, and charmed by the loftiness of his own human spirit, he prostrates himself before some impersonal ideal, of which in self-adoration he deems himself to be the worshipful incarnation. But whatever may be the various stages in the progress of this egoistic religion, it never overcomes its subjective character, remaining always a religion *for the sake of man.* Men are religious in order to conjure the spirits hovering behind the veil of Nature, to free themselves from the oppressive sway of the cosmos. It matters not whether the Lama priest confines the evil spirits in his jugs, whether the nature-gods of the Orient are invoked to afford shelter against the forces of nature, whether the loftier gods of Greece are worshipped in their ascendency above nature, or whether, finally, idealistic philosophy presents the spirit of man himself as the real object of adoration;—in all these different forms it is and remains a religion fostered for man's sake, aiming at his safety, his liberty, his elevation, and partly also at his triumph over death. And even when a religion of this kind has developed itself into monotheism, the god whom it worships remains invariably a god who exists in order to help man, in order to secure good order and tranquility for the State, to furnish assistance and deliverance in time of need, or to strengthen the nobler and higher impulse of the human heart in its ceaseless struggle with the degrading influences of sin. The consequence of this is that all such religion thrives in time of famine and pestilence, it flourishes among the poor and oppressed, and it expands among the humble and the feeble; but it pines away in the days of prosperity, it fails to attract the well-to-do, it is abandoned by those who are more highly cultured. As soon as the more civilized classes enjoy tranquility and comfort, and by the progress of science feel more and more delivered from the pressure of the cosmos, they throw away the crutches of religion, and with a sneer at everything holy go stumbling forward on their own poor legs. This is the fatal end of egoistic religion;— it becomes superfluous and disappears as soon as the egoistic interests are satisfied. This was the course of religion among all non-Christian nations, in earlier times, and the same phenomenon is repeating itself in our own century, among nominal Christians of the higher, more prosperous and more cultured classes of society.

Now the position of Calvinism is diametrically opposed to all this. It does not deny that religion has also its human and subjective side; it does not dispute the fact that religion is promoted, encouraged and strengthened by our disposition to seek help in time of need and spiritual elevation in the face of sensual passions; but it maintains that it reverses the proper order of things to seek, in these accidental motives, the *essence* and the very *purpose* of religion. The Calvinist values all of these as *fruits* which are produced by religion, or as props which gave it support, but he refuses to honor them as the reason for its existence. Of course, religion, as such, produces *also* a blessing for man, but it does not exist for the sake of man. It is not God who exists for the sake of His creation;—the creation exists for the sake of God. For, as the Scripture says, He has created all things for Himself.

For this reason God even impressed a religious expression on the whole of unconscious nature,—on plants, on animals and also on children. "The whole earth is full of His glory." "How excellent is Thy Name, God, in all the earth." "The Heavens declare the glory of God and the firmament sheweth His handiwork." "Out of the mouths of babes and sucklings Thou hast ordained praise." Frost and hail, snow and vapor, the abyss and the hurricane—everything does praise God. But just as the entire creation reaches its culminating point in man, so also religion finds its clear expression only in man who is made in the image of God, and this not because man seeks it, but because God Himself implanted in man's nature the real essential religious expression, by means of the "seed of religion" (*semen religionis*), as Calvin defines it, sown in our human heart.*

God Himself makes man religious by means of the *sensus divinitatis,* i.e., the sense of the Divine, which He causes to strike the chords on the harp of his soul. A sound of need interrupts the pure harmony of this divine melody, but only in consequence of sin. In its original form, in its natural condition, religion is exclusively a sentiment of *admiration* and *adoration* which elevates and unites, not a feeling of dependence which severs and depresses. Just as the anthem of the Seraphim around the throne is one uninterrupted cry of *"Holy,—Holy,—Holy!,"* so also the religion of man upon this earth should consist in one echoing of God's glory, as our Creator and Inspirer. The starting-point of every motive in religion is God and not Man. Man is the instrument and means, God alone is here the goal, the point of departure and the point of arrival, the fountain, from which the waters flow, and at the same time, the ocean into which they finally return. To be irreligious is to forsake the highest aim of our existence, and on the other hand to covet no other existence than for the sake of God, to long for nothing but for the will of God, and to be wholly absorbed in the glory of the name of the Lord, such is the pith and kernel of all true religion. "Hallowed be thy Name. Thy kingdom come. Thy Will be done," is the threefold petition, which gives utterance to all true religion. Our watchword must be,—"Seek first the kingdom of God," and after that, think of your own need. First stands the confession of the absolute Sovereignty of the Triune God; for of Him, through Him, and unto Him are all things. And therefore our prayer remains the deepest expression of all religious life. This is the fundamental conception of religion as maintained by Calvinism, and hitherto, no one has ever found a higher conception. For no higher conception *can* be found. The fundamental thought of Calvinism, at the same time

---

* Calvin's *Institutes,* Eng. Edinburgh translation, Vol. I, Book I, Chapter 3: "That there exists in the human mind and indeed by natural instinct, some *sense of Deity* we hold to be beyond dispute . . ." Chapter 4, § 1. "But though experience testifies that a *seed of religion* is divinely sown in all, scarcely one in a hundred is found who cherishes it in his heart, and not one in whom it grows to maturity, so far it is from yielding fruit in its season. In no part of the world can genuine godliness be found."

the fundamental thought of the Bible, and of Christianity itself, leads, in the domain of religion, to the realization of the highest ideal. Nor has the philosophy of religion in our own century, in its most daring flights, ever attained a higher point of view nor a more ideal conception.

The second principal question in all religion is whether it must be *direct,* or *mediate.* Must there stand a church, a priest, or, as of old, a sorcerer, a dispenser of sacred mysteries, between God and the soul, or shall all intervening links be cast away, so that the bond of religion shall bind the soul directly to God? Now we find that in all non-Christian religions, without any exception, human intercessors are deemed necessary, and in the domain of Christianity itself the intercessor intruded again upon the scene, in the Blessed Virgin, in the host of angels, in the saints and martyrs, and in the priestly hierarchy of the clergy; and although Luther took the field against all priestly mediation, yet the church which is called by his name, renewed by its title of *"ecclesia docens"* the office of mediator and steward of mysteries. On this point also it was Calvin, and he alone, who attained to the full realization of the ideal of pure spiritual religion. Religion, as he conceived it, must *"nullis mediis interpositis,"* i.e., without any creaturely intercession, realize the direct communion between God and the human heart. Not because of any hatred against priests, as such, not because of any undervaluing of the martyrs, nor underestimating the significance of angels, but solely because Calvin felt bound to vindicate the essence of religion and the glory of God in that essence, and absolutely devoid of all yielding or wavering, he waged war, with holy indignation, against everything that interposed itself between the soul and God. Of course he clearly perceived that in order to be fitted for the true religion fallen man needs a Mediator, but such a mediator could not be found in any fellow-man. Only the God-man,—only God Himself could be such a mediator. And this mediatorship could be confirmed not by us, but only from the side of God, by the indwelling of God the Holy Spirit in the heart of the regenerated.

In all religion God Himself must be the active power. He must *make* us religious, He must *give* us the religious disposition, nothing being left to us but the power to give form and expression to the deep religious sentiment which He, Himself, stirred in the depth of our heart. There we see the mistake of those who regarded Calvin as only an *Augustinus redivivus*. Notwithstanding his sublime confession of God's holy grace, Augustine remained *the Bishop*. He kept his intermediate position between the Triune God and the layman. And although prominent among the most pious men of his time, he had so little insight into the real claims of thorough-going religion on behalf of laymen that in his dogmatics he lauds the church as the mystical Purveyor, into whose bosom God caused all grace to flow and from whose treasure all men had to accept it. Only he, therefore, who superficially confines his attention to predestination can confuse Augustinianism and Calvinism. Religion *for the sake of man* carries with it the position that man has to act as a mediator for his fellow-man. Religion *for the sake of God* inexorably excludes every human mediatorship. As long as it remains the chief purpose of religion to help man, and as long as man is understood to deserve grace by his devotion, it is perfectly natural that the man of inferior piety should invoke the mediation of the holier man. Another must procure for him what he cannot procure for himself. The fruit on the branches hangs too high, and, therefore, the higher-reaching man has to pluck it, and hand it down to his helpless comrade. If, on the contrary, the demand of religion is that *every* human heart must give glory to God, no man can appear before God on behalf of another. Then every single human being must appear personally, for himself, and religion achieves its aim only in the *general priesthood of believers*. Even the new-born babe must have received the seed of religion from God Himself; and in case it dies without being baptized, it must not be sent off to a *limbus innocentium*, but, if elected, enter, even as the long-lived, into personal communion with God, for all eternity.

The importance of this second point, in the question of religion, culminating, as it does, in the confession of personal election, is incalcuable. On the one hand, all religion must tend *to make man free,* that by a clear utterance he may express that general religious impression stamped, by God Himself, upon unconscious nature. On the other hand, every appearance of an interposing priest or enchanter in the domain of religion fetters the human spirit in a chain which presses the more woefully the more the piety increases in fervor. In the Church of Rome, even at the present day, the *bons catholiques* are most closely confined in the fetters of the clerus. Only the Roman Catholic whose piety has decreased is able to secure for himself a partial liberty by loosening more than halfway the tie which connects him with his church. In the Lutheran churches the clerical fetters are less confining, yet far from being loosened, entirely. And only in churches which take their stand in Calvinism, do we find that spiritual independence which enables the believer to oppose, if need be, and for God's sake, even the most powerful office-bearer in his church. Only he who personally stands before God on his own account, and enjoys an uninterrupted communion with God, can properly display the glorious wings of liberty. And both in Holland and in France, in England as well as in America, the historic result affords most undeniable evidence of the fact that despotism has found no more invincible antagonists, and liberty of conscience no braver, no more resolute champions than the followers of Calvin. In the last analysis, the cause of this phenomenon lies in the fact that the effect of every clerical interposition invariably was, and must be, to make religion external and to smother it with sacerdotal forms. Only where all priestly intervention disappears, where God's sovereign election from all eternity binds the inward soul directly to God Himself, and where the ray of divine light enters straightway into the depth of our heart,—only there does religion, in its most absolute sense, gain its ideal realization.

This leads me, naturally, to the third religious question: Is religion *partial,* or is it all-subduing, and comprehensive,—*universal* in the strict sense of the word? Now, if the aim of religion be found in man himself and if its realization be made dependent on clerical mediators, religion cannot be but *partial*. In that case it follows logically that every man confines his religion to those occurrences of his life by which his religious needs are stirred, and to those cases in which he finds human intervention at his disposal. The partial character of this sort of religion shows itself in three particulars: in the religious *organ* through which, in the *sphere* in which, and in the *group of persons* among which, religion has to thrive and flourish.

Recent controversy affords a pertinent illustration of the first limitation. The wise men of our generation maintain that religion has to retire from the precinct of the human intellect. It must seek to express itself either by means of the mystical feelings, or else by means of the practical will. Mystical and ethical inclinations are hailed with enthusiasm, in the domain of religion, but in that same domain the intellect, as leading to metaphysical hallucinations, must be muzzled. Metaphysics and Dogmatics are increasingly tabooed, and Agnosticism is ever more loudly acclaimed as the solution of the great enigma. On the rivers of sentiment and of feeling, navigation is made duty-free, and ethical activity is becoming the only touch-stone for testing the religious gold; but Metaphysics is avoided as drowning us in a swamp. Whatsoever announces itself with the pretension of an axiomatic dogma, is rejected as irreligious contraband. And although that same Christ whom these very scholars honor as a religious genius has taught us most emphatically: "Thou shalt love God, not only with all thy heart and with all thy strength, but also *with all thy mind*," yet they, on the contrary, venture to dismiss our mind, or intellect, as unfit for use, in this holy domain, and as not fulfilling the requirements of a religious organ.

Thus the religious organ being found, not in the whole of our being, but in part of it, being confined to our feelings and our will, consequently also *the sphere* of religious life must assume in consequence the same *partial character*. Religion is excluded from science, and its authority from the domain of public life; henceforth the inner chamber, the cell for prayer, and the secrecy of the heart should be its exclusive dwelling place. By his *du Sollst*, Kant limited the sphere of religion to the ethical life. The mystics of our own times banish religion to the retreats of sentiment. And the result is that, in many different ways, religion, once the central force of human life, is now placed alongside of it; and, far from the thriving of the world, is understood to hide itself in a distant and almost private retreat.

This brings us naturally to the third characteristic note of this partial view of religion,—religion as pertaining not to all, but only to *the group of pious people* among our generation. Thus the limitation of the *organ* of religion brings about the limitation of its sphere, and the limitation of its sphere consequently brings about the limitation of its group or *circle* among men. Just as art is understood to have an *organ* of its own, a *sphere* of its own, and therefore, also, its own *circle* of devotees, so also, according to this view, must it be with religion. It so happens that the great bulk of the people are almost devoid of mystical feeling, and energetic strength of will. For this reason they have either no perception of the glow of mysticism, or are incapable of really pious deeds. But there are also those whose inner life is overflowing with a sense of the Infinite, or who are full of holy energy, and among such it is that piety and religion flourish most brilliantly both in their imaginative power, and in their realizing capability.

From a quite different standpoint, Rome gradually and increasingly came to favor the same partial views. She knew religion only as it existed in her own Church, and considered the influence of religion to be confined to that portion of life which she had consecrated. I fully acknowledge that she tried to draw all human life as far as possible into the holy sphere, but everything outside this sphere, everything not touched by baptism, nor aspersed by her holy water, was devoid of all genuine religious efficiency. And just as Rome drew a boundary line between the consecrated and the profane sides of life, she also subdivided her own sacred precincts according to different degrees of religious intensity,—the clergy and the cloister constituting the *Holy of Holies,* the pious laity forming the *Holy Place,* thus leaving the *Outer Court* to those who, although baptized, continued to prefer to church-devotion the often sinful pleasures of the world,—a system of limitation and division, which for those in the *Outer Court,* ended in setting nine tenths of practical life outside of all religion. So religion was made partial, by carrying it from ordinary days to days of festival, from days of prosperity to times of danger and sickness, and from the fulness of life to the time of approaching death. A dualistic system which has found its most emphatic expression in the praxis of the Carnival, giving Religion a full sway over the soul during the weeks of Lent, but leaving to the flesh a fair chance, before descending into this vale of gloom, to empty to the dregs the full cup of pleasure, if not of mirth and folly.

Now this whole view of the matter is squarely antagonized by Calvinism, which vindicates for religion its full universal character, and its complete universal application. If everything that is, exists for the sake of God, then it follows that the whole creation must give glory to God. The sun, moon, and stars in the firmament, the birds of the air, the whole of Nature around us, but, above all, man himself, who, priestlike, must concentrate to God the whole of creation, and all life thriving in it. And although sin has deadened a large part of creation to the glory of God, the demand,—the ideal, remains unchangeable, that *every* creature must be immersed in the stream of religion, and end by lying as a religious offering on the altar of the Almighty. A religion confined to feeling or will is therefore unthinkable to the Calvinist. The sacred anointing of the priest of creation must reach down to his beard and to the hem of his garment. His whole being, including all his abilities and powers, must be pervaded by the *sensus divinitatis,* and how then could he exclude his rational consciousness,—the λο'γος which is in him,—the light of thought which comes from God Himself to irradiate him? To possess his God for the underground world of his feelings, and in the outworks of the exertion of his will, but not in his inner self, in the very center of his consciousness, and his thought; to have fixed starting-points for the study of nature and axiomatic strongholds for practical life, but to have no fixed support in his thoughts about the Creator Himself,—all of this was, for the Calvinist, the very denying of the Eternal Logos.

The same character of universality was claimed by the Calvinist for the *sphere* of religion and its *circle* of influence among men.

Everything that has been created was, in its creation, furnished by God with an unchangeable law of its existence. And because God has fully ordained such laws and ordinances for all life, therefore the Calvinist demands that all life be consecrated to His service, in strict obedience. A religion confined to the closet, the cell, or the church, therefore, Calvin abhors. With the Psalmist, he calls upon heaven and earth, he calls upon all peoples and nations to give glory to God. God is present in all life, with the influence of His omnipresent and almighty power, and no sphere of human life is conceivable in which religion does not maintain its demands that God shall be praised, that God's ordinances shall be observed, and that every *labora* shall be permeated with its *ora* in fervent and ceaseless prayer. Wherever man may stand, whatever he may do, to whatever he may apply his hand, in agriculture, in commerce, and in industry, or his mind, in the world of art, and science, he is, in whatsoever it may be, constantly standing before the face of his God, he is employed in the service of his God, he has strictly to obey his God, and above all, he has to aim at the glory of his God. Consequently, it is impossible for a Calvinist to confine religion to a single group, or to some circles among men. Religion concerns the whole of our human race. This race is the product of God's creation. It is His wonderful workmanship, His absolute possession. Therefore the whole of mankind must be imbued with the fear of God,—old as well as young,—low as well as high,—not only those who have become initiated into His mysteries, but also those who still stand afar off. For not only did God create all men, not only is He all for all men, but His grace also extends itself, not only as a special grace, to the elect, but also as a common grace (*gratia communis*) to all mankind. To be sure, there is a concentration of religious light and life in the Church, but then in the walls of this church there are wide open windows, and through these spacious windows the light of the Eternal has to radiate over the whole world. Here is a city, set upon a hill, which every man can see afar off. Here is a holy salt that penetrates in every direction, checking all corruption. And even he who does not yet imbibe the higher light, or maybe shuts his eyes to it, is nevertheless admonished, with equal emphasis, and in all things, to give glory to the name of the Lord. All partial religion drives the wedges of dualism into life, but the true Calvinist never forsakes the standard of religious monism. One supreme calling must impress the stamp of *one-ness* upon *all* human life, because one God upholds and preserves it, just as He created it all.

This brings us, without any further transition, to our fourth main question, viz., Must religion be *normal* or abnormal, i.e., *soteriological*? The distinction which I have in mind here is concerned with the question, whether in the matter of religion we must reckon *de facto* with man in his present condition as *normal*, or as having fallen into sin, and having therefore become *abnormal*. In the latter case religion must necessarily assume a soteriological character. Now the prevailing idea, at present, favors the view that religion has to start from man as being *normal*. Not of course as though our race as a whole should conform already to the highest religious norm. This nobody affirms. Everyone knows better than to make such an absurd statement. As a matter of fact, we meet with much irreligiousness, and imperfect religious development continues to be the rule. But precisely in this slow and gradual progress from the lowest forms to the highest ideals, the development demanded by this normal view of religion contends that it has found confirmation. According to this view, the first traces of religion are found in animals. They are seen in the dog who adores his master, and as the *homo sapiens* develops out of the chimpanzee, so religion only enters upon a higher stage. Since that time religion has passed through all the notes of the gamut. At present it is engaged in loosening itself from the bands of Church and dogma, to pass on to what is again considered a higher stage, namely, *the unconscious feeling for the Unknown Infinite*. Now, this whole theory is opposed by that other and entirely different theory, which, without denying the preformation of so much that is human, in the animal, or the fact that (if you will allow me to say so) animals were created after the image of man, just as man was created after the image of God, nevertheless maintains that the first man was created in perfect relations to his God, *i.e.*, as imbued by a pure and genuine religion, and consequently explains the many low, imperfect and absurd forms of religion found in Paganism, not as the result of his creation but as the outcome of his Fall. These low and imperfect forms of religion are not to be understood as a process that leads from a lower to a higher, but as a lamentable degeneration,—a degeneration, which, in the nature of the case, makes the restoration of the true religion possible only in the soteriological way. Now in the choice between these two theories Calvinism allows no hesitation. Standing himself, with this question, too, before the face of God, the Calvinist was so impressed with the holiness of God that the consciousness of guilt immediately lacerated his soul, and the terrible nature of sin pressed on his heart as with an intolerable weight. Every attempt to explain sin as an incomplete stage on the way to perfection, aroused his wrath, as an insult to the majesty of God. He confessed, from the beginning, the same truth which Buckle has demonstrated empirically in his "History of Civilization in England," *viz.*, that the *forms* in which sin makes its appearance may show us a gradual refinement, but that the moral condition of the human heart, as such, has remained the same throughout all the centuries. To the *de profundis* with which, thirty centuries ago, the soul of David cried unto God, the troubled soul of every child of God in the sixteenth century still sounded a response with undiminished power. The conception of the corruption of sin as the source of all human misery was nowhere more profound than in Calvin's environment. Even in the assertions which the Calvinist made, in accordance with Holy Scripture, concerning hell and damnation, there is no coarseness, no rudeness, but only that clearness which is the result of the utmost seriousness of life, and the undaunted courage of a deep-rooted conviction of the holiness of the most High. Did not He, from whose lips flowed the most tender, and the most winning words,—did not He, Himself, also speak most decidedly and repeatedly of an "outer darkness," of a "fire that cannot be quenched," and of a "worm that dieth not"? And in this, also, Calvin was right, for to refuse to assent to these words is nothing but a lack of thoroughgoing consistency. It shows a want of sincerity in our confession of the holiness of God, and of the destructive power of sin. And on the contrary, in this spiritual experience of sin, in this empirical

consideration of the misery of life, in this lofty impression of the
holiness of God, and in this staunchness of his convictions, which
led him to follow his conclusions to the bitter end, the Calvinist
found the roots of the necessity first of *Regeneration,* for real
existence; and secondly, the necessity of *Revelation,* for clear
consciousness.

Now my subject does not induce me to speak in detail of regeneration, as that immediate act by which God, as it were, sets
right again the crooked wheel of life. But it is necessary that I
say a few words concerning Revelation, and the authority of the
Holy Scriptures. Very improperly, the Scriptures have been represented, by Schweizer and others, as only the *formal* principle
of the Reformed confession. The conception of genuine Calvinism
lies much deeper. The meaning of Calvin was expressed in what
he called the *necessitas S. Scripturae;* i.e , the need of Scriptural
revelation. This *necessitas S. S.* was for Calvin the unavoidable
expression for the all-dominating authority of the Holy Scriptures, and even now it is this very dogma which enables us to understand why it is that the Calvinist of today considers the critical
analysis and the application of the critical solvent to the Scriptures as tantamount to an abandoning of Christianity itself. In
Paradise, before the Fall, there was no Bible, and there will be no
Bible in the future Paradise of glory. When the transparent light,
kindled by Nature, addresses us directly, and the inner word of
God sounds in our heart in its original clearness, and all human
words are sincere, and the function of our inner ear is perfectly
performed, why should we need a Bible? What mother loses herself in a treatise upon the "love of our children" the very moment that her own dear ones are playing about her knee, and God
allows her to drink in their love with full draughts? But, in our
present condition, this immediate communion with God by means
of nature, and of our own heart is lost. Sin brought separation instead, and the opposition which is manifest nowadays against the
authority of the Holy Scriptures is based on nothing else than the
false supposition that, our condition being still normal, our religion need not be soteriological. For of course, in that case, the
Bible is not wanted, it becomes, indeed, a hindrance, and grates

upon your feelings, since it interposes a book between God and your heart. Oral communication excludes writing. When the sun shines in your house, bright and clear, you turn off the electric light, but when the sun disappears below the horizon, you feel the *necessitas luminis artificiosi,* i.e., the need of artificial light, and the artificial light is kindled in every dwelling. Now this is the case in matters of religion. When there are no mists to hide the majesty of the divine light from our eyes, what need is there then for a lamp unto the feet, or a light upon the path? But when history, experience and consciousness all unite in stating the fact that the pure and full light of Heaven *has* disappeared, and that we are groping about in the dark, then, a different, or if you will, an artificial light *must* be kindled for us,—and such a light God has kindled for us in His Holy Word.

For the Calvinist, therefore, the necessity of the Holy Scriptures does not rest in ratiocination, but on the immediate testimony of the Holy Spirit,—on the *testimonium Spiritus Sancti.* Our theory of inspiration is the product of historical deduction, and so is also every canonical declaration of the Scriptures. But the magnetic power with which the Scripture influences the soul, and draws it to herself, just as the magnet draws the steel, is not derived, but immediate. All of this takes place in a manner which is not magical, nor unfathomably mystical, but clear, and easy to be understood. God regenerates us,—that is to say, He rekindles in our heart the lamp sin had blown out. The necessary consequence of this regeneration is an irreconcilable conflict between the inner world of our heart and the world outside, and this conflict is ever the more intensified the more the regenerative principle pervades our consciousness. Now, in the Bible, God reveals, to the regenerate, a world of thought, a world of energies, a world of full and beautiful life, which stands in direct opposition to his ordinary world, but which proves to agree in a wonderful way with the new life that has sprung up in his heart. So the regenerate begins to guess the identity of what is stirring in the depth of his own soul, and of what is revealed to him in Scripture, thereby learning both the inanity of the world around him, and the divine reality of the world of the Scriptures, and as soon as this has become a certainty to him, he has personally received the *testimony* of the *Holy Spirit*. Everything that is in him thirsted for the Father of all Lights and Spirits. Outside the Scripture, he discovered only vague shadows. But now as he looked upward, through the prism of the Scriptures, he rediscovers his Father and his God. For this reason he puts no shackles on science. If a man wants to criticize, let him criticize. Such criticism even holds the promise that it will deepen our own insight into the structure of the scriptural edifice. Only no Calvinist ever allows the critic to dash out of his hand, for a moment, the *prism itself* which breaks up the divine ray of light into its brilliant tints and colors. No appeal to the grace bestowed inwardly, no pointing to the fruits of the Holy Ghost, can enable him to dispense with the *necessitas* which the soteriological standpoint of religion among sinners carries with it. As mere *entities* we share our life with plants and animals. *Unconscious* life we share with the children, and with the sleeping man, and even with the man who has lost his reason. That which distinguishes us, as higher beings, and as wide awake men, is our *full self-consciousness,* and therefore, if religion, as the highest vital function, is to operate also in that highest sphere of self-consciousness, it must follow that soteriological religion, next to the *necessitas* of inward *palingenesis,* demands also the *necessitas* of an assistant light, of revelation to be kindled in our twilight. And this assistant light coming from God Himself, but handed to us by human agency, beams upon us in His holy Word.

Summing up the results of our investigations thus far, I may express my conclusion as follows. In each one of the four great problems of religion, Calvinism has expressed its conviction in an appropriate dogma and each time has made that choice which even now, after three centuries, satisfies the most ideal wants, and leaves the way open for an ever-richer development. *First,* it regards religion, not in an utilitarian, or eudæmonistic sense, as existing for the sake of man, but for God, and for God alone. This is its dogma of *God's Sovereignty. Secondly,* in religion there must be no intermediation of any creature between God and the soul,—

all religion is the immediate work of God Himself, in the inner heart. This is the doctrine of *Election*. *Thirdly*, religion is not partial but universal,—this is the dogma of *common or universal grace*. And, finally, in our sinful condition, religion cannot be normal, but has to be *soteriological*,—this is its position in the two-fold dogma of the necessity of Regeneration, and of the *necessitas S. Scripturae*.

Having considered Religion as such, and coming now *to the Church*, as its organized form, or its phenomenal appearance, I shall present, in three successsive stages, the Calvinistic concep- of the *essence,* the *manifestation* and the *purpose* of the Church of Christ upon earth.

In its essence, for the Calvinist, the Church is a sp'.itual organ-ism, including heaven and earth, but having at present its center, and the starting-point for its action, not upon earth, but in heaven. This is to be understood thus: God created the Cosmos geocen-trically, i.e., He placed the spiritual center of this Cosmos on our planet, and caused all the divisions of the kingdoms of nature, on this earth, to culminate in man, upon whom, as the bearer of His image He called to consecrate the Cosmos to His glory. In God's creation, therefore, man stands as the prophet, priest and king, and although sin has disturbed these high designs, yet God pushes them onward. He so loves His world that He has given Himself to it, in the person of His Son, and thus He has again brought our race, and through our race, His whole Cosmos, into a renewed contact with eternal life. To be sure, many branches and leaves fell off the tree of the human race, yet the tree itself shall be saved; on its new root in Christ, it shall once more blossom gloriously. For regeneration does not save a few isolated individuals, finally to be joined together mechanically as an aggregate heap. Regen-eration saves the organism, itself, of our race. And therefore all regenerate human life forms one organic body, of which Christ is the Head, and whose members are bound together by their mysti-cal union with Him. But not before the second Advent shall this

new all-embracing organism manifest itself as the center of the
cosmos. At present it is hidden. Here, on earth, it is only as it were
its silhouette that can be dimly discerned. In the Future, *this new
Jerusalem* shall descend from God, out of heaven, but at present it
withdraws its beams from our sight in the mysteries of the invisible. And therefore the true sanctuary is now *above*. On high are
both the Altar of Atonement, and the incense-Altar of Prayer;
and on high is Christ, as the only priest who, according to Melchizedek's ordinance, ministers at the Altar, in the sanctuary, before
God.

Now, in the middle ages, the Church had more and more lost
sight of this celestial character,—she had become worldly in her
nature. The Sanctuary was again brought back to earth, the altar
was rebuilt of stone, and a priestly hierarchy had reconstituted itself for the ministrations of the altar. Next of course it was necessary to renew the tangible sacrifice on earth, and this at last brought
the church to create the unbloody offering of the Mass. Now
against all this, Calvinism opposed itself, not to contend against
priesthood on principle, or against altars as such, or against sacrifice in itself, because the office of priest cannot perish, and everyone knowing the fact of sin realizes in his own heart the absolute need of a propitiatory sacrifice; but in order to do away
with all this worldly paraphernalia, and to call believers to lift up
their eyes again, on high, to the real sanctuary, where Christ, our
only priest, ministers at the only real altar. The battle was waged,
not against *sacerdotium,* but against *sacerdotalism**, and Calvin
alone fought this battle through to the end, with thorough consistency. Lutherans and Episcopalians *rebuilt* a kind of altar, on
earth; Calvinism alone dared to put it away, entirely. Consequently, among the Episcopalians the earthly priesthood was retained,
even in the form of a hierarchy; in Lutheran lands the sovereign
became *summus episcopus* and the divisions of ecclesiastical ranks
were imitated; but Calvinism proclaimed the absolute equality of
all who engaged in the service of the church, and refused to ascribe
to its leaders and officebearers any other character than that of

---

* *Sacerdotium* denotes priesthood; *sacerdotalism* is the doctrine that the priest
offers sacrifice in Eucharist.

Ministers (i.e., *servants*). That which, under the shadows of the Old Testament dispensation, furnished intuitive instruction by types and symbols, now the types were fulfilled, had become to Calvin a detriment to the glory of Christ, and lowered the heavenly nature of the Church. Therefore, Calvinism could not rest until this worldly tinsel had ceased to charm and attract the eye. Only when the last grain of the sacerdotal leaven had been eliminated, could the Church on earth again become the outer court, from which believers could look up and onward to the real sanctuary of the living God in heaven.

The Westminster Confession beautifully sets forth this heavenly all-embracing nature of the Church, when it says: "The Catholic or Universal Church, which is invisible, consists of the whole number of the elect that have been, are or shall be, gathered into one, under Christ the Head, thereof; and is the spouse, the body, the fulness of Him that filleth all in all." Only thus was the dogma of the invisible church religiously consecrated and apprehended in its cosmological, and enduring significance. For, of course, the reality and fulness of the Church of Christ cannot exist on earth. Here is found, at most, one generation of believers at a time, in the portal of the Temple,—all previous generations, from the beginning and foundation of the world, had left this earth, and had gone up on high. Therefore, those who remained here, were, *eo ipso, pilgrims,* meaning thereby that they were marching from the portal unto the Sanctuary itself, no possibility of salvation after death remaining for those who had not been united to Christ during this present life. No room could be left for masses for the dead, nor for a call to repentance on the other side of the grave, as German Theologians are now advocating. For all such processional and gradual transitions were regarded by Calvin as destroying the absolute contrast between the essence of the Church in Heaven, and its imperfect form, here on earth. The Church on earth does not send *up* its light to heaven, but the Church in heaven must send its light *down* to the Church on earth. There is now, as it were, a curtain stretched before the eye, which hinders it from penetrating while on earth into the real essence of the Church. Therefore, all that remains possible to us on earth is first, a mystical communion with that real Church, by means of the Spirit, and in the second place, the enjoyment of the shadows which are displaying themselves on the transparent curtain before us. Accordingly, no child of God should imagine that the real Church is here on earth, and that behind the curtain there is only an ideal product of our imagination; but, on the contrary, he has to confess that Christ in human form, in our flesh, has entered into the invisible, behind the curtain; and that, with Him, around Him, and in Him, our Head, is the real Church, the real and essential sanctuary of our salvation.

After having thus clearly grasped the nature of the Church, in its bearing upon the re-creation both of our human race and of the Cosmos as a whole, let us now turn our attention to its *form of manifestation,* here on earth. As such it displays, unto us, different *local congregations of believers,* groups of *confessors,* living in some ecclesiatical union, in obedience to the ordinances of Christ Himself. The Church on earth is not an institution for the dispensation of grace, as if it were a dispensary of spiritual medicines. There is no mystical, spiritual order gifted with mystical powers to operate with a magical influence upon laymen. There are only *regenerated and confessing individuals,* who, in accordance with the Scriptural command, and under the influence of the sociological element of all religion, have formed a society, and are endeavoring to live together in subordination to Christ as their king. This, alone, is the Church on earth.—not the building,—not the institution,—not a spiritual order. For Calvin, the Church is found in the *confessing individuals themselves,* — not in each individual separately, but in all of them taken together, and united, not as they themselves see fit, but according to the ordinances of Christ. In the Church on earth, the universal priesthood of believers must be realized. Do not misunderstand me. I do not say: The Church consists of pious persons united in groups for religious purposes. That, in itself, would have nothing in common with the Church. The real, heavenly, invisible Church must manifest itself *in* the earthly Church. If not, you will have a society, but no church.

Now the real essential Church is and remains the body of Christ, of which regenerate persons are members. Therefore the Church on earth consists only of those who have been incorporated into Christ, who bow before Him, live in His Word, and adhere to His ordinances; and for this reason the Church on earth has to preach the Word, to administer the sacraments, and to exercise discipline, and in everything to stand before the face of God.

This at the same time determines the form of government of this Church on earth. This government, like the Church itself, originates in Heaven, in Christ. *He* most effectually rules, governs His Church by means of the Holy Spirit, by whom He works in His members. Therefore, all being equal under Him, there can be no distinctions of rank among believers; there are only ministers, who serve, lead and regulate; a thoroughly Presbyterian form of government; the Church power descending directly from Christ Himself, into the congregation, concentrated from the congregation in the ministers, and by them being administered unto the brethren. So the sovereignty of Christ remains absolutely monarchial, but the government of the Church on earth becomes democratic to its bones and marrow; a system leading logically to this other sequence, that all believers and all congregations being of an equal standing, no Church may exercise any dominion over another, but that all local churches are of equal rank, and as manifestations of one and the same body, can only be united synodically, i.e., by way of *confederation.*

Now let me draw your attention to another most important consequence of this same principle, *viz.,* to the multiformity of denominations as the necessary result of the differentiation of the churches, according to the different degrees of their purity. If the Church is considered to be an institute of grace, independent of the believers, or an institute in which a hierarchial priesthood distributes the treasury of grace entrusted to it, the result must be that this hierarchy itself extends through all nations, and imparts the same stamp to all forms of ecclesiastical life. But if the Church consists in the *congregation of believers,* if the churches are formed by the union of confessors, and are united only in the way of confederation, then the differences of climate and of nation, of historical past, and of disposition of mind come in to exercise a widely variegating influence, and multiformity in ecclesiastical matters must be the result. A result, therefore, of very far-reaching importance, because it annihilates the absolute character of every visible church, and places them all side by side, as differing in degrees of purity, but always remaining in some way or other a manifestation of one holy and catholic Church of Christ in Heaven.

I do not say that Calvinistic theologians have proclaimed this full consequence from the beginning. The desire for ruling power lurked also at the door of their heart, and even apart from this dangerous disposition it was right and natural for them theoretically to judge each church according to the standard of their own ideals. But this does not in the least detract from the great significance of the fact that by regarding their church, not as a hierarchy or institution, but as the gathering of individual confessors, they started for the life of the church, as well as for the life of the state, and civil society, from the principle not of compulsion, but of liberty. For, of course, by virtue of this starting-point, there was no other church-power superior to the local churches, save only what the churches themselves constituted, by means of their confederation. Hence it followed of necessity that the natural and historic differences between men should also, wedge-like, force their way into the phenomenal life of the church upon earth. National differences of morals, differences of disposition and of emotions, different degrees in depth of life and insight, necessarily resulted in emphasizing first one, and then another side of the same truth. Hence the numerous sects and denominations into which the external church-life has fallen by virtue of this principle. So on our side there are denominations which may have departed from the rich, deep and full Calvinistic Confession, in no small degree, even such as bitterly oppose more than one capital article of our Confession; yet they all owe their origin to a deep-rooted opposition to sacerdotalism, and to the acknowledgment of the Church as the "congregation of believers," the truth in which Calvinism expressed its fundamental conception. And although this fact unavoidably led to much unholy rivalry, and even to sinful errors of conduct; yet, after an experience of three centuries it must be confessed that this multiformity, which is inseparably connected with the fundamental thought of Calvinism, has been much more favorable to the growth and prosperity of religious life than the compulsory uniformity in which others sought the very basis of its strength. And fruit is to be expected more abundantly still in the future, provided only that the principle of ecclesiastical liberty does not degenerate into indifference, and that no church, which, in its name and confession still upholds the Calvinistic banner, omits to fulfil its holy mission of recommending to others the superiority of its principles.

Still another point must be brought forward in this connection. The conception of the Church as the "congregation of believers" might lead to the conception that it included the believers only, without their children. This, however, is by no means the teaching of Calvinism; its teaching on the subject of infant baptism showing quite the contrary. Believers who meet together do not thereby sever the natural bond that binds them to their offspring. On the contrary, they consecrate this bond, and by baptism incorporate their children in the communion of their church, and these minors are kept in this Church communion until, when of age, they become themselves confessors, or sever themselves from the church by their unbelief. This is the all-important Calvinistic dogma of the *Covenant;* a prominent article of our confession, showing that the waters of the Church do not flow outside the natural stream of human life, but cause the life of the Church to proceed hand in hand with the natural organic reproduction of mankind in its succeeding generations. *Covenant* and Church are inseparable,—the Covenant binding the Church to the race, and God Himself sealing in it the connection between the life of grace and the life of nature. Of course, Church discipline must come in here, in order to preserve the purity of this Covenant as soon as the interpermeation of grace by nature tends to lower the purity of the Church. From the Calvinistic point of view, therefore, it is impossible to speak of a national Church as being destined to embrace all the inhabitants of a whole country. A national Church, i.e., a Church comprising only one nation, and that nation entirely, is a Heathen, or at most, a Jewish conception. The Church of Christ is not national but ecumenical. Not one single state, but the whole world is its domain. And when the Lutheran Reformers at the instigation of their sovereigns, nationalized their churches, and Calvinistic churches allowed themselves to deviate into the same track, they did not ascend to a higher conception than that of Rome's world-church, but descended to distinctly lower ground. Happily I may conclude by bearing witness that both our Synod of Dordt, and your not less venerable Westminster Assembly, have honored again the ecumenical character of our Reformed Churches, thereby censuring as unpardonable, every deviation from the only right principle.

Having thus far given an outline of the *nature* of the Church, and the *form* of its *manifestation*, let me now draw your attention in the last place to the purpose of its appearance on earth. I shall not say anything for the present on the separation of Church and State. This will naturally find place in the next Lecture. At present I confine myself to the *purpose* that has been assigned to the Church in its pilgrimage through the world. That purpose cannot be human or egoistic, *to prepare the believer for Heaven*. A regenerate child, dying in the cradle, goes straight to Heaven, without any further preparation and wheresoever the Holy Ghost has kindled the spark of Eternal life in the soul, the perseverance of the saints assures the certainty of eternal salvation. Nay, upon earth also, the Church exists merely *for the sake of God*. Regeneration is sufficient for the elect man, to make him sure of his eternal destiny, but it is not enough to satisfy the glory of God in His work among men. For the glory of our God it is necessary to have regeneration followed by conversion, and to this conversion the Church must contribute, by means of the preaching of the Word. In the regenerate man glows the spark, but only in the converted man does the spark burst into a blaze, and that blaze radiates the light from the Church into the world, that, according to our Lord's commandment, our Father, which is in Heaven, may be glorified. And both our conversion and our sanctification in good works are only then marked by the lofty character which Jesus demands, when we make them serve, in the first place, not as the guarantee of our own salvation, but rather the glorifying of God. In the second place, the Church must fan this blaze, and make it brighten, by the communion of the saints and by the Sacraments. Only when hundreds of candles are burning from one candelabrum, can the full brightness of the soft candlelight strike us, and in the same way it is the communion of saints which has to unite the many small lights of the single believers so that they may mutually increase their brightness, and Christ, walking in the midst of the seven candlesticks, may sacramentally purify the glow of their brightness to a still more brilliant fervour. Thus the purpose of the Church does not lie in us, but in God, and in the glory of His name.

From this solemn purpose originates, in the same way, the severely spiritual cultus which Calvinism tried to restore in the services of the Church. Even Von Hartman, the far-from-Christian philosopher, perceived that cultus becomes more religious just in proportion as it has the courage to despise all external show, and the energy to evolve itself from symbolism, in order to clothe itself in beauty of a much higher order,—*the inward, spiritual beauty of the worshipping soul.* Sensual church services tend to soothe and flatter *man* religiously, and only the purely spiritual service of Calvinism aims at the pure worship of God, and at adoration of Him in spirit and truth.—The same tendency leads our church discipline, that indispensable element of every genuine Calvinistic church activity. Church discipline was also instituted in the first place, not to prevent scandals, not even primarily to prune the wild branches, but rather *to preserve the sanctity of the Cove nant of God,* and ever to impress upon the outside world the solemn fact that God is too pure to look upon evil.—Finally we have the service of Church *philanthropy,* in the Diaconate which Calvin alone understood, and restored to its primordial honor. Neither Rome nor the Greek Church, neither the Lutheran nor the Episcopal Church, caught the real meaning of the Diaconate. Calvinism alone has restored the Diaconate to its place of honor, as an indispensable and constitutive element of ecclesiastical life. But, in this Diaconate, also, the lofty principle must prevail that it may not glorify those who give alms, but only the name of Him who moves the hearts of the people to liberality. The Deacons are not *our* servants, but servants of Christ. That which we commit to them we simply give back to Christ, as stewards of what is His property; and in His name it must be distributed to His poor,— our brothers and sisters. The poor church-member, who thanks the

Deacon and the giver, but not Christ, actually denies Him Who is the real and divine Giver, and Who through His Deacons, purposes to make it manifest that for the whole man, and for the whole of life He is the *Christus Consolator*, the Heavenly Redeemer, anointed and appointed by God Himself, for our fallen race, from all eternity. And so, as you see, the result proves incontestably that in Calvinism, the fundamental conception of the *Church* fits perfectly to the fundamental idea of *Religion*. All egoism and eudæmonism are excluded from both, even unto the end. Always and ever we have a *Religion*, and a *Church*, for the sake of God, and not for the sake of man. The origin of the Church is in God, its form of manifestation is from God, and from beginning to end, its purpose is and remains *to magnify God's glory*.

Now finally, I come to the fruit of religion in our *practical life,* or the position taken by Calvinism in the *question of morals,*—the third and last division, with which this lecture on *Calvinism and Religion* will naturally conclude.

Here, the first thing that attracts our attention is the apparent contradiction between a confession, which, it is alleged, blunts the edge of moral incentives, and a practice, which, in moral earnestness exceeds the practice of all other religions. The Antinomian and the Puritan seemed to be mingled in this field like tares and wheat, so that at first sight it seemed as though the Antinomian were the logical result of the Calvinistic confession, and as though it were only by a fortunate inconsistency that the Puritan could infuse the warmth of his moral earnestness into the all-congealing chill emanating from the dogma of predestination. Romanists, Lutherans, Arminians and Libertines have ever charged against Calvinism that its absolute doctrine of predestination, culminating in the perseverance of saints, must necessarily result in a too easy conscience and a dangerous laxity of morals. But Calvinism answers this charge, not by opposing reasoning against reasoning, but by putting a fact of world-wide reputation over against this false deduction of fictitious consequences. It simply asks: "What rival moral fruits have other religions to oppose if we point to the high moral earnestness of the Puritans?" "Shall we continue in sin that grace may abound" is the old diabolical whisper which the evil spirit hurled against the Holy Apostle himself in the childhood of the Christian Church. And when, in the sixteenth century the Heidelberg Catechism had to defend Calvinism against the shameful charge: "Does not this doctrine lead to careless and ungodly lives?" Ursinus and Olevianus had to deal with nothing less than the echoing and monotonous repetition of the same old slander. Certainly the ungodly lust to persist in, and even to foster, indwelling sin, yea, even Antinomianism itself, again and again abused the Calvinistic confession, seizing it like a shield, to hide the carnal appetites of the unconverted heart. But as little as the mechanical repetition of a written confession had ever anything in common with genuine religion, just so little may the Calvinistic Confession be made responsible for those reverberating stone pillars, echoing Calvin's formulæ, but without a grain of Calvinistic earnestness in their heart. He only is the real Calvinist, and may raise the Calvinistic banner, who in his own soul, personally, has been struck by the Majesty of the Almighty, and yielding to the overpowering might of his eternal Love, has dared to proclaim this majestic love, over against Satan and the world, and the worldliness of his own heart, in the personal conviction of being chosen by God Himself, and therefore of having to thank Him and Him alone, for every grace everlasting. Such an one could not but tremble before the might and the majesty of God, as a matter of course accepting His Word as the ruling principle of His conduct in life—a principle which has led so far that for its strong attachment to the Scriptures, Calvinism has been censured as being a *nomistic* religion, but without any warrant. *Nomistic* is the appropriate name for a religion which proclaims *salvation* to be attained by the fulfilment of the law, while Calvinism, on the other hand, in a thoroughly soteriological sense, never derived salvation but from Christ and the atoning fruit of His merits.

But it remained the special trait of Calvinism that it placed the believer *before the face of God,* not only in His church, but also in his personal, family, social, and political life. The majesty of God, and the authority of God press upon the Calvinist in the whole of his human existence. He is a pilgrim, not in the sense that he is marching through a world with which he has no concern, but in the sense that at every step of the long way he must remember his responsibility to that God so full of majesty, who awaits him at his journey's end. In front of the Portal which opens for him, on the entrance into Eternity, stands the *Last Judgment*; and that judgment shall be one broad and comprehensive test, to ascertain whether the long pilgrimage has been accomplished with a heart that aimed at God's glory, and in accordance with the ordinances of the Most High.

What now does the Calvinist mean by his faith in the ordinances of God? Nothing less than the firmly rooted conviction that all life has first been in the *thoughts* of God, before it came to be realized in *Creation*. Hence all created life necessarily bears in itself a law for its existence, instituted by God Himself. There is no life outside us in Nature, without such divine ordinances,—ordinances which are called the laws of Nature—a term which we are willing to accept, provided we understand thereby, not laws originating *from* Nature, but laws imposed *upon* Nature. So, there are ordinances of God for the firmament above, and ordinances for the earth below, by means of which this world is maintained, and, as the Psalmist says, These ordinances are the servants of God. Consequently there are ordinances of God for our bodies, for the blood that courses through our arteries and veins, and for our lungs as the organs of respiration. And even so are there ordinances of God, in logic, to regulate our thoughts; ordinances of God for our imagination, in the domain of æsthetics; and so, also, strict ordinances of God for the whole of human life in the *domain of morals*. Not moral ordinances in the sense of summary general laws, which leave the decision in concrete and detailed instances to ourselves, but just as the ordinance of God determines the course of the smallest asteroid, as well as the orbit of the mightiest star, so also these moral ordinances of God descend to the smallest and most particular details, stating to us what in every case is to be considered as the will of God. And those ordinances of God, ruling both the mightiest problems and the smallest trifles, are urged upon us, not like the statutes of a law-book, not like rules which may be read from paper, not like a codification of life, which could even for a single moment, exercise any authority of itself—but they are urged upon us as the constant will of the Omnipresent and Almighty God, who at every instant is determining the course of life, ordaining its laws and continually binding us by His divine authority. The Calvinist does not, like Kant, ascend in his reasoning from the *"Du sollst"* (Thou shalt) to the idea of a lawgiver, but, because he stands before the face of God, because he sees God, and walks with God, and feels God in the whole of his being and existence, therefore he cannot withdraw his ear from that never silenced *"Thou shalt,"* which proceeds continually from his God, in nature, in his body, in his reason, and in his action.

Thence it follows that the true Calvinist adjusts himself to these ordinances not by force, as though they were a yoke of which he would like to rid himself, but with the same readiness with which we follow a guide through the desert, recognizing that *we* are ignorant of the path, which the guide knows, and therefore acknowledging that there is no safety but in closely following in his footsteps. When our respiration is disturbed, we try irresistibly and immediately to remove the disturbance, and to make it normal again, *i.e.,* to restore it, by bringing it again into accordance with the ordinances which God has given for man's respiration. To succeed in this gives us a feeling of unspeakable relief. Just so, in every disturbance of the normal life the believer has to strive as speedily as possible to restore his spiritual respiration, according to the moral commands of his God, because only after this restoration can the inward life again thrive freely in his soul, and renewed energetic action become possible. Therefore every distinction between general moral ordinances, and more special *Christian* commandments is unknown to him. Can we imagine that at one time God willed to rule things in a certain moral order, but that now, in Christ, He wills to rule it otherwise? As though He were not the Eternal, the Unchangeable, Who, from the very hour of creation, even unto all eternity, had willed, wills, and shall will and maintain, one and the same firm moral world-order! Verily Christ has swept away the dust with which man's sinful limitations had covered up this world-order, and has made it glitter again in its original brilliancy. Verily Christ, and He alone, has disclosed to us the eternal love of Christ which was, from the beginning, the moving principle of this world-order. Above all, Christ has strengthened in us the ability to walk in this world-order with a firm, unfaltering step. But the world-order itself remains just what it was from the beginning. It lays full claim, not only to the believer (as though less were required from the unbeliever), but to every human being and to all human relationships. Hence Calvinism does not lead us to philosophize on a so-called moral life, as though *we* had to create, to discover, or to regulate this life. Calvinism simply places us under the impress of the majesty of God, and subjects us to His eternal ordinances and unchangeable commandments. Hence it is that, for the Calvinist, all ethical study is based on the Law of Sinai, not as though at that time the moral world-order began to be fixed, but to honor the Law of Sinai, as the divinely authentic summary of that original moral law which God wrote in the heart of man, at his creation, and which God is re-writing on the tables of every heart at its conversion. The Calvinist is led to submit himself to the conscience, not as to an individual lawgiver, which every person carries about in himself, but as to a direct *sensus divinitatis,* through which God Himself stirs up the inner man, and subjects him to His judgment. He does not hold to religion, with its *dogmatics,* as a *separate entity,* and then place his moral life with its ethics as a *second entity* alongside of religion, but he holds to religion as placing him in the presence of God Himself, Who thereby embues him with His divine will. Love and adoration are, to Calvin, themselves the motives of every spiritual activity, and thus the fear of God is imparted to the whole of life as a reality—into the family, and into society, into science and art, into personal life, and into the political career. A redeemed man who in *all* things and in *all* the choices of life is controlled solely by the most searching and heart-stirring reverence for a God Who is ever present to his consciousness, and Who ever holds him in His eye—thus does the Calvinistic type present itself in history. Always and in all things the deepest, the most sacred reverence for the ever-present God as the rule of life—this is the only true picture of the original Puritan.

The avoidance of the world has never been the Calvinistic mark, but the shibboleth of the Anabaptist. The specific, anabaptistical dogma of "avoidance" proves this. According to this dogma, the Anabaptists, announcing themselves as "saints," were severed from the world. They stood in opposition to it. They refused to take the oath; they abhorred all military service; they condemned the holding of public offices. Here already, they shaped a new world, in the midst of this world of sin, which however had nothing to do with this our present existence. They rejected all obligation and responsibility towards the old world, and they avoided it systematically, for fear of contamination, and contagion. But this is just what the Calvinist always disputed and denied. It is not true that there are two worlds, a bad one and a good, which are fitted into each other. It is one and the same person whom God created perfect and who afterwards fell, and became a sinner—and it is this same "ego" of the old sinner who is born again, and who enters into eternal life. So, also, it is one and the same world which once exhibited all the glory of Paradise, which was afterwards smitten with the curse, and which, since the Fall, is upheld by common grace; which has now been redeemed and saved by Christ, in its center, and which shall pass through the horror of the judgment into the state of glory. For this very reason the Calvinist cannot shut himself up in his church and abandon the world to its fate. He feels, rather, his high calling to push the development of this world to an even higher stage, and to do this in constant accordance with God's ordinance, for the sake of God, upholding, in the midst of so much painful corruption, everything that is honorable, lovely, and of good report among men. Therefore it is that we see in History (if I may be permitted to speak of my own ancestors) that scarcely had Calvinism been firmly established in the Netherlands for a quarter of a century when there was a rustling of life in all directions, and an indomitable energy was fermenting in every department of human activity, and their commerce and trade, their handicrafts and industry, their agriculture and horticulture, their art and science, flourished with a brilliancy previously unknown, and imparted a new impulse for an entirely new development of life, to the whole of Western Europe.

This admits of only one exception, and this exception I wish both to maintain and to place in its proper light. What I mean is this. Not *every* intimate intercourse with the unconverted world is deemed lawful, by Calvinism, for it placed a barrier against the too unhallowed influence of this world by putting a distinct "veto" upon three things, *card playing, theatres,* and *dancing*—three forms of amusement which I shall first treat separately, and then set forth in their combined significance.

Card-playing has been placed under a ban by Calvinism, not as though games of all kinds were forbidden, nor as though something demoniacal lurked in the cards themselves, but because it fosters in our heart the dangerous tendency to look away from God, and to put our trust in *Fortune* or *Luck*. A game which is decided by keenness of vision, quickness of action, and range of experience, is ennobling in its character, but a game like cards, which is chiefly decided by the way in which the cards are arranged in the pack, and blindly distributed, induces us to attach a certain significance to that fatal imaginative power, outside of God, called *Chance* or *Fortune*. To this kind of unbelief, every one of us is inclined. The fever of stock-gambling shows daily how much more strongly people are attracted and influenced by the nod of Fortune, than by solid application to their work. Therefore the Calvinist judged that the rising generation ought to be guarded against this dangerous tendency, because by means of card-playing it would be fostered. And since the sensation of God's ever-enduring presence was felt by Calvin and his adherents as the never-failing source from which they drew their stern seriousness of life, they could not help loathing a game which poisoned this source by placing Fortune above the disposition of God, and the hankering after chance above the firm confidence in His will. To fear God, and to bid for the favors of Fortune, seemed to him as irreconcilable as fire and water.

Entirely different objections were entertained against *Theatre-going*. In itself there is nothing sinful in fiction—the power of the imagination is a precious gift of God Himself. Neither is there any special evil in *dramatic* imagination. How highly did Milton appreciate Shakespeare's Drama, and did not he himself write in dramatic form? Nor did the evil lie in public theatrical representations, as such. Public performances were given for all the people at Geneva, in the Market Place, in Calvin's time, and with his approval. No, that which offended our ancestors was not the comedy or tragedy, nor should have been the opera, in itself, but the *moral sacrifice* which as a rule was demanded of actors and actresses for the amusement of the public. A theatrical troop, in those days especially, stood, morally, rather low. This low moral standard resulted partly from the fact that the constant and ever-changing presentation of the character of another person finally hampers the moulding of your personal character; and partly because our modern Theaters, unlike the Greek, have introduced the presence of women on the stage, the prosperity of the Theater being too often gauged by the measure in which a woman jeopardizes the most sacred treasures God entrusts to her, her stainless name, and irreproachable conduct. Certainly, a strictly normal Theater is very well conceivable; but with the exception of a few large cities, such Theaters would neither be sufficiently patronized nor could exist financially; and the actual fact remains that, taking all the world over, the prosperity of a Theater often increases in proportion to the moral degradation of the actors. Too often therefore—Hall Caine in his *"Christian"* corroborated once more the sad truth—the prosperity of Theaters is purchased at the cost of manly character, and of female purity. And the purchase of delight for the ear and the eye at the price of such a moral hecatomb, the Calvinist, who honored whatever was human in man for the sake of God, could not but condemn.

Finally, so far as the *dance* is concerned, even worldly papers, like the Parisian *"Figaro,"* at present justify the position of the Calvinist. Only recently an article in this paper called attention to the moral pain with which a father takes his daughter into the ball-room for the first time. This moral pain, it declared, is evident, in Paris at least, to all who are familiar with the whisperings, indecent looks and actions prevalent in those pleasure-loving circles. Here, also, the Calvinist does not protest against the Dance itself, but exclusively against the impurity to which it is often in danger of leading.

With this I return to the barrier of which I spoke. Our fathers perceived excellently well that it was just these three: Dancing, Card-playing, and Theater going, with which the world was madly in love. In worldly circles these pleasures were not regarded as secondary trifles, but honored as all-important matters: and whoever dared to attack them exposed himself to the bitterest scorn and enmity. For this very reason, they recognized in these three the *Rubicon* which no true Calvinist could cross without sacrificing his earnestness to dangerous mirth, and the fear of the Lord to often far from spotless pleasures. And now may I ask, has not the result justified their strong and brave protest? Even yet, after a lapse of three centuries, you will find, in my Calvinistic country, in Scotland, and in your own States, entire social circles into which this worldliness is never allowed to enter, but in which the richness of human life has turned, from without, inward, and in which, as the result of a sound spiritual concentration, there has been developed such a deep sense of everything high, and such an energy for everything holy, as to excite the envy even of our antagonists. Not only has the wing of the butterfly in those circles been preserved intact, but even the golddust upon this wing shines as brilliantly as ever.

This now is the proof to which I invite your respectful attention. Our age is far ahead of the Calvinistic age in its overflowing mass of ethical essays and treatises and learned expositions. Philosophers and Theologians really vie with one another in discovering for us (or in *hiding* from us, just as you may be pleased to put it) the straight road in the domain of morals. But there is something that all this host of learned scholars have *not* been able to do. They have not been able to restore *moral firmness* to the enfeebled public conscience.

Rather must we complain that ever more and more the foundations of our moral building are gradually being loosened and unsettled, until finally there remains not one stronghold left of which the people in their wider ranks can feel that it guarantees *moral certainty* for the Future. Statesmen and Jurists are openly proclaiming the right of the strongest; the ownership of property is called stealing; free love has been advocated; and honesty is ridiculed. A pantheist has dared to put Jesus and Nero on the same footing; and Nietzsche, going further still, deemed Christ's blessing of the meek to be the curse of humanity.

Now compare with all this the marvelous results of three centuries of Calvinism. Calvinism understood that the world was not to be saved by ethical philosophizing, but only by the restoration of tenderness of conscience. Therefore it did not indulge in reasoning, but appealed directly to the soul, and placed it face to face with the Living God, so that the heart trembled at His holy majesty, and in that majesty, discovered the glory of His love. And when, going back in this historical review, you observe how thoroughly corrupt and rotten Calvinism found the world, to what depth moral life at that time had sunk, in the courts, and among the people, in the clergy and among the leaders of science, among men and women, among the higher and the lower classes of society—then what censor among you will dare to deny the palm of moral victory to Calvinism, which in one generation, though nunted from the battlefield to the scaffold, created, throughout five nations at once, wide serious groups of noble men, and still nobler women, hitherto unsurpassed in the loftiness of their ideal conceptions and unequalled in the power of their moral self-control.

THIRD LECTURE

CALVINISM AND POLITICS

MY third lecture leaves the sanctuary of religion and enters upon the domain of the State—the first transition from the sacred circle to the secular field of human life. Only now therefore we proceed, summarily and in principle, to combat the unhistorical suggestion that Calvinism represents an exclusively ecclesiastical and dogmatic movement.

The religious momentum of Calvinism has placed also beneath political Society a fundamental conception, all its own, just because it not merely pruned the branches and cleaned the stem, but reached down to the very root of our human life.

That this *had to be so* becomes evident at once to everyone who is able to appreciate the fact that no political scheme has ever become dominant which was not founded in a specific religious or anti-religious conception. And that this *has* been the fact, as regards Calvinism, may appear from the political changes which it has effected in those three historic lands of political freedom, the Netherlands, England and America.

Every competent historian will without exception confirm the words of Bancroft: "The fanatic for Calvinism was a fanatic for liberty, for in the moral warfare for freedom, his creed was a part of his army, and his most faithful ally in the battle."[1] And Groen van Prinsterer has thus expressed it: "In Calvinism lies the origin and guarantee of our constitutional liberties." That Calvinism has led public law into new paths, first in Western Europe, then in two Continents, and today more and more among all civilized nations, is admitted by all scientific students, if not yet fully by public opinion.

---

1) BANCROFT, *History of the United States of America*. Fifteenth Edition; Boston, 1853; I, 464; Ed. New York, 1891, I, 319.

But for the purpose I have in view, the mere statement of this important fact is insufficient.

In order that the influence of Calvinism on our political development may be felt, it must be shown for what fundamental political conceptions Calvinism has opened the door, and how these political conceptions sprang from its root principle.

This dominating principle was not, soteriologically, justification by faith, but, in the widest sense cosmologically, *the Sovereignty of the Triune God over the whole Cosmos,* in all its spheres and kingdoms, visible and invisible. A *primordial* Sovereignty which eradiates in mankind in a threefold deduced supremacy, *viz.,* 1. The Sovereignty in the *State*; 2. The Sovereignty in *Society*; and 3. The Sovereignty in the *Church.*

Allow me to argue this matter in detail by pointing out to you how this threefold deduced Sovereignty was understood by Calvinism.

First then a deduced Sovereignty in that political sphere, which is defined as *the State.* And then we admit that the impulse to form states arises from man's social nature, which was expressed already by Aristotle, when he called man a "ζῷον πολιτικο'ν." God might have created men as disconnected individuals, standing side by side and without genealogical coherence. Just as Adam was separately created, the second and third and every further man might have been individually called into existence; but this was *not* the case.

Man is created from man, and by virtue of his birth he is organically united with the whole race. Together we form *one humanity,* not only with those who are living now, but also with all the generations behind us and with all those who shall come after us—pulverized into millions though we may be. All the human race is from *one blood.* The conception of *States,* however, which subdivide the earth into continents, and each continent into morsels, does not harmonize with this idea. Then only would the organic unity of our race be realized politically, if *one State* could embrace all the world, and if the whole of humanity were associated in one world empire. Had sin not intervened, no doubt this would actually have been so. If sin, as a disintegrating force, had not divided humanity into different sections, nothing would have marred or broken the organic unity of our race. And the mistake of the Alexanders, and of the Augusti, and of the Napoleons, was not that they were charmed with the thought of the *One World-empire,* but it was this—that they endeavored to realize this idea notwithstanding that the force of sin had dissolved our unity.

In like manner the international cosmopolitan endeavors of the Social-democracy present, in their conception of union, an ideal, which on this very account charms us, even when we are aware that they try to reach the unattainable, in endeavoring to realize this high and holy ideal, now and in a sinful world. Nay, even Anarchy, conceived as the attempt to undo all mechanical connections among men, together with the undoing of all human authority, and to encourage, in their stead, the growth of a new organic tie, arising from nature itself—I say, all this is nothing but a looking backward after a lost paradise.

For, indeed, without sin there would have been neither magistrate nor state-order; but political life, in its entirety, would have evolved itself, after a patriarchal fashion, from the life of the family. Neither bar of justice nor police, nor army, nor navy, is conceivable in a world without sin; and thus every rule and ordinance and law would drop away, even as all control and assertion of the power of the magistrate would disappear, were life to develop itself, normally and without hindrance, from its own organic impulse. Who binds up, where nothing is broken? Who uses crutches, where the limbs are sound?

Every State-formation, every assertion of the power of the magistrate, every mechanical means of compelling order and of guaranteeing a safe course of life is therefore always something unnatural; something against which the deeper aspirations of our nature rebel; and which, on this very account, may become the source both of a dreadful abuse of power, on the part of those who exercise it, and of a continuous revolt on the part of the multitude. Thus originated the battle of the ages between *Authority* and *Liberty,* and in this battle it was the very innate thirst for liberty which proved itself the God-ordained means to bridle the authority wheresoever it degenerated into despotism. And thus all true conception of the nature of the State and of the assumption of authority by the magistrate, and on the other hand all true conception of the right and duty of the people to defend liberty, depends on what Calvinism has here placed in the foreground, as the primordial truth—*that God has instituted the magistrates, by reason of sin.*

In this one thought are hidden both the *light-side* and the *shady-side* of the life of the State. The *shady-side* for this multitude of states ought not to exist; there should be only one world-empire. These magistrates rule mechanically and do not harmonize with our nature. And this authority of government is exercised by sinful *men,* and is therefore subject to all manner of despotic ambitions. But the *light-side* also, for a sinful humanity, without division of states, without law and government, and without ruling authority, would be a veritable hell on earth; or at least a repetition of that which existed on earth when God drowned the first degenerate race in the deluge. Calvinism has, therefore, by its deep conception of sin laid bare the true root of state-life, and has taught us two things: first—that we have gratefully to receive, from the hand of God, the institution of the State with its magistrates, as a means of preservation, now indeed indispensable. And on the other hand also that, by virtue of our natural impulse, we must ever watch against the danger which lurks, for our personal liberty, in the power of the State.

But Calvinism has done more. In Politics also it taught us that the *human* element—here *the people*—may not be considered as the principal thing, so that God is only dragged in to help this people in the hour of its need; but on the contrary that God, in His Majesty, must flame before the eyes of every nation, and that all nations together are to be reckoned before Him as a drop in a bucket and as the small dust of the balances. From the ends of the earth God cites all nations and peoples before His high judgment seat. For God created the nations. They exist for Him. They are His own. And therefore all these nations, and in them humanity, must exist for His glory and consequently after his ordinances, in order that in their well-being, when they walk after His ordinances, His divine wisdom may shine forth.

When therefore humanity falls apart through sin, in a multiplicity of separate peoples; when sin, in the bosom of these nations, separates men and tears them apart, and when sin reveals itself in all manner of shame and unrighteousness—the glory of God demands that these horrors be bridled, that order return to this chaos, and that a compulsory force, from without, assert itself to make human society a possibility.

This right is possessed by God, and by Him alone.

No man has the right to rule over another man, otherwise such a right necessarily, and immediately becomes the *right of the strongest*. As the tiger in the jungle rules over the defenceless antelope, so on the banks of the Nile a Pharaoh ruled over the progenitors of the fellaheen of Egypt.

Nor can a group of men, by contract, from their own right, compel you to obey a fellow-man. What binding force is there for me in the allegation that ages ago one of my progenitors made a "Contrat Social," with other men of that time? As man I stand free and bold, over against the most powerful of my fellow-men.

I do not speak of the family, for here organic, natural ties rule; but in the sphere of the State I do not yield or bow down to anyone, who is man, as I am.

Authority over men cannot arise from men. Just as little from a majority over against a minority, for history shows, almost on every page, that very often the *minority was right*. And thus to the first Calvinistic thesis that *sin alone has necessitated the institution of governments,* this second and no less momentous thesis is added that: *all authority of governments on earth originates from the Sovereignty of God alone.* When God says to me, "obey," then I humbly bow my head, without compromising in the least my personal dignity, as a man. For, in like proportion as you degrade yourself, by bowing low to a child of man, whose breath is in his nostrils; so, on the other hand do you raise yourself, if you submit to the authority of the Lord of heaven and earth.

Thus the word of Scripture stands: "By Me kings reign," or as the apostle has elsewhere declared: "The powers, that be, are ordained of God. Therefore he that resisteth the power, withstandeth the ordinance of God." The magistrate is an instrument of "common grace," to thwart all license and outrage and to shield the good against the evil. But he is more. Besides all this he is instituted by God as *His Servant,* in order that he may preserve the glorious work of God, in the creation of humanity, from total destruction. Sin attacks God's handiwork, God's plan, God's justice, God's honor, as the supreme Artificer and Builder. Thus God, ordaining the powers that be, in order that, through their instrumentality, He might maintain His justice against the strivings of sin, has given to the magistrate the terrible right of life and death. Therefore all the powers that be, whether in empires or in republics, in cities or in states, rule *"by the grace of God."* For the same reason justice bears a holy character. And from the same motive every citizen is bound to obey, not only from dread of punishment, but for the sake of conscience.

Further Calvin has expressly stated that authority, as such, is in no way affected by the question how a government is instituted and in what form it reveals itself. It is well known that personally he preferred *a republic*, and that he cherished no predilection for a monarchy, as if this were the divine and ideal form of government. This indeed would have been the case in a sinless state. For had sin not entered, God would have remained the sole king of all men, and this condition will return, in the glory to come, when God once more will be all and in all. God's own direct government is absolutely *monarchial*; no monotheist will deny it. But Calvin considered a co-operation of many persons under mutual control, i.e., *a republic*, desirable, now that a mechanical institution of government is necessitated by reason of sin.

In his system, however, this could only amount to a gradual difference in practical excellency, but never to a fundamental difference, as regards the essence of authority. He considers a monarchy and an aristocracy, as well as a democracy, both possible and practicable forms of government; provided it be unchangeably maintained, that no one on earth can claim authority over his fellow-men, unless it be laid upon him *"by the grace of God"*; and therefore, the ultimate duty of obedience is imposed upon us not by man, but by God Himself.

The question how those persons, who by divine authority are to be clothed with power, are indicated, cannot, according to Calvin, be answered alike for all peoples and for all time. And yet he does not hesitate to state, in an ideal sense, that the most desirable conditions exist, *where the people itself chooses its own magistrates.*

Where such a condition exists he thinks that the people should gratefully recognize therein a favor of God, precisely as it has been expressed in the preamble of more than one of your constitutions; —"Grateful to almighty God that He gave us the power to choose our own magistrates." In his Commentary on Samuel, Calvin therefore admonishes such peoples:—"And ye, O peoples, to whom God gave the liberty to choose your own magistrates, see to it, that ye do not forfeit this favor, by electing to the positions of highest honor, rascals and enemies of God."

I may add that the popular choice gains the day, as a matter of course, where no other rule exists, or where the existing rule falls away. Wherever new States have been founded, except by conquest or force, the first government has always been founded by popular choice; and so also where the highest authority had fallen into disorder, either by want of a determination of the right of succession, or through the violence of revolution, it has always been the people who, through their representatives, claimed the right to restore it. But with equal decision, Calvin asserts that God has the sovereign power, in the way of His dispensing Providence, to take from a people this most desirable condition, or never to bestow it at all, when a nation is unfit for it, or, by its sin, has utterly forfeited the blessing.

The historic development of a people shows, as a matter of course, in what other ways authority is bestowed. This bestowal may flow from the right of inheritance, as in a hereditary monarchy. It may result from a hard-fought war, even as Pilate had power over Jesus, "given him from above." It may proceed from electors, as it did in the old German empire. It may rest with the States of the country, as was the case in the old Dutch republic. In a word it may assume a variety of forms, because there is an endless difference in the development of nations. A form of government like your own could not exist one day in China. Even now, the people of Russia are unfit for any form of constitutional government. And among the Kaffirs and Hottentots of Africa, even a government, such as exists in Russia, would be wholly inconceivable. All this is determined and appointed by God, through the hidden counsel of His providence.

All this, however, is no *theocracy*. A theocracy was only found in Israel, because in Israel, God intervened immediately. For both by *Urim and Thummim* and by *Prophecy;* both by His saving miracles, and by His chastising judgments, He held in His own hand the jurisdiction and the leadership of His people. But the Calvinistic confession of the Sovereignty of God holds good for *all* the world, is true for all nations, and is of force in all authority, which man exercises over man; even in the authority which parents possess over their children. It is therefore a political faith which may be summarily expressed in these three theses: 1. God only—and never any creature—is possessed of sovereign rights, in the destiny of the nations, because God alone created them, maintains them by His Almighty power, and rules them by His ordinances. 2. Sin has, in the realm of politics, broken down the direct government of God, and therefore the exercise of authority, for the purpose of government, has subsequently been invested in men, as a mechanical remedy. And 3. In whatever form this authority may reveal itself, man never possesses power over his fellow-man in any other way than by an authority which descends upon him from the majesty of God.

Directly opposed to this Calvinistic confession there are two other theories. That of the *Popular-sovereignty,* as it has been antitheistically proclaimed at Paris in 1789; and that of *State-sovereignty,* as it has of late been developed by the historicopantheistic school of Germany. Both these theories are at heart identical, but for the sake of clearness they demand a separate treatment.

What was it that impelled and animated the spirits of men in the great French revolution? Indignation at abuses, which had crept in? A horror of a crowned despotism? A noble defense of the rights and liberties of the people? In part certainly, but in all this there is so little that is sinful, that even a Calvinist gratefully recognizes, in these three particulars, the divine judgment, which at that time was executed in Paris.

But the impelling force of the French Revolution did not lie in this hatred of abuses. When Edmund Burke compares the "glorious Revolution" of 1688 with the principle of the Revolution of 1789, he says: "Our revolution and that of France are just the reverse of each other, in almost every particular, and in the whole spirit of the transaction."*

This same Edmund Burke, so bitter an antagonist of the French revolution, has manfully defended your own rebellion against England, as "arising from a principle of energy, showing itself in this good people the main cause of a free spirit, the most adverse to all implicit submission of mind and opinion."

The three great revolutions in the Calvinistic world left untouched the glory of God, nay, they even proceeded from the acknowledgement of His majesty. Every one will admit this of our rebellion against Spain, under William the Silent. Nor has it even been doubted of the "glorious Revolution," which was crowned by the arrival of William III of Orange and the overthrow of the Stuarts. But it is equally true of your own Revolution. It is expressed in so many words in the *Declaration of Independence,* by John Hancock, that the Americans asserted themselves by virtue— "of the law of nature and of nature's God"; that they acted—"as endowed by the Creator with certain unalienable rights"; that they appealed to—"the Supreme Judge of the world for the rectitude of their intention";[1] and that they sent forth their "declaration of Independence"—"With a firm reliance on the protection of Divine Providence."[2] In the "Articles of Confederation" it is confessed in the preamble,—"that it hath pleased the great Governor of the world to incline the hearts of the legislators."[3] It is also declared in the preamble of the Constitution of many of the States:— "Grateful to Almighty God for the civil, political and religious liberty, which He has so long permitted us to enjoy and looking unto Him, for a blessing upon our endeavors."[4] God is there honored as "the Sovereign Ruler,"[5] and the "Legislator of the Universe"[6] and it is there specifically admitted, that from God alone the people received "the right to choose their own form of government."[7] In one of the meetings of the Convention, Franklin

---

* BURKE, *Works,* III, p. 25, Ed. McLean, London.
1. *American Constitutions,* by FRANKLIN B. HUGH; Albany; Weed, Parsons & Co.; 1872. Vol. I, p. 5.
2. *Ibidem,* p. 8.
3. *Ibidem,* p. 19.
4. *Ibidem,* II, p. 549.
5. *Ibidem,* p. 555.
6. *Ibidem,* p. 555.
7. *Ibidem,* p. 549.

proposed, in a moment of supreme anxiety, that they should ask wisdom from God in prayer. And if any one should still doubt whether or not the American revolution was homogeneous with that of Paris, this doubt is fully set at rest by the bitter fight in 1793 between Jefferson and Hamilton. Therefore it remains as the German historian Von Holtz stated it: "Es wäre Thorheit zu sagen dass die Rousseauschen Schriften einen Einfluss auf die Entwicklung in America ausgeübt haben."[1] ("Mere madness would it be to say that the American revolution borrowed its impelling energy from Rousseau and his writings.") Or as Hamilton himself expressed it, that he considered "the French Revolution to be no more akin to the American Revolution than the faithless wife in a French novel is like the Puritan matron in New England."[2]

The French Revolution is in principle distinct from all these *national* revolutions, which were undertaken with praying lips and with trust in the help of God. The French Revolution ignores God. It opposes God. It refuses to recognize a deeper ground of political life than that which is found in nature, that is, in this instance, in man himself. Here the first article of the confession of the most absolute infidelity is—"ni Dieu ni maitre." The sovereign God is dethroned and man with his free will is placed on the vacant seat. It is the will of man which determines all things. All power, all authority proceeds from man. Thus one comes from the individual man to the many men; and in those many men conceived as *the people,* there is thus hidden the deepest fountain of all sovereignty. There is no question, as in your Constitution, of a sover-

---

1. Von Holz, *Verfassung und Democratie der Vereinigten Staten von America;* Dusseldorf, 1873; I, p. 96.

2. John F. Morse, *Thomas Jefferson;* Boston, 1883; p. 147. In a positively *Christian* sense Hamilton proposed in a letter to Bayard (April, 1801) the founding of "A Christian Constitutional Society," and wrote in another letter, quoted by Henry Cabot Lodge, *Alexander Hamilton;* Boston, 1892; p. 256: "When I find the doctrines of Atheism openly advanced in the Parisian Convention, and heard with loud applause; when I see the sword of fanaticism extended to force a political creed upon citizens, who were invited to submit to the arms of France as the harbingers of Liberty; when I behold the hand of rapacity outstretched to prostrate and ravish the monuments of religious worship, I acknowledge, that I am glad to believe, that *there is no real resemblance between what was the cause of America and the cause of France.*"

eignty derived from God, which He, under certain conditions, implants in the people. Here an original sovereignty asserts itself, which everywhere and in all states can only proceed from the people itself, having no deeper root than in the human will. It is a sovereignty of the people therefore, which is perfectly identical with atheism. And herein lies its self-abasement. In the sphere of Calvinism, as also in your *Declaration,* the knee is bowed to God, while over against man the head is proudly lifted up. But here, from the standpoint of the sovereignty of the people, the fist is defiantly clenched against God, while man grovels before his fellow-men, tinseling over this self-abasement by the ludicrous fiction that, thousands of years ago, men, of whom no one has any remembrance, concluded a political contract, or, as they called it, *"Contrat Social."* Now, do you ask for the result? Then, let History tell you how the rebellion of the Netherlands, the "glorious Revolution" of England and your own rebellion against the British Crown have brought liberty to honor; and answer for yourself the question: Has the French Revolution resulted in anything else but the shackling of liberty in the irons of State-omnipotence? Indeed, no country in our 19th century has had a sadder State-history than France.

No wonder that scientific Germany has broken away from this fictitious sovereignty of the people, since the days of De Savigny and Niebuhr. The Historical school, founded by these eminent men, has pilloried the a-prioristic fiction of 1789. Every historical connoisseur now ridicules it. Only that which they recommended instead of it, bears no better stamp.

Now it was to be not the sovereignty of the people, but the *Sovereignty of the State,* a product of Germanic philosophical pantheism. Ideas are incarnated in the reality, and among these the idea of the State was the highest, the richest, the most perfect idea of the relation between man and man. Thus the State became a mystical conception. The State was considered as a mysterious being, with a hidden *ego*; with a State-*consciousness,* slowly developing; and with an increasing potent State-*will,* which by a slow process endeavored to blindly reach the highest State-*aim*. The people was not understood as with Rousseau, to be the sum total of the individuals. It was correctly seen that a people is no aggregate, but an organic whole. This organism must of necessity have its organic members. Slowly these organs arrived at their historic development. By these organs the will of the State operates, and everything must bow before this will. This sovereign State-will might reveal itself in a republic, in a monarchy, in a Cæsar, in an Asiatic despot, in a tyrant as Philip of Spain, or in a dictator like Napoleon. All these were but forms, in which the one State-idea incorporated itself; the stages of development in a never-ending process. But in whatever form this mystical being of the State revealed itself, the idea remained supreme: the State shortly asserted its sovereignty and for every member of the State it remained the touchstone of wisdom to give way to this State-apotheosis.

Thus all transcendent right in God, to which the oppressed lifted up his face, falls away. There is no other right, but the immanent right which is written down in the law. The law is right, not because its contents are in harmony with the eternal principles of right, but because *it is law*. If on the morrow it fixes the very opposite, this also must be right. And the fruit of this deadening theory is, as a matter of course, that the consciousness of right is blunted, that all fixedness of right departs from our minds, and that all higher enthusiasm for right is extinguished. That which exists is good, because it exists; and it is no longer the will of God, of Him Who created us and knows us, but it becomes the ever-changing will of the State, which, having no one above itself, actually becomes *God,* and has to decide how our life and our existence shall be.

And when you further consider that this mystical State expresses and enforces its will only through men—what further proof is demanded that this state-sovereignty, even as popular sovereignty, does not outgrow the abasing subjection of man to his fellow-man and never ascends to a duty of submission which finds its cogency in the conscience?

Therefore in opposition both to the atheistic popular-sovereignty of the Encyclopedians, and the pantheistic state-sovereignty of German philosophers, the Calvinist maintains the Sovereignty of God, as the source of all authority among men. The Calvinist upholds the highest and best in our aspirations by placing every man and every people before the face of our Father in heaven. He takes cognizance of the fact of sin, which erstwhile was juggled away in 1789, and which now, in pessimistic extravagance, is accounted the essence of our being. Calvinism points to the difference between the natural concatenation of our organic society and the mechanical tie, which the authority of the magistrate imposes. It makes it easy for us to obey authority, because, in all authority, it causes us to honor the demand of divine sovereignty. It lifts us from an obedience born of dread of the strong arm, into an obedience for conscience sake. It teaches us to look upward from the existing law to the source of the eternal Right in God, and it creates in us the indomitable courage incessantly to protest against the unrighteousness of the law in the name of this highest Right. And however powerfully the State may assert itself and oppress the free individual development, above that powerful State there is always glittering, before our soul's eye, as infinitely more powerful, the majesty of the King of kings, Whose righteous bar ever maintains the right of appeal for all the oppressed, and unto Whom the prayer of the people ever ascends, to bless our nation and, in that nation, us and our house!

So much for the sovereignty of the State. We now come to *sovereignty in the sphere of Society*.

In a Calvinistic sense we understand hereby, that the family, the business, science, art and so forth are all social spheres, which do not owe their existence to the state, and which do not derive the law of their life from the superiority of the state, but obey a high authority within their own bosom; an authority which rules, by the grace of God, just as the sovereignty of the State does.

This involves the antithesis between *State* and *Society*, but upon this condition, that we do not conceive this society as a conglomerate, but as analyzed in its organic parts, to honor, in each of these parts, the independent character, which appertains to them.

In this independent character a special *higher authority* is of necessity involved and this highest authority we intentionally call —*sovereignty in the individual social spheres,* in order that it may be sharply and decidedly expressed that these different developments of social life have *nothing above themselves but God,* and that the State cannot intrude here, and has nothing to command in their domain. As you feel at once, this is the deeply interesting question of our civil liberties.[1]

It is here of the highest importance sharply to keep in mind the difference in grade between the *organic* life of society and the *mechanical* character of the government. Whatever among men originates directly from creation is possessed of all the data for its development, in human nature as such. You see this at once in the family and in the connection of blood relations and other ties. From the duality of man and woman marriage arises. From the original existence of *one* man and *one* woman monogamy comes forth. The children exist by reason of the innate power of reproduction. Naturally the children are connected as brothers and sisters. And when by and by these children, in their turn, marry again, as a matter of course, all those connections originate from blood-relationship and other ties, which dominate the whole family-life. In all this there is nothing mechanical. The development is spontaneous, just as that of the stem and the branches of a plant. True, sin here also has exerted its disturbing influence and has distorted much which was intended for a blessing into a curse. But this fatal efficiency of sin has been stopped by common grace. Free-love may try to dissolve, and the concubinate to desecrate, the holiest tie, as it pleases; but, for the vast majority of our race, marriage remains the foundation of human society and the family retains its position as the primordial sphere in sociology.

The same may be said of the other spheres of life.

Nature about us may have lost the glory of paradise by reason of sin, and the earth may bear thorns and thistles so that we can

---

1. Cf. Dr. A. Kuyper, *Calvinism the Source and Guarantee of Our Constitutional Liberties,* 1873; and Dr. A. Kuyper, *Sovereignty in the Spheres of Society,* 1880.

eat our bread only in the sweat of our brow; notwithstanding all this the chief aim of all human effort remains what it was by virtue of our creation and before the fall,—namely *dominion over nature*. And this dominion cannot be acquired except by the exercise of the powers, which, by virtue of the ordinances of creation, are innate in nature itself. Accordingly all Science is only the application to the cosmos of the powers of investigation and thought, created within us; and Art is nothing but the natural productivity of the potencies of our imagination. When we admit therefore that sin, though arrested by "common grace," has caused many modifications of these several expressions of life, which originated only after paradise was lost, and will disappear again, with the coming of the Kingdom of glory;—we still maintain that the fundamental character of these expressions remains as it was originally. All together they form the life of creation, in accord with the ordinances of creation, and therefore are *organically* developed.

But the case is wholly different with the assertion of the powers of government. For though it be admitted that even without sin the need would have asserted itself of combining the many families in a higher unity, this unity would have *internally* been bound up in the Kingship of God, which would have ruled regularly, directly and harmoniously in the hearts of all men, and which would *externally* have incorporated itself in a patriarchial hierarchy. Thus no States would have existed, but only one organic world-empire, with God as its King; exactly what is prophesied for the future which awaits us, when all sin shall have disappeared.

But it is exactly this, which sin has now eliminated from our human life. This unity does no longer exist. This government of God can no longer assert itself. This patriarchal hierarchy has been destroyed. A world-empire neither cannot be established nor ought it to be. For in this very desire consisted the contumacy of the building of Babel's tower. Thus peoples and nations originated. These peoples formed States. And over these States God appointed *governments*. And thus, if I may be allowed the expression, it is not a natural head, which organically grew from the body of the people, but a *mechanical* head, which from without has been placed upon the trunk of the nation. A mere remedy, therefore, for a wrong condition supervening. A stick placed beside the plant to hold it up, since without it, by reason of its inherent weakness, it would fall to the ground.

The principal characteristic of government is the right of life and death. According to the apostolic testimony the magistrate bears the sword, and this sword has a threefold meaning. It is the sword of *justice,* to mete out corporeal punishment to the criminal. It is the sword of *war* to defend the honor and the rights and the interests of the State against its enemies. And it is the sword of *order,* to thwart at home all forcible rebellion. Luther and his co-Reformers have correctly pointed out that the institution proper and the full investiture of the magistrate with power were only brought about after the flood, when God commanded that capital punishment should fall upon him who shed man's blood. The right of taking life belongs only to Him, who can give life, *i.e.,* to God; and therefore no one on earth is invested with this authority, except it be God-given. On this account, Roman law, which committed the *jus vitae et necis* to the father and to the slave-owner, stands intrinsically much lower than the law of Moses, which knows no other capital punishment but that by the magistrate and at his command.

The highest duty of the government remains therefore unchangeably that of *justice,* and in the second place it has to care for the people as a unit, partly *at home,* in order that its unity may grow ever deeper and may not be disturbed, and partly *abroad,* lest the national existence suffer harm. The consequence of all this is that on the one hand, in a people, all sorts of *organic* phenomena of life arise, from its *social* spheres, but that, high above all these, the *mechanical* unifying force of the government is observable. From this arises all friction and clashing. For the government is always inclined, with its *mechanical* authority, to invade social life, to subject it and mechanically to arrange it. But on the other hand social life always endeavors to shake off the authority of the government, just as this endeavor at the present time again culminates in social-democracy and in anarchism, both of which aim at nothing less than the total overthrow of the institution of authority. But leaving these two extremes alone, it will be admitted that all healthy life of people or state has ever been the historical consequence of the struggle between these two powers. It was the so-called "constitutional government," which endeavored more firmly to regulate the mutual relation of these two. And in this struggle Calvinism was the first to take its stand. For just in proportion as it honored the authority of the magistrate, instituted by God, did it lift up that *second sovereignty,* which had been implanted by God in the social spheres, in accordance with the ordinances of creation.

It demanded for both independence in their own sphere and regulation of the relation between both, not by the executive, but *under the law.* And by this stern demand, Calvinism may be said to have generated constitutional public law, from its own fundamental idea.

The testimony of history is unassailable that this constitutional public law has not flourished in Roman Catholic or in Lutheran States, but among the nations of a Calvinistic type. The idea is here fundamental therefore that the sovereignty of God, in its descent upon men, separates itself into two spheres. On the one hand the mechanical sphere of *State-authority,* and on the other hand the organic sphere of the authority of the *Social circles.* And in both these spheres the inherent authority is sovereign, that is to say, it has above itself nothing but God.

Now for the mechanically coercing authority of the government any further explanation is superfluous, not so, however, for the organic social authority.

Nowhere is the dominating character of this organic social authority more plainly discernable than in the sphere of Science. In the introduction to an edition of the "Sententiæ" of Lombard and of the "Summa Theologica" of Thomas Aquinas, the learned Thomist wrote: "The work of Lombard has ruled one hundred and fifty years and his produced Thomas, and after him the 'Summa' of Thomas has ruled all Europe (totam Europam rexit) during five full centuries and has generated all the subsequent theologians."[1] Suppose we admit that this language is overbold, yet the idea, here expressed, is unquestionably correct. The dominion of men like Aristotle and Plato, Lombard and Thomas, Luther and Calvin, Kant and Darwin, extends, for each of them, over a field of ages. Genius is a *sovereign* power; it forms schools; it lays hold on the spirits of men, with irresistible might; and it exercises an immeasurable influence on the whole condition of human life. This sovereignty of genius is a gift of God, possessed only by His grace. It is subject to no one and is responsible to Him alone Who has granted it this ascendancy.

The same phenomenon is observable in the sphere of Art. Every *maëstro* is a king in the Palace of Art, not by the law of inheritance or by appointment, but only by the grace of God. And these maëstros also impose authority, and are subject to no one, but rule over all and in the end receive from all the homage due to their artistic superiority.

And the same is to be said of the sovereign power of personality. There is no equality of persons. There are weak, narrow-minded persons, with no broader expanse of wings than a common sparrow; but there are also broad, imposing characters, with the wing-stroke of the eagle. Among the last you will find a few of royal grandeur, and these rule in their own sphere, whether people draw back from them or thwart them; usually waxing all the stronger, the more they are opposed. And this entire process is carried out in all the spheres of life. In the labor of the mechanic, in the shop, or on the exchange, in commerce, on the sea, in the field of benevolence and philanthropy. Everywhere one man is more powerful than the other, by his personality, by his talent and by circumstances. Dominion is exercised everywhere; but it is a dominion which works organically; not by virtue of a State-investiture, but from life's sovereignty itself.

In relation herewith, and on entirely the same ground of organic superiority, there exists, side by side with this personal sov-

---

1. Edition of Migne at Paris, 1841. Tome 1, proof 1.

ereignty, the sovereignty of *the sphere*. The University exercises
scientific dominion; the Academy of fine arts is possessed of art-
power; the guild exercised a technical dominion; the trades-union
rules over labor—and each of these spheres or corporations is conscious of the power of exclusive independent judgment and authoritative action, within its proper sphere of operation. Behind
these organic spheres, with intellectual, æsthetical and technical
sovereignty, the sphere of the family opens itself, with its right of
marriage, domestic peace, education and possession; and in this
sphere also the natural head is conscious of exercising an inherent
authority,—not because the government allows it, but because
God has imposed it. Paternal authority roots itself in the very life-
blood and is proclaimed in the fifth Commandment. And so also
finally it may be remarked that the social life of cities and villages
forms a sphere of existence, which arises from the very necessities
of life, and which therefore must be autonomous.

In many different directions we see therefore that sovereignty
in one's own sphere asserts itself — 1. In the social sphere, by personal superiority. 2. In the corporative sphere of universities,
guilds, associations, etc. 3. In the domestic sphere of the family
and of married life, and 4. In communal autonomy.

In all these four spheres the State-government cannot impose
its laws, but must reverence the innate law of life. God rules in
these spheres, just as supremely and sovereignly through his chosen *virtuosi,* as He exercises dominion in the sphere of the State
itself, through his chosen *magistrates.*

Bound by its own mandate, therefore, the government may
neither ignore nor modify nor disrupt the divine mandate, under
which these social spheres stand. The sovereignty, by the grace of
God, of the government is here set aside and limited, for God's
sake, by another sovereignty, which is equally divine in origin.
Neither the life of science nor of art, nor of agriculture, nor of industry, nor of commerce, nor of navigation, nor of the family, nor
of human relationship may be coerced to suit itself to the grace of
the government. The State may never become an octopus, which
stifles the whole of life. It must occupy its own place, on its own

root, among all the other trees of the forest, and thus it has to honor and maintain every form of life which grows independently in its own sacred autonomy.

Does this mean that the government has no right *whatever* of interference in these autonomous spheres of life? Not at all.

It possesses the threefold right and duty: 1. Whenever different spheres clash, to compel mutual regard for the boundary-lines of each; 2. To defend individuals and the weak ones, in those spheres, against the abuse of power of the rest; and 3. To coerce all together to bear *personal* and *financial* burdens for the maintenance of the natural unity of the State. The decision cannot, however, in these cases, *unilaterally* rest with the magistrate. The Law here has to indicate the rights of each, and the rights of the citizens over their own purses must remain the invincible bulwark against the abuse of power on the part of the government.

And here exactly lies the starting-point for that cooperation of the sovereignty of the government, with the sovereignty in the social sphere, which finds its regulation in the Constitution. According to the order of things, in his time, this became to Calvin the doctrine of the "magistratus inferiores." Knighthood, the rights of the city, the rights of guilds and much more, led then to the self-assertion of *social* "States," with their own civil authority; and so Calvin wished the law to be made by the cooperation of these with the High magistrates.

Since that time these medieval relations, which in part arose from the feudal system, have become totally antiquated. These corporations or social orders are now no longer invested with ruling power, their place is taken by Parliament, or whatever name the general house of representatives may bear in different countries, and now it remains the duty of those Assemblies to maintain the popular rights and liberties, of all and in the name of all, *with* and if need be *against* the government. A united defence which was preferred to individual resistance, both to simplify the construction and operation of State institutions and to accelerate their functions. But in whatever way the form may be modified, it remains essentially the old Calvinistic plan, to assure to the people, in all its classes and orders, in all its circles and spheres, in all its corporations and independent institutions, a legal and orderly influence in the making of the law and the course of government, in a healthy democratic sense. And the only difference of opinion is yet on the important question whether we shall continue in the now prevailing solution of the special rights of those social spheres in the *individual* right of franchise; or whether it is desirable to place by its side a *corporative* right of franchise, which shall enable the different circles to make a separate defence. At present a new tendency to organization reveals itself even in the spheres of commerce and industry and not less in that of labor, and even from France voices, like that of Benoit, arise, which clamor for the juncture of the right of franchise with these organizations.

I for one, would welcome such a move, provided its application were not one-sided, much less exclusive; but I may not linger over these side issues. Let it suffice to have shown that Calvinism protests against State-omnipotence; against the horrible conception that no right exists above and beyond existing laws; and against the pride of absolutism, which recognizes no constitutional rights, except as the result of princely favor.

These three representations, which find so dangerous a nourishment in the ascendancy of Pantheism, are death to our civil liberties. And Calvinism is to be praised for having built a dam across this absolutistic stream, not by appealing to popular force, nor to the hallucination of human greatness, but by deducing those rights and liberties of social life from the same source from which the high authority of the government flows—even the *absolute sovereignty of God*. From this *one* source, in God, *sovereignty in the individual sphere,* in the family and in every social circle, is just as directly derived as the *supremacy of State authority*. These two must therefore come to an understanding, and both have the same sacred obligation to maintain their God-given sovereign authority and to make it subservient to the majesty of God.

A people therefore which abandons to State Supremacy the rights of the family, or a University which abandons to it the rights of science, is just as guilty before God as a nation which lays its hand upon the rights of the magistrates. And thus the struggle for liberty is not only declared permissible, but is made a duty for each individual in his own sphere. And this not as was done in the French Revolution, by setting God aside and by placing man on the throne of God's Omnipotence; but on the contrary, by causing all men, the magistrates included, to bow in deepest humility before the majesty of God Almighty.

As third and last part of this lecture, the discussion remains of a question yet more difficult than the previous one, namely how we must conceive of *the Sovereignty of the Church* in the State.

I call this a difficult problem, not because I am in doubt as to the conclusions, or because I doubt your assent to these conclusions. For, as far as regards American life, all uncertainty in this respect is removed by what your Constitution at first declared — and has later been modified in your Confessions—concerning the liberty of worship and the coordination of Church and State. And as far as I am personally concerned, more than a quarter of a century ago I wrote above my Weekly paper the motto—"A free Church in a free State." In a hard struggle this motto has ever been lifted on high by me, and our Netherland churches also are about to reconsider the article in our Confession which touches on this matter.

The difficulty of the problem lies elsewhere. It lies in the pile and fagots of Servetus. It lies in the attitude of the Presbyterians toward the Independents. It lies in the restrictions of liberty of worship and in the "civil disabilities," under which for centuries even in the Netherlands the Roman Catholics have suffered. The difficulty lies in the fact that an article of our old Calvinistic Confession of Faith entrusts to the government the task "of defending against and of extirpating every form of idolatry and false religion and to protect the sacred service of the Church." The difficulty lies in the unanimous and uniform advice of Calvin and his epigonies, who demanded intervention of the government in the matter of religion.

The accusation is therefore a natural one that, by choosing in favor of liberty of religion, we do not pick up the gauntlet for Calvinism, but that we directly oppose it.

In order to shield myself from this undesirable suspicion, I advance the rule—that a system is not known in what it has in common with other preceding systems; but that it is distinguished by that in which it differs from those preceding systems.

The duty of the government to extirpate every form of false religion and idolatry was not a find of Calvinism, but dates from Constantine the Great, and was the reaction against the horrible persecutions which his pagan predecessors on the imperial throne had inflicted upon the sect of the Nazarene. Since that day this system had been defended by all Romish theologians and applied by all Christian princes. In the time of Luther and Calvin, it was a universal conviction that that system was the true one. Every famous theologian of the period, Melanchthon first of all, approved of the death by fire of Servetus; and the scaffold, which was erected by the Lutherans at Leipzig for Krell,* the thorough Calvinist, was infinitely more reprehensible when looked at from a Protestant standpoint.

But whilst the Calvinists, in the age of Reformation, yielded their victims, by tens of thousands, to the scaffold and the stake (those of the Lutherans and Roman Catholics being hardly worth counting), history has been guilty of the great and far-reaching unfairness of ever casting in their teeth this one execution of fire of Servetus, as a *crimen nefandum.*

Notwithstanding all this, I not only deplore that one stake, but I unconditionally disapprove of it; yet not as if it were the expression of a special characteristic of Calvinism, but on the contrary as the fatal after-effect of a system, grey with age, which Calvinism found in existence, under which it had grown up, and from which it had not yet been able entirely to liberate itself.

If I desire to know what in this respect must follow from the specific principles of Calvinism, then the question must be put quite differently. Then we must see and acknowledge that this system of bringing differences in religious matters under the criminal jurisdiction of the government resulted directly from the con-

---

* Nicholas Crellius, chancellor of Christian I, leader in the crypto-calvinistic struggle in Germany. Beheaded in 1601, after ten years of harsh imprisonment. He had become much hated by the nobles. The process which led to his death sentence as traitor was conducted very arbitrarily.

viction that the Church of Christ on earth could express itself only in *one* form and as *one* institution. This *one* Church alone, in the Middle Ages, was the Church of Christ, and everything, which differed from her, was looked upon as inimical to this one true Church. The government, therefore, was not called upon to judge, or to weigh or to decide for itself. There *was* only one Church of Christ on earth, and it was the task of the Magistrate to protect that Church from schisms, heresies and sects.

But break that one Church into fragments, admit that the Church of Christ can reveal itself in many forms, in different countries; nay, even in the same country, in a multiplicity of institutions; and immediately everything which was deduced from this unity of the visible church drops out of sight. And therefore, if it cannot be denied that Calvinism itself *has* ruptured the unity of the Church, and that in Calvinistic countries a rich variety of all manner of church-formations revealed itself, then it follows that we must not seek the true Calvinistic characteristic in what, for a time, it has retained of the old system, but rather in that, which, new and fresh, has sprung up from its own root.

Results have shown that, even after the lapse of three centuries, in all distinctively Roman Catholic countries, even in the South American Republics, the Roman Catholic church is and remains the State Church, precisely as does the Lutheran Church in Lutheran countries. And the free churches have exclusively flourished in those countries which were touched by the breath of Calvinism, *i.e.,* in Switzerland, the Netherlands, England, Scotland, and the United States of North America.

In Roman Catholic countries, the identification of the invisible and the visible Church, under Papal unity, is still maintained. In Lutheran countries, with the aid of "curius regio eius religio," the Court-confession has been monstrously imposed on the people as the land-confession; there the Reformed were treated harshly, they were exiled and outraged, as enemies of Christ. In the Calvinistic Netherlands, on the contrary, all those who were persecuted for religion's sake, found a harbor of refuge. There the Jews were hospitably received; there the Lutherans were in honor; there the Mennonites flourished; and even the Arminians and Roman Catholics were permitted the free exercise of their religion at home and in secluded churches. The Independents, driven from England, have found a resting place in the Calvinistic Netherlands; and from this same country the Mayflower sailed forth to transport the Pilgrim Fathers to their new fatherland.

I do not build therefore on subterfuge, but I appeal to clear historical facts. And here I repeat the underlying characteristic of Calvinism must be sought, not in what it has adopted from the past, but in what it has newly created. It is remarkable, in this connection, that, from the very beginning, our Calvinistic Theologians and jurists have defended liberty of conscience against the Inquisition. Rome perceived very clearly how liberty of conscience must loosen the foundations of the unity of the visible Church, and therefore she opposed it. But on the other hand it must be admitted that Calvinism, by praising aloud liberty of conscience, has in principle abandoned every absolute characteristic of the visible Church.

As soon as in the bosom of one and the same people the conscience of one half witnessed against that of the other half, the breach had been accomplished, and placards were no longer of any avail. As early as 1649 it was declared that persecution, for faith's sake, was—"A spiritual murder, an assassination of the soul, a rage against God himself, the most horrible of sins." And it is evident that Calvin himself wrote down the premises of the correct conclusion, by his acknowledgment that against atheists even the Catholics are our allies; by his open recognition of the Lutheran Church; and still more emphatically by his pertinent declaration: "Scimus tres esse errorum gradus, et quibusdam fatemur dandam esse veniam, aliis modicam castigationem sufficere, ut tantum manifesta impietas capitali supplitio plectatur.[1] That is to say: "There exists a threefold departure from the Christian truth; a slight one, which had better be left alone; a moderate one, which must be restored by a moderate chastisement; and only manifest godlessness must be capitally punished." I admit that this is a harsh decision, but yet a decision in which in principle the *visible unity* is discarded; and where that unity is broken, there liberty will dawn as a matter of course. For here lies the solution of the

---

1. Tome VIII, p. 516c; Ed. Schippers.

problem: With Rome the system of persecution issued from the identification of the visible with the invisible Church, and from *this* dangerous line Calvin departed. But what he still persevered in defending was the identification of his Confession of the Truth with the absolute Truth itself, and it only wanted fuller experience to realize that also this proposition, true as it must ever remain in our personal conviction, may never be imposed by force upon other people.

So much for the facts. Now let us put the theory itself to the test and look successively at the duty of the magistrate in things spiritual: 1. towards *God,* 2. towards the *Church,* and 3, towards *individuals.* As regards the first point, the magistrates are and remain—"God's servants." They have to recognize God as Supreme Ruler, from Whom they derive their power. They have to serve God, by ruling the people according to *His* ordinances. They have to restrain blasphemy, where it directly assumes the character of an affront to the Divine Majesty. And God's supremacy is to be recognized by confessing His name in the Constitution as the Source of all political power, by maintaining the Sabbath, by proclaiming days of prayer and thanksgiving, and by invoking His Divine blessing.

Therefore in order that they may govern, according to His holy ordinances, every magistrate is in duty bound to investigate the rights of God, both in the natural life and in His Word. Not to subject himself to the decision of any Church, but in order that he himself may catch the light which he needs for the knowledge of the Divine will. And as regards blasphemy, the *right* of the magistrate to restrain it rests in the God-consciousness innate in every man; and the *duty* to exercise this right flows from the fact that God is the Supreme and Sovereign Ruler over every State and over every Nation. But for this very reason the fact of blasphemy is only then to be deemed established, when the intention is apparent contumaciously to affront this majesty of God *as Supreme Ruler of the State.* What is then punished is not the religious offence, nor the impious sentiment, but the attack upon the foundation of public law, upon which both the State and its government are resting.

Meanwhile there is in this respect a noteworthy difference between States which are absolutely governed by a monarch, and States which are governed constitutionally; or in a republic, in a still wider range, by an extensive assembly.

In the absolute monarch the consciousness and the personal will are *one,* and thus this one person is called to rule his people after his own personal conception of the ordinances of God. When on the contrary the consciousness and the will of many cooperate, this unity is lost and the subjective conception of the ordinances of God, by these many, can only be indirectly applied. But whether you are dealing with the will of a single individual, or with the will of many men, in a decision arrived at by a vote, the principal thing remains that the government has to judge and to decide independently. Not as an appendix to the Church, nor as its pupil. The sphere of State stands itself under the majesty of the Lord. In that sphere therefore an independent responsibility to God is to be maintained. The sphere of the State is not profane. But both Church and State must, each in their own sphere, obey God and serve His honor. And to that end in either sphere *God's Word* must rule, but in the sphere of the State only through the conscience of the persons invested with authority. The first thing of course is, and remains, that all nations shall be governed in a Christian way; that is to say, in accordance with the principle which, for all statecraft, flows from the Christ. But this can never be realized except through the subjective convictions of those in authority, according to their personal views of the demands of that Christian principle as regards the public service.

Of an entirely different nature is the second question, what ought to be the relation between the government and the *visible Church*. If it had been the will of God to maintain the formal unity of this visible Church, this question would have to be answered quite differently from what is now the case. That this unity was originally sought is natural. Unity of religion has great value for the life of a people and not a little charm. And only narrowmindedness can feel itself offended by the rage of despair wherewith Rome in the 16th century fought for the maintenance of that unity. It can also be easily understood that this unity was originally established. The lower a people stands in the scale of development, the less difference of opinion is revealed. We see therefore that nearly all nations begin with unity of religion. But it is equally natural that this unity is split up, where the individual life, in the process of development, gains in strength, and where multiformity asserts itself as the undeniable demand of a richer development of life. And thus we are confronted with the fact that the visible Church has been split up, and that in no country whatever the absolute unity of the visible Church can be any longer maintained.

What then is the duty of the government?

Must it—for the question may be reduced to this—must it now form an individual judgment, as to which of those many Churches is the true one? And must it maintain this one over against the others? Or is it the duty of the government to suspend its own judgment and to consider the multiform complex of all these denominations as the totality of the manifestation of the Church of Christ on earth?

From a Calvinistic standpoint we must decide in favor of the latter suggestion. Not from a false idea of neutrality, nor as if Calvinism could ever be indifferent to what is true and what false, *but because the government lacks the data of judgment,* and because every magisterial judgment here *infringes the sovereignty of the Church.* For otherwise, if the government be an absolute monarchy, you get the "cuius regio eius religio" of the Lutheran princes, which has ever been combated from the side of Calvinism. Or if the government rests with a plurality of persons, the Church which yesterday was counted the false one, is today considered the true one, according to the decision of the vote; and thus all continuity of state-administration and church-position is lost.

Hence it is that the Calvinists have always struggled so proudly and courageously for the liberty, that is to say, for the sovereignty, of the Church, within her own sphere, in distinction from the Lutheran theologians. In Christ, they contended, the Church has her own King. Her position in the State is not assigned her by the permission of the Government, but *jure divino*. She has her own organization. She possesses her own office-bearers. And in a similar way she has her own gifts to distinguish truth from the lie. It is therefore her privilege, and not that of the State, to determine her own characteristics as the true Church, and to proclaim her own confession as the confession of the truth.

If in this position she is opposed by other Churches, she will fight against these her spiritual battle, with spiritual and social weapons; but she denies and contests the right of everyone whomsoever, and therefore also of the government, to pose as a power above these different institutions and to render a decision between her and her sister-churches. The government bears the sword which wounds; not the sword of the Spirit, which decides in spiritual questions. And for this reason the Calvinists have ever resisted the idea to assign to the government a *patria potestas*. To be sure a father regulates in his family the religion of that family. But when the government was organized, the family was not set aside, but remained; and the government received only a limited task, which is defined by the sovereignty in the individual sphere, and not least of all by the sovereignty of Christ in His Church. Only let us guard here against exaggerated Puritanism and let us not refuse, in Europe at least, to reckon with the effects of historical conditions. It is an entirely different matter whether one puts up a new building on a free lot or whether one must restore a house which is standing.

But this can in no regard break the fundamental rule that the government must honor the complex of Christian churches as the multiform manifestation of the Church of Christ on earth. That the magistrate has to respect the liberty, *i.e.*, the sovereignty, of the Church of Christ in the individual sphere of these churches. That Churches flourish most richly when the government allows them to live from their own strength on the voluntary principle. And that therefore neither the Cœsaropapy of the Czar of Russia; nor the subjection of the State to the Church, taught by Rome; nor the "Cuius regio eius religio" of the Lutheran jurists; nor the irreligious neutral standpoint of the French revolution; but that only the system of a free Church, in a free State, may be honored from a Calvinistic standpoint.

The sovereignty of the State and the sovereignty of the Church exist side by side, and they mutually limit each other.

Of an entirely different nature, on the contrary, is the last question to which I referred, namely, the duty of the government as regards the *sovereignty of the individual person.*

In the second part of this lecture I have already indicated that the developed man also possesses an individual sphere of life, with sovereignty in his own circle. Here I do not refer to the family, for this is a social bond between several individuals. I have reference to that which is thus expressed by Prof. Weitbrecht: "Ist doch vermöge seines Gewissens jeder ein König, ein Souverain, der über jede Verantwortung exhaben is."[1] ("Every man stands a king in his conscience, a sovereign in his own person, exempt from all responsibility.") Or that which Held has formulated in this way: "In gewisser Beziehung wird jeder Mensch supremus oder Souverain sein, denn jeder Mensch muss eine Sphäre haben, und hat sie auch wirklich, in welcher er der Oberste ist."[2] (In some respects every man is a sovereign, for everybody must have and has a sphere of life of his own, in which he has no one above him, but God alone.) I do not point to this to over-estimate the importance of conscience, for whosoever wishes to liberate conscience, where God and His Word are concerned, I meet as an opponent, not as an ally. This, however, does not prevent my maintaining the sovereignty of conscience as the palladium of all personal liberty, in this sense—that conscience is never subject to man but always and ever to God Almighty.

This need of the personal liberty of conscience, however, does not immediately assert itself. It does not express itself with emphasis in the child, but only in the mature man; and in the same way it mostly slumbers among undeveloped peoples, and is irresistible only among highly developed nations. A man of ripe and rich development will rather become a voluntary exile, will rather suffer imprisonment, nay, even sacrifice life itself, than tolerate constraint in the forum of his conscience. And the deeply rooted

---

1. WEITBRECHT, *Woher und Wohin*; Stuttgart, 1877; p. 103.
2. HELD, *Verfassungsysteem*, I, p. 234.

repugnance against the Inquisition, which for three long centuries would not be assuaged, grew up from the conviction that its practices violated and assaulted human life in man. This imposes on the government a twofold obligation. In the first place, it must cause this liberty of conscience to be respected by the Church; and in the second place, it must give way itself to the sovereign conscience.

As regards the first, the sovereignty of the Church finds its natural limitation in the sovereignty of the free personality. Sovereign within her own domain, she has no power over those who live outside of that sphere. And wherever, in violation of this principle, transgression of power may occur, the government has to respect the claims on protection of every citizen. The Church may not be forced to tolerate as a member one whom she feels obliged to expel from her circle; but on the other hand no citizen of the State must be compelled to remain in a church which his conscience forces him to leave.

Meantime what the government in this respect demands of the churches, it must practice itself, by allowing to each and every citizen liberty of conscience, as the primordial and inalienable right of all men.

It has cost a heroic struggle to wrest this greatest of all human liberties from the grasp of despotism; and streams of human blood have been poured out before the object was attained. But for this very reason every son of the Reformation tramples upon the honor of the fathers, who does not assiduously and without retrenching, defend this palladium of our liberties. In order that it may be able to rule *men,* the government must respect this deepest ethical power of our human existence. A nation, consisting of citizens whose consciences are bruised, is itself broken in its national strength.

And even if I am forced to admit that our fathers, in theory, had not the courage of the conclusions which follow from this liberty of conscience, for the *liberty of speech,* and the *liberty of worship*; even if I am well aware that they made a desperate effort to hinder the spread of literature which they disliked, by censure and refusal of publication—all this does not set aside the fact that the free expression of thought, by the spoken and printed word, has first achieved its victory in the Calvinistic Netherlands. Whosoever was elsewhere straightened, could first enjoy the liberty of ideas and the liberty of the press on Calvinistic ground. And thus the logical development of what was enshrined in the liberty of conscience, as well as that liberty itself, first blessed the world from the side of Calvinism.

For it is true that, in Roman lands, spiritual and political despotism have been finally vanquished by the French Revolution, and that in so far we have gratefully to acknowledge that this revolution also began by promoting the cause of liberty. But whosoever learns from history that the guillotine, all over France, for years and years could not rest from the execution of those who were of a different mind; whosoever remembers how cruelly and wantonly the Roman Catholic clergy were murdered, because they refused to violate their conscience by an unholy oath; or whosoever, like myself, by a sad experience, knows the spiritual tyranny which liberalism and conservatism on the European Continent have applied, and are still applying, to those who have chosen different paths,—is forced to admit that liberty in Calvinism and liberty in the French Revolution are two quite different things.

In the French Revolution a civil liberty for every Christian *to agree with the unbelieving majority*; in Calvinism, a liberty of conscience, which enables every man to serve God *according to his own conviction and the dictates of his own heart.*

FOURTH LECTURE

CALVINISM AND SCIENCE

IN MY fourth lecture allow me to draw your attention to the nexus between *Calvinism and Science*. Not, of course, in order to exhaust in one lecture such a weighty subject. Four points of it only I submit to your thoughtful consideration; first, that Calvinism fostered and could not but foster *love for science*; secondly, that it restored to science *its domain*; thirdly, that it delivered science from *unnatural bonds*; and fourthly, in what manner it sought and found a solution for the unavoidable *scientific conflict*.

First of all then: There is found hidden in Calvinism an impulse, an inclination, an incentive, to scientific investigation. *It is a fact* that science has been fostered by it, and its principle demands the scientific spirit. One glorious page from the history of Calvinism may suffice to prove the fact, before we enter more fully upon the discussion of the incentive to scientific investigation found in Calvinism as such. The page from the history of Calvinism, or let us rather say of mankind, matchless in its beauty, to which I refer, is the siege of Leyden, more than three hundred years ago. This siege of Leyden was in fact a struggle between Alva and Prince William about the future course of the history of the world; and the result was that in the end Alva had to withdraw, and that William the Silent was enabled to unfurl the banner of liberty over Europe. Leyden, defended almost exclusively by its own citizens, entered the lists against the best troops of what was looked upon at that time as the finest army of the world. Three months after the commencement of the siege, the supply of food became exhausted. A fearful famine began to rage. The apparently doomed citizens managed to live on dogs and rats. This black famine was soon followed by the black death or the plague, which carried off a third part of the inhabitants. The Spaniards offered peace and

110

pardon to the dying people; but Leyden, remembering the bad faith of the enemy in the treatment of Naarden and Haarlem, answered boldly and with pride: If it is necessary, we are ready to consume our left arms, and to defend with our right arms our wives, our liberty and our religion against thee, O tyrant. Thus they persevered. They patiently waited for the coming of the Prince of Orange to raise the siege, . . . but . . . the prince had to wait for God. The dikes of the province of Holland had been cut through; the country surrounding Leyden was flooded; a fleet lay ready to hasten to Leyden's aid; but the wind drove the water back, preventing the fleet from passing the shallow pools. God tried his people sorely. At last however, on the first of October, the wind turned towards the West, and, forcing the waters upward, enabled the fleet to reach the beleaguered city. Then the Spaniards fled in haste to escape the rising tide. On the 3rd of October the fleet entered the port of Leyden, and the siege being raised, Holland and Europe were saved. The population, all but starved to death, could scarcely drag themselves along, yet all to a man limped as well as they could to the house of prayer. There all fell on their knees and gave thanks to God. But when they tried to utter their gratitude in psalms of praise, they were almost voiceless, for there was no strength left in them, and the tones of their song died away in grateful sobbing and weeping.

Behold what I call a glorious page in the history of liberty, written in blood, and if you now ask me, what has this to do with *science,* see here the answer: In recognition of such patriotic courage, the States of Holland did not present Leyden with a handful of knightly orders, or gold, or honor, but with a *School of the Sciences,*—the University of Leyden, renowned through the whole world. The German is surpassed by none in pride of his scientific glory, and yet no less a man than Niebuhr has testified, "that the Senate chamber of Leyden's University is the most memorable hall of science." The ablest scholars were induced to fill the amply endowed chairs. Scaliger was conveyed from France in a man-of-war. Salmasius came to Leyden under convoy of a whole squadron. Why should I give you the long list of names of the princes of science, of the giants in learning, who have filled Leyden with the lustre of their renown, or tell you how this love for science, going forth from Leyden, permeated the whole nation? You know the Lipsii, the Hemsterhuizen, the Boerhaves.* You know that in Holland were invented the telescope, the microscope and the thermometer;** and thus empirical science, worthy of its name, was made possible. It is an undeniable fact, that the Calvinistic Netherlands *had* love for science and fostered it. But the most evident, the most convincing proof is doubtless found in the establishment of Leyden's University. To receive as the highest reward a University of the Sciences in a moment, when, in a fearful struggle, the course of the history of the world was turned by your heroism is only conceivable among a people in whose very life-principle love for science is involved.

And now I approach the principle itself. For it is not enough to be acquainted with the fact, I must also show you why it is that Calvinism cannot but foster love for science. And do not think it strange, when I point to the Calvinistic dogma of predestination as the strongest motive in those days for the cultivation of science in a higher sense. But in order to prevent misunderstanding let me first explain what the term "science" here means.

I speak of human science as a whole, not of what is called among you "sciences," or as the French express it "sciences exactes." Especially do I deny that mere empiricism in itself ever is perfect science. Even the minutest microscopic, the farthest reaching telescopic investigation is nothing but *perception* with strengthened eyes. This is transformed into science when you discover in the specific phenomena, perceived by empiricism, a universal *law,* and thereby reach *the thought* which governs the whole constellation

---

* Justus Lipsius, 1547-1606, linguist, critic, and humanist R. C. He was in turn Lutheran, Reformed, and again Roman Catholic. At his death he was historian of the king of Spain. Tiberius Hemsterhuis, philologist, 1685—1766; F. Hemsterhuis, nephew of Tiberius, 1721—1790, philosopher, moralist. Herman Boerhave, very famous as physician, 1668—1738.

** The invention of the telescope is attributed to Lipperhey of Middelburg, about 1600; of the microscope to Z. Jansen (1590), and of the thermometer, as well as the barometer, to C. Drebbel. Drebbel in 1619 exhibited Jansen's compound microscope to James I. Anton van Leeuwenhoek, 1632—1723, was one of the most successful pioneer microscopists.

of phenomena.* In this wise the special sciences originate; but even in them the human mind cannot acquiesce. The subject-matter of the several sciences must be grouped under one head and brought under the sway of one principle by means of theory or hypothesis, and finally Systematics, as the queen of sciences, comes forth from her tent to weave all the different results into one organic whole. It is true, I know, that Dubois Raymond's winged word *Ignorabimus* has been used by many to make it seem impossible that our thirst for science in the highest sense will ever be quenched, and that Agnosticism, drawing a curtain across the background and over the abysses of life, is satisfied with a study of the phenomena of the several sciences; but some time ago, the human mind began to take its revenge on this spiritual vandalism. The question about the origin, interconnection and destiny of everything that exists cannot be suppressed; and the *veni, vidi, vici,* wherewith the theory of evolution with full speed occupied the ground in all the circles, inimical to the Word of God, and especially among our naturalists, is a convincing proof how much we need unity of view.

How, now, can we prove that love for science in that higher sense, which aims at unity in our cognizance of the entire cosmos, is effectually secured by means of our Calvinistic belief in God's fore-ordination? If you want to understand this you have to go back from predestination to God's decree in general. This is not a matter of choice; on the contrary, it *must* be done. Belief in predestination is nothing but the penetration of God's decree into your own personal life; or, if you prefer it, the personal heroism to apply the sovereignty of God's decreeing will to your own existence. It means that we are not satisfied with a mere profession of words, but that we are willing to stand by our confession in regard both to this life and the life to come. It is a proof of honesty, unmovable firmness and solidity in our expressions concerning the unity of God's Will, and the certainty of His operations. It is a deed of high courage because it brings you under the suspicion of

* In his *Encyclopedia of Theology,* II, p. 29, Dr. K. defines science as an impulse in the human spirit that the cosmos to which he is related organically, may be reflected plastically in us, according to its moments, (causes, originating things), and may be comprehended logically, in its relations. Cf. p. 168.

high-mindedness. But if you now proceed to the decree of God, what else does God's fore-ordination mean than the certainty that the existence and course of all things, *i.e.*, of the entire cosmos, instead of being a plaything of caprice and chance, obeys law and order, and that there exists a firm will which carries out its designs both in nature and in history? Now do you not agree with me that this forces upon our mind the indissoluble conception of one all-comprehensive unity, and the acceptance of one principle by which everything is governed? It forces upon us the recognition of something that is general, hidden and yet expressed in that which is special. Yea, it forces upon us the confession that there must be stability and regularity ruling over everything. Thus you recognize that the cosmos, instead of being a heap of stones, loosely thrown together, on the contrary presents to our mind a monumental building erected in a severely consistent style. Do you abandon this point of view, then it is uncertain at any moment, what is to happen, what course things may take, what every morning and evening may have in store for you, your family, your country, the world at large. Man's capricious will is then the principal concern. Every man may then choose and act every moment in a certain way, but it is also possible that he may do just the reverse. If this were so, you could count upon nothing. There is no interconnection, no development, no continuity; a chronicle, but no history. And now tell me, what becomes of science under such conditions? You may yet speak of the study of nature, but the study of human life has been made ambiguous and uncertain. Nothing but bare facts may then be historically ascertained, interconnection and plan have no longer a place in history. History dies away.

I do not for a moment propose to enter just now into a discussion about man's free will. We have no time for it. But it is a fact that the more thorough development of science in our age has almost unanimously decided in favor of Calvinism with regard to the antithesis between the unity and stability of God's decree, which Calvinism professes, and the superficiality and looseness, which the Arminians preferred. The systems of the great modern philosophers are, almost to one, in favor of unity and stability. Buckle's *History of the Civilization in England* has succeeded in proving the firm order of things in human life with astonishing, almost mathematical demonstrative force. Lombroso, and his entire school of criminalists, place themselves on record in this respect as moving on Calvinistic lines. And the latest hypothesis, that the laws of heredity and variation, which control the whole organization of nature, admit of no exception in the domain of human life, has already been accepted as "the common creed" by all evolutionists. Though I abstain at present from any criticism either of these philosophical systems or of these naturalistic hypotheses, so much at least is very clearly demonstrated by them, that the entire development of science in our age presupposes a cosmos which does not fall a prey to the freaks of chance, but exists and develops from one principle, according to a firm order, aiming at one fixed plan. This is a claim which is, as it clearly appears, diametrically opposed to Arminianism, and in complete harmony with Calvinistic belief that there is one Supreme will in God, the cause of all existing things, subjecting them to fixed ordinances and directing them towards a pre-established plan. Calvinists have never thought that the idea of the cosmos lay in God's foreordination as an aggregate of loosely conjoined decrees, but they have always maintained that the whole formed one organic programme of the entire creation and the entire history. And as a Calvinist looks upon God's decree as the foundation and origin of the natural laws, in the same manner also he finds in it the firm foundation and the origin of every moral and spiritual law; both these, the natural as well as the spiritual laws, forming together one high order, which exists according to God's command and wherein God's counsel will be accomplished in the consummation of His eternal, all-embracing plan.

Faith in such an *unity, stability* and *order* of things, personally, as predestination, cosmically, as the counsel of God's decree, could not but awaken as with a loud voice, and vigorously foster love for science. Without a deep conviction of this unity, this stability and this order, science is unable to go beyond mere conjectures, and only when there is faith in the organic interconnection of the Universe, will there be also a possibility for science to ascend from the empirical investigation of the special phenomena to the general, and from the general to the law which rules over it, and from that law to the principle, which is dominant over all. The data, which are absolutely indispensable for all higher science, are at hand only under this supposition. Remember the fact that in those days when Calvinism cleared for itself a path in life, tottering semi-pelagianism had blunted this conviction of unity, stability and order to such an extent that even Thomas Aquinas lost a great deal of his influence, while Scotists, Mystics and Epicureans vied with one another in their endeavors to deprive the human mind of its steady course. And who is there who does not perceive what entirely new impulse to undertake scientific investigations had to grow out of the new-born Calvinism, which with one powerful grasp brought order out of chaos, putting under discipline so dangerous a spiritual licentiousness, making an end to that halting between two or more opinions, and showing us instead of rising and falling mists, the picture of a powerfully-rushing mountain stream, taking its course through a well-regulated bed towards an ocean which waits to receive it. Calvinism has gone through many fierce struggles on account of its clinging to the counsel of God's decree. Again and again it seemed to be near the brink of destruction. Calvinism has been reviled and slandered on account of it, and when it refused to exclude even our sinful action from God's plan, because without it the programme of the order of the world would again be rent to pieces, our opponents did not shrink from accusing us of making God the author of sin. They knew not what they did. Through evil report and good report Calvinism has firmly maintained its confession. It has not allowed itself to be deprived by scoff and scorn of the firm conviction that our entire life must be under the sway of *unity, solidity* and *order,* established by God himself. This accounts for its need of unity of insight, firmness of knowledge, order in its world-view, fostered among us, even in the wide circles of the common people, and this manifest need is the reason that a thirst for knowledge was quickened, which in those days was nowhere satisfied in a more abundant measure than in Calvinistic countries. This explains why it is that in the writings of those days you meet with such a determination, such an energy of thought, such a comprehensive view of life. I even venture to say, that in the memoirs of noble women of that century and in the correspondence of the unlettered, a unity of world-view and life-view is manifest, which impressed a scientific stamp on their whole existence. Intimately connected with this is also the fact that they never favored the so-called primacy of the will. They demanded, in their practical life, the bridle of a clear conscience-ness, and in this consciousness the leadership could not be entrusted to humor or whim, to fancy or chance, but only to the majesty of the highest principle, wherein they found the explanation of their existence and to which their whole life was consecrated.

I now leave my first point, that Calvinism fostered *love for science,* in order to proceed to the second, that Calvinism restored to science *its domain.* I mean to say that cosmical science originated in the Græco-Roman world; that in the middle ages the cosmos vanished behind the horizon to draw the attention of all to the distant sights of future life, and that it was Calvinism which, without losing sight of the spiritual, led to a rehabilitation of the cosmic sciences. If we were forced to choose between the beautiful cosmic taste of Greece with its blindness for things eternal, and the middle ages with their blindness for cosmical things, but with their mystic love for Christ, then certainly every child of God on his death-bed would tender the palm to Bernard of Clairvaux and Thomas Aquinas rather than to Heraclitus and Aristotle. The pilgrim who wanders through the world without concerning himself about its preservation and destiny, presents to us a more ideal figure than the Greek worldling who sought religion in the worship of Venus, or Bacchus, and who flattered himself in hero-worship, debased his honor as a man in the veneration of prostitutes, and at last sank lower than the brutes in pederasty. Let it be quite understood therefore that I do not in any way over-rate the classical world, to the detraction of the heavenly lustre which sparkled through all the haze of the middle ages. But notwithstanding all this I assert and maintain that the one Aristotle knew more of the cosmos than all the church-fathers taken together; that under the dominion of Islam, better cosmic science flourished than in the cathedral- and monastic-schools of Europe; that the recovery of the writings of Aristotle was the first incentive to renewed though rather deficient study; and that Calvinism alone, by means of its dominating principle, which constantly urges us to go back from the Cross to Creation, and no less by means of its doctrine of *common grace*, threw open again to science the vast field of the cosmos, now illumined by the Sun of Righteousness, of Whom the Scriptures testify that in Him are hid all the treasures of wisdom and knowledge. Let us pause then to consider first that *general principle* of Calvinism and afterwards the dogma of *"common grace."*

All agree that the Christian religion is substantially soteriological. "What must I do to be saved?" remains throughout all the ages the question of the anxious inquirer, to which above all else an answer must be given. This question is unintelligible for those who refuse to view time in the light of eternity, and who are accustomed to think of this earth without organic and moral connection with the life to come. But of course, wherever two elements appear, as in this case the sinner and the saint, the temporal and the eternal, the terrestrial and the heavenly life, there is always danger of losing sight of their interconnection and of falsifying both by error or onesidedness. Christendom, it must be confessed, did not escape this error. A dualistic conception of regeneration was the cause of the rupture between the life of nature and the life of grace. It has, on account of its too intense contemplation of celestial things, neglected to give due attention to the world of God's creation. It has, on account of its exclusive love of things eternal, been backward in the fulfilment of its temporal duties. It has neglected the care of the body because it cared too exclusively for the soul. And this one-sided, inharmonious conception in the course of time has led more than one sect to a mystic worshipping of Christ alone, to the exclusion of God the Father Almighty, *Maker of heaven and earth.* Christ was conceived exclusively as the Savior, and His *cosmological* significance was lost out of sight.

This dualism, however, is by no means countenanced by the Holy Scriptures. When John is describing the Savior, he first tells us that Christ is the "eternal Word, by Whom all things are made, and who is the life of men." Paul also testifies that "all things were created by Christ and consist by Him;" and further, that the object of the work of redemption is not limited to the salvation of individual sinners, but extends itself to the redemption *of the world,* and to the organic reunion of all things in heaven and on earth under Christ as their original head. Christ himself does not speak only of the regeneration of the earth, but also of a regeneration of the cosmos (Matt. 19:28). Paul declares: "The whole creation groaneth waiting for the bursting forth of the glory of the children of God." And when John on Patmos listened to the hymns of the Cherubim and the Redeemed, all honor, praise and thanks were given to God, "Who has created the heaven and *the* earth." The Apocalypse returns to the starting-point of Gen. 1:1— "In the beginning God created the heaven and *the earth."* In keeping with this, the final outcome of the future, foreshadowed in the H. Scriptures, is not the merely spiritual existence of saved souls, but *the restoration of the entire cosmos,* when God will be all in all under the renewed heaven on the renewed earth. Now this wide, comprehensible, cosmical meaning of the gospel has been apprehended again by Calvin, apprehended not as a result of a dialectic process, but of the deep impression of God's majesty, which had moulded his personal life.

Certainly our salvation is of substantial weight, but it cannot be compared with the much greater weight of the glory of our God, Who has revealed His majesty in His wondrous creation. This creation is His handiwork, and being marred by sin, the way was opened, it is true for a still more glorious revelation in its restoration, yet restoration is and ever will be the salvation of that which was first created, the theodicy of the original handiwork of our God. The mediatorship of Christ is and ever will be the burden of the grand hymn of the tongues of men and the voices of angels, but even this mediatorship has for its final end the glory of the Father; and however grand the splendor of Christ's kingdom may be, He will at last surrender it to God and the Father. He is still our Advocate with the Father, but the hour is coming when His prayer for us will cease, because we shall know in that day that the Father loves us. Thereby of course Calvinism puts an end once and for all to contempt for the world, neglect of temporal and un-

der-valuation of cosmical things. Cosmical life has regained its
worth not at the expense of things eternal, but by virtue of its
capacity as God's handiwork and as a revelation of God's attributes.

Two facts may suffice to impress you with the truth of this. During the terrible plague which once devastated Milan, Cardinal
Borromeo's* heroic love shone brightly in the courage he manifested in his ministrations to the dying; but during the plague,
which in the 16th century tormented Geneva, Calvin acted better
and more wisely, for he not only cared incessantly for the spiritual needs of the sick, but at the same time introduced hitherto unsurpassed hygienic measures whereby the ravages of the plague
were arrested. The second fact to which I draw your attention is
not less remarkable. The Calvinistic preacher Peter Plancius** of
Amsterdam was an eloquent sermonizer, a pastor unrivalled in his
consecration to his work, foremost in the ecclesiastical struggle of
his days, but at the same time he was the oracle of shipowners and
sea-captains on account of his extensive geographical knowledge.
The investigation of the lines of longitude and latitude of the
terrestrial globe formed in his estimation one whole with the investigation of the length and breadth of the love of Christ. He saw
himself placed before two works of God, the one in creation, the
other in Christ, and in both he adored that majesty of Almighty
God, which transported his soul into ecstasy. In this light it is de-
serving of notice that our best Calvinistic Confessions speak of
two means whereby we know God, *viz.*, the Scriptures *and Nature*. And still more remarkable it is that Calvin, instead of simply
treating Nature as an accessorial item as so many Theologians were
inclined to do, was accustomed to compare the Scriptures to a
pair of spectacles, enabling us to decipher again the divine
Thoughts, written by God's Hand in the book of *Nature*, which
had become obliterated in consequence of the curse. Thus vanished every dread possibility that he who occupied himself with nature was wasting his capacities in pursuit of vain and idle things.

---

* Frederick Borromeo (1564—1631) cardinal, archbishop of Milan. During the
famine and pest at Milan he fed 2,000 poor daily.

** Petrus Plancius, 1622, St. Steven called him "le tres-docte geograph."

It was perceived, on the contrary, that for God's sake, our attention may not be withdrawn from the life of nature and creation; the study of the body regained its place of honor beside the study of the soul; and the social organization of mankind on earth was again looked upon as being as well worthy an object of human science as the congregation of the perfect saints in heaven. This also explains the close relation existing between Calvinism and Humanism. In as far as Humanism endeavored to substitute life in this world for the eternal, every Calvinist opposed the Humanist. But in as much as the Humanist contented himself with a plea for a proper acknowledgment of secular life, the Calvinist was his ally.

Now I proceed to consider the dogma of *"common grace,"* that natural outcome of the general principle, just presented to you, but in its special application to *sin,* understood as corruption of our nature. Sin places before us a riddle, which in itself is insoluble. If you view sin as a deadly poison, as enmity against God, as leading to everlasting condemnation, and if you represent a sinner as being "wholly incapable of doing any good, and prone to all evil," and on this account salvable only if God by regeneration changes his heart, then it seems as if of necessity all unbelievers and unregenerate persons ought to be wicked and repulsive men. But this is far from being our experience in actual life. On the contrary the unbelieving world excels in many things. Precious treasures have come down to us from the old heathen civilization. In Plato you find pages which you devour. Cicero fascinates you and bears you along by his noble tone and stirs up in you holy sentiments. And if you consider your own surroundings, that which is reported to you, and that which you derive from the studies and literary productions of professed infidels, how much there is which attracts you, with which you sympathize and which you admire. It is not exclusively the spark of genius or the splendor of talent, which excites your pleasure in the words and actions of unbelievers, but it is often their beauty of character, their zeal, their devotion, their love, their candor, their faithfulness and their sense of honesty. Yea, we may not pass it over in silence, not unfrequently you entertain the desire that certain believers might have more of this attractiveness, and who among us has not himself been put to the blush occasionally by being confronted with what is called the "virtues of the heathen"?

It is thus a fact, that your dogma of total depravity by sin does not always tally with your experience in life. Yet, if you now run to the opposite direction and proceed from these experimental facts, you must not forget that your entire Christian confession falls to the ground, for then you look upon human nature as good and incorrupt; the criminal villains have to be pitied as ethically-insane; regeneration is entirely superfluous in order to live honorably; and your imagination of higher grace seems to be nothing else than playing with a medicine, which often proves entirely ineffectual. True, some people save themselves from this awkward position by speaking of the virtues of unbelievers as "splendid vices," and, on the other hand, by charging the sins of believers to old Adam, yet you feel, yourselves, that this is a subterfuge, which lacks earnestness.

Rome tried to find a better way of escape in the well-known doctrine of the *pura naturalia*. Romanists taught that there existed two spheres of life, the earthly or the merely human here below, and the heavenly, higher than the human as such; the latter offering celestial enjoyments in the vision of God. Now, Adam, according to this theory, was well prepared by God for both spheres, for the common sphere of life by the nature He gave him, and for the extra-common by granting him the supra-natural gift of original righteousness. In this wise Adam was doubly furnished for the natural as well as the celestial life. By the fall he lost the latter, not the former. His natural equipment for his earthly life remained almost unimpaired. It is true, human nature was weakened, but as a whole it remained in its integrity. Adam's natural endowments remained his possession after the fall. This explains to them why it is that fallen man often excels in the natural order of life, which is in fact merely human. You perceive that this is a system which tries to reconcile the dogma of the fall with the real state of things round about us, and on this remarkable anthropology is founded the entire Roman catholic religion. Two things only are faulty in this system, on the one hand it lacks the deep Scriptural conception of sin, and on the other it errs by the undervaluation of human nature to which it leads. This is the false dualism, to which a previous Lecture pointed, in the carnival. At that time the world is once more fully enjoyed, before one enters upon the *Caro vale,* but after the Carnival, in order to save the ideal, follows, for a short time, spiritual elevation into the higher spheres of life. For this reason the clergy, severing the earthly tie in celibacy, rank higher than the laity, and again, the monk, who turns away from earthly possessions also and sacrifices his own will, stands, ethically considered, on a higher level than the clergy. And finally the highest perfection is reached by the stylite, who, mounting his pillar, severs himself from everything earthly, or by the yet more silent penitent who causes himself to be immured in his subterranean cave. Horizontally, if I may use this expression, the same thought finds embodiment in the separation between sacred and secular ground. Everything uncountenanced and uncared for by the church is looked upon as being of a lower character, and exorcism in baptism tells us that these lower things are really meant to be unholy. Now, it is evident that such a standpoint did not invite Christians to make a study of earthly things. Nothing but a study appertaining to the sphere of heavenly things and contemplation could attract those who under such a banner had mounted guard over the sanctuary of the ideal.

This conception of the moral condition of fallen man has been opposed in principle by Calvinism, on the one hand by taking our conception of sin in the most absolute sense, and on the other by explaining that which is good in fallen man by the dogma of *common grace.* Sin, according to Calvinism, which is in full accord with the Holy Scriptures, sin unbridled and unfettered, left to itself, would forthwith have led to a total degeneracy of human life, as may be inferred from what was seen in the days before the flood. But God arrested sin in its course in order to prevent the complete annihilation of His divine handiwork, which naturally would have followed. He has interfered in the life of the individual, in the life of mankind as a whole, and in the life of nature itself by His common grace. This grace, however, does not kill the core of sin, nor does it save unto life eternal, but it arrests the complete effectuation of sin, just as human insight arrests the fury of wild beasts. Man can prevent the beast from doing damage: 1st, by putting it behind bars; 2nd, he can subject it to his will by taming it; and 3rd, he can make it attractive by domesticating it, *e.g.,* by transforming the originally wild dog and cat into domestic animals. In a similar manner God by His "common grace" restrains the operation of sin in man, partly by breaking its power, partly by taming his evil spirit, and partly by domesticating his nation or his family. Common grace has thus led to the result that an unregenerated sinner may captivate and attract us by much that is lovely and full of energy, just as our domestic animals do, but this of course after the manner of man. The nature of sin, however, remains as venomous as it was. This is seen in the cat, which, brought back to the woods, returns to its former wild state after two generations, and a similar experience has been made with regard to human nature, just now, in Armenia and Cuba. He who reads an account of the massacres of St. Bartholomew is easily inclined to place these horrors to the account of the low state of culture in those days, but behold! our nineteenth century has surpassed these horrors by the massacres in Armenia. And he who has read a description of the cruelties committed by the Spaniards in the 16th century in the villages and cities of the Netherlands against defenceless old men, women and children, and then heard the news of what occurred now in Cuba, cannot help acknowledging that, what was a disgrace in the 16th, has been repeated in the 19th century. Where evil does not come to the surface, or does not manifest itself in all its hideousness, we do not owe it to the fact that our nature is not so deeply corrupt, but to God alone, Who by His "common grace" hinders the bursting forth of the flames from the smoking fire. And if you ask how it is possible, that in such a way out of restrained evil something may come forth which attracts, pleases and interests you, take then as an illustration the ferry-boat. This boat is put in motion by the current, which would carry it swiftly as an arrow down stream and ruin it; but by means of the chain, to which it is fastened, the boat arrives safely on the opposite side, pressed forward by the same power, which would otherwise have demolished it. In this wise God restrains the evil, and it is He who brings forth good out of evil; and meanwhile we Calvinists, never remiss in accusing our sinful nature, yet praise and thank God for making it possible for men to dwell together in a well-ordered society, and for restraining us personally from horrible sins. Moreover, we thank Him for bringing to light all the talents, hidden in our race, developing, by means of a regular process, the history of mankind, and securing by the same grace, for His church on earth, a place for the sole of her foot.

This confession, however, places the Christian in a quite different position over against life. For then, in his judgment, not only *the church,* but also *the world* belongs to God and in both has to be investigated the masterpiece of the supreme Architect and Artificer.

A Calvinist who seeks God, does not for a moment think of limiting himself to theology and contemplation, leaving the other sciences, as of a lower character, in the hands of unbelievers; but on the contrary, looking upon it as his task to know God in *all* his works, he is conscious of having been called to fathom with all the energy of his intellect, things *terrestrial* as well as things *celestial*; to open to view both the order of creation, and the "common grace" of the God he adores, in nature and its wondrous character, in the production of human industry, in the life of mankind, in sociology and in the history of the human race. Thus you perceive how this dogma of "common grace" suddenly removed the interdict, under which secular life had laid bound, even at the peril of coming very near a reaction in favor of a one-sided love for these secular studies.

It was now understood that it was the "common grace" of God, which had produced in ancient Greece and Rome the treasures of philosophic light, and disclosed to us treasures of art and justice, which kindled the love for classical studies, in order to renew to us the profit of so splendid an heritage. It was not clearly seen that the history of mankind is not so much an aphoristic spectacle of cruel passions as a coherent process with the Cross as its center; a process in which every nation has its special task, and the knowledge of which may be a fountain of blessing for every people. It was apprehended that the science of politics and national economy deserved the careful attention of scholars and men of thought. Yea, it was intuitively conceived, that there was nothing either in the life of nature round about us, or in human life itself, which did not present itself as an object worthy of investigation, which might throw new light on the glories of the entire cosmos in its visible phenomena and its invisible operations. And if on a different standpoint, progress in thorough scientific knowledge on these lines often led to pride and estranged the heart from God, we owe it to this glorious dogma of common grace that in Calvinistic circles the most profound investigator never ceased to acknowledge himself a guilty sinner before God, and to ascribe to God's mercy alone, his splendid understanding of the things of the world.

Having proved that Calvinism has fostered *love for science* and restored to science *its domain,* allow me now in the third place to show in what manner it has advanced its *indispensable liberty.* Liberty is for genuine science what the air we breathe is for us. This does not mean that science is entirely untrammeled in the use of its liberty and need obey no laws. On the contrary, a fish lying on dry land is perfectly free, *viz.,* to die and to perish, while a fish, which really shall be free to live and to thrive must be entirely surrounded by water and guided by its fins. In the same manner every science has to keep up the closest connection with its subject, and strictly to obey the claims of its proper method; and only when strictly bound by this double tie, can science move freely on. For the liberty of science does not consist in licentiousness or lawlessness, but in its being freed from all unnatural bonds, unnatural because they are not rooted in its vital principle. Now in order fully to understand the position Calvin took, we should abstain from any wrong conception of university-life in the middle ages. State universities were not known in those days. The universities were free corporations, and in so far prototypes of most of the universities in America. It was the general opinion in those days that science called into existence a *respublica litterarum,* "a commonwealth of learned men," which has to live upon its own spiritual capital or to die of lack of talent and energy. The encroachment upon the liberty of science in those days came not from the State but from an entirely different quarter. For ages two dominant powers, only, had been known in the life of mankind, the *Church* and the *State.* The dichotomy of body and soul was reflected in this view of life. The Church was the *soul,* the State the *body*; a third power was unknown. Church-life was centralized in the *Pope,* while the political life of the nations found its point of union in the *Emperor,* and it was the endeavor to resolve this dualism into a higher unity, that kindled the flames of the fierce struggle for the supremacy of the imperial crown or the papal tiara, as seen in the conflict between the Hohenstaufen and the Guelphs. Since then, however, science as a third power, thanks to the *Renaissance,* had pushed itself in between them. Before the thirteenth century elapsed, Science had found in the rising university-life an embodiment of its own, and claimed an existence independent of pope and emperor.

The only remaining question was whether this new power also was to create a hierarchial center in order to unveil itself as the third great potentate at the side of the pope and the emperor.

On the contrary, the republican character of the university demanded the exclusion of all monarchical aspirations. But it was just as natural for Pope and Cæsar, who had partitioned among themselves the entire domain of life, to watch with suspicion the growth of a third, entirely independent power, and to try everything in order to subject the universities to their rule. If all the then existing universities had taken a firm stand such a plan would never have succeeded. But as is often the case among free corporations, competition allured the weaker to seek support from without and so they turned for help to the Vatican. This compelled the stronger Universities to follow, and rather soon the favor of the Pope was universally coveted, in order to secure special privileges. Herein is found the fundamental evil. In this wise Science surrendered its independent character. It was overlooked that the intellectual reception into, and the reflection from, our consciousness of the cosmos wherein all science consists, forms a sphere entirely different from the Church. Now this evil has been checked by the Reformation, and mastered especially by Calvinism. Formally mastered, because in the Church itself the monarchical hierarchy being abandoned, and under the monarchical authority of Christ a republican and federal organization having been introduced, a spiritual Church-head, whose task it would be to rule over universities, no longer existed for our Calvinists. For Lutherans such a visible head was at hand in the ruler of the land, whom they honored as "first Bishop"; but not for Calvinistic nations, which kept Church and State separate as two different spheres of life. A doctor's diploma, in their system, might not derive its significance from public opinion, neither from papal consent, nor from an ecclesiastical ordinance, but solely from the scientific character of the institution.

To this must be added a second point. Without regarding the Papal auspices over the University as such, the Church exercised pressure upon Science by harassing, accusing and persecuting the innovators on account of their expressed opinions and published writings. Rome did oppose, not only *in* the Church, what was right, but also beyond its boundaries, the freedom of the word. Truth alone, not error, had the right to propagate itself in society and truth was expected to keep its ground, not by conquering error in honest conflict, but by arraigning it at the bar of justice. This impaired the liberty of Science, because it submitted scientific questions which could not be settled by ecclesiastical jurisdiction to the judgment of the civil Court. He who shrunk from conflicts kept silence or submitted to circumstances; and he, who being of more heroic mettle defied opposition, was punished by having his wings clipped; and if he nevertheless tried to fly with clipped wings, had his neck wrung. He who published a book, betraying too bold opinions, was considered a criminal, and came at last in contact with the Inquisition and the scaffold. The right of free inquiry was unknown. Firmly believing that everything knowable and worthy of being known *was* known already, and known firmly and well, the Church in those days had no idea of the immense task, reserved for science, just awaking from its mediæval slumber, nor of the "struggle for life," which was to be the indispensable rule in the execution of its task. The Church was unable to hail, in the dawn of science, a rosy morn, heralding to the horizon the rising of a new sun, but saw in its glittering rather the smouldering sparks, which threatened to set the world on fire; and therefore she considered herself justified and in duty bound to quench this fire and to extinguish these flames wherever an outbreak occurred. This position, when we place ourselves back in those times, we can understand, but not without firmly condemning its underlying principle, for it would have smothered nascent science in its very cradle, if all the world had persisted in favoring it. Glory, therefore, to Calvinism, which first of all abandoned this pernicious position with effectual results; theoretically by its discovery of the sphere of common grace, and, before long, practically, by offering a safe harbor to all who were caught in a storm elsewhere. It is true, Calvinism, as always happens in such cases, did by no means immediately understand the full bearing of its opposition, for it began by leaving the duty to extirpate error untouched in its own code, and yet the invincible idea, which was bound to lead and in the course of time has led to freedom of the word found its absolute expression in the principle that the church has to retire to the domain of *particular* grace, and that exempted from her rule lies the wide and free domain of "*common* grace." The result of this was that the penalties of criminal law were gradually reduced to a dead letter, and that, to instance only one case, Des Cartes, who had to leave Roman Catholic France, found among the Calvinists of the Netherlands, of course, a scientific antagonist in Voetius, but in the republic a safe retreat.

To this I must add that in order to cause science to flourish *a demand for science* had to be created, and to that end the public mind had to be made free. As long, however, as the Church stretched out her *velum* over the entire drama of public life, the state of bondage naturally continued, because the only object of life was to merit heaven and to enjoy as much of the world as the Church considered to be consistent with this main end. From this point of view it was unimaginable that any one should be willing to devote himself with sympathy and with the investigator's love to the study of our earthly existence. The seeking love of all was directed towards eternal life, and it could not be realized that Christianity, besides its yearning for eternal salvation, has to perform on earth, by divine commission, a grand task with regard to the cosmos. This new conception was first introduced by Calvinism when it cut at the root in the most absolute sense of every idea, that life on earth were ever destined to merit the blessedness of heaven. This blessedness, for every true Calvinist, grows out of regeneration, and is sealed by the perseverance of the saints. Where in this manner the "certainty of faith" supplanted the traffic of indulgences, Calvinism called Christendom back to the order of creation: "Replenish the earth, subdue it and have dominion over everything that lives upon it." Christian life as a pilgrimage was not changed, but the Calvinist became a pilgrim, who, while on his way to our eternal home, had yet to perform on earth an important task. The cosmos, in all the wealth of the kingdom of nature, was spread out before, under, and above man. This entire limitless field had to be worked. To this labor the Calvinist consecrated himself with enthusiasm and energy. For the earth with all that is in it, had, according to God's Will, to be subjected to man. Thus flourished, in those days, in my native country, agriculture and industry, commerce and navigation as never before. This new-born national life awakened new needs. In order to subdue the earth, a knowledge of the earth was indispensable, knowledge of its oceans, of its nature, and of the attributes and laws of this nature. And so it came to pass that the people itself, who had until now refrained from encouraging science, by a new and sparkling energy, suddenly called it into action, spurring it on to a sense of liberty, hitherto entirely unknown.

———

And now I approach my last point, *viz.,* the assertion that the emancipation of Science must inevitably lead to a sharp *conflict of principles*, and that, for this conflict, also, Calvinism alone offered the *ready solution*. You understand which conflict I have in view. Free investigation leads to collisions. One draws the lines on the map of life differently from his neighbor. The result is the origin of schools and tendencies. Optimists and pessimists. A school of Kant, and a school of Hegel. Among jurists the determinists oppose the moralists. Among medical men the homeopaths oppose the allopaths. Plutonists and Neptunists, Darwinists and anti-Darwinists compete with one another in the natural sciences. Wilhelm van Humboldt, Jacob Grimm and Max Mueller form different schools in the domain of Linguistics. Formalists and Realists pick quarrels with one another within the classical walls of the philological temple. Everywhere contention, conflict, struggle, sometimes vehement and keen, not seldom mixed with personal asperity. And yet, although the energy of the difference of principle lies at the root of all these disputes, these subordinate conflicts are entirely put in the shade by the *principal conflict,* which in *all* countries perplexes the mind most vehemently, the powerful conflict between those who cling to the confession of the Triune God and His Word, and those who seek the solution of the world-problem in Deism, Pantheism and Naturalism.

Notice that I do not speak of a conflict between faith and science. Such a conflict does not exist. Every science in a certain degree starts *from faith,* and, on the contrary, faith, which does not lead to science, is mistaken faith or superstition, but real, genuine faith it is not. Every science presupposes faith in self, in our self-consciousness; presupposes faith in the accurate working of our senses; presupposes faith in the correctness of the laws of thought; presupposes faith in something universal hidden behind the special phenomena; presupposes faith in life; and especially presupposes faith in the principles, from which we proceed; which signifies that all these indispensable axioms, needed in a productive scientific investigation, do not come to us by proof, but are established in our judgment by our inner conception and *given with our self-consciousness.* On the other hand every kind of faith has in itself an impulse to speak out. In order to do this it needs words, terms, expressions. These words must be the embodiment of thoughts. Those thoughts must be connected reciprocally not only with themselves but also with our surroundings, with time and eternity, and as soon as faith thus beams forth in our consciousness, the need of science and demonstration is born. Hence it follows that the conflict is not between faith and science, but between the assertion that the cosmos, as it exists today, is either in a *normal* or *abnormal* condition. If it is *normal*, then it moves by means of an eternal evolution from its potencies to its ideal. But if the cosmos in its present condition is *abnormal*, then a *disturbance* has taken place in the past, and only a *regenerating* power can warrant it the final attainment of its goal. This, and no other is the principal antithesis, which separates the thinking minds in the domain of Science into two opposite battle-arrays.

The *Normalists* refuse to reckon with other than natural data, do not rest until they have found an identical interpretation of all phenomena, and oppose with the utmost vigor, at every turn of the line, all attempts to break or to check the logical inferences of cause and effect. Therefore, they also honor faith in a *formal* sense but only as far as it remains in harmony with the general data of the human consciousness and this be considered as normal. *Materially,* however, they reject the very idea of creation, and can only accept evolution,—an evolution without a point of departure in the past, and eternally evolving itself in the future, until lost in the boundless infinite. No species, not even the species *Homo sapiens,* originated as such, but within the circle of natural data developed out of lower and preceding forms of life. Especially no miracles, but instead of them the natural law, dominating in an inexorable manner. No sin, but evolution from a lower to a higher moral position. If they tolerate the Holy Scriptures at all, they do it on condition that all those parts which cannot be logically explained as a human production be exscinded. A Christ, if necessary, but such a one as is the product of the human development of Israel. And in the same manner a God, or rather a Supreme Being, but after the manner of the Agnostics, concealed behind the visible Universe, or pantheistically hiding in all existing things, and conceived of as the ideal reflection of the human mind.

The *Abnormalists,* on the other hand, who do justice to relative evolution, but adhere to primordial creation over against an *evolutio in infinitum,* oppose the position of the Normalists with all their might; they maintain inexorably the conception of man as an independent species, because in him alone is reflected the image of God; they conceive of sin as the destruction of our original nature, and consequently as rebellion against God; and for that reason they postulate and maintain the miraculous as the only means to restore the abnormal; the miracle of regeneration; the miracle of the Scriptures; the miracle in the Christ, descending as God with His own life into ours; and thus, owing to this regeneration of the abnormal, they continue to find the ideal norm not in the natural but in the Triune God.

Not faith and science therefore, but *two scientific systems* or if you choose, two scientific elaborations, are opposed to each other, *each having its own faith.* Nor may it be said that it is here *science* which opposes *theology,* for we have to do with two absolute forms of science, *both* of which claim the whole domain of human knowledge, and both of which have a suggestion about the supreme Being of their own as the point of departure for their world-view. Pantheism as well as Deism is a system about God, and without reserve the entire modern theology finds its home in the science of the Normalists. And finally, these two scientific systems of the Normalists and the Abnormalists are not relative opponents, walking together half way, and, further on, peaceably suffering one another to choose different paths, but they are both in earnest, disputing with one another *the whole domain of life,* and they cannot desist from the constant endeavor to pull down to the ground *the entire edifice* of their respective controverted assertions, all the supports included, upon which their assertions rest. If they did not try this, they would thereby show on both sides that they did not honestly believe in their point of departure, that they were no serious combatants, and that they did not understand the primordial demand of science, which of course claims *unity of conception.*

A Normalist, who retains in his system the slightest possibility of creation, of a specific image of God in man, of sin as a fall, of Christ in so far as he transcends the human, of regeneration, as different from evolution, of the Scriptures, as bringing us real oracles of God,—is an amphibious scholar and forfeits the name of scientist. But on the other side, he, who, as Abnormalist, transforms creation to a certain extent into evolution; who does not see in the animal a protoplastic creature, made in the image of man, but man's origin; who surrenders the creation of man in original righteousness; and who moreover tries every way to explain Regeneration, Christ, and the Scriptures as the result of merely human causes, instead of clinging with all the energy of his soul to *the Divine cause,* as dominating in all this over all human data, must as decidedly be banished from our ranks as an amphibious and unscientific man. The *normal* and the *abnormal* are two absolutely differing starting-points, which have nothing in common in their origin. Parallel lines never intersect. You have to choose either the one or the other. But whatever you may choose, whatever you are as a scientific man, you have to be it consistently, not only in the faculty of theology, but in all faculties; in your entire world- and life-view; in the full reflection of the whole world-picture from the mirror of your human consciousness.

Chronologically, it is true, we Abnormalists, for many ages in succession, have been the speakers, hardly ever having been challenged, while our opponents had scarcely any opportunity to dispute our principles. With the decay of the old heathen, and the rise of the Christian world-view, the general conviction soon took deep root among all students that everything has been created by God, that the species of beings have been brought into existence by special creative acts, and that among these species of beings man has been created as image-bearer of God in original righteousness; further, that the original harmony has been broken by intervening sin; and that, in order to restore this abnormal state of affairs to its primitive condition, God introduced the abnormal means of Regeneration, of Christ as our Mediator and of the Holy Scriptures. There were of course through all ages, even in large numbers, scoffers who derided these facts, and indifferent people who took no interest in them; but the very few who during ten centuries scientifically opposed this universal conviction, you may count at once on your fingers' ends. The Renaissance doubtless favored the rise of an infidel tendency, which was felt even in the Vatican, and Humanism created enthusiasm for Græco-Roman ideals; but granted, that after the close of the middle ages, the opposition of the Normalists made a beginning, it yet remains a fact, that the large host of philologians, jurists, physicians and physicists, for centuries afterwards left untouched these foundations, on which the very old conviction rested. It was during the eighteenth century that the opposition made a change of front by leaving the circumference and taking up a position at the center; and it was the newer philosophy which, for the first time, on a general scale, set out with the declaration that the principles of the Christian world-view were utterly untenable. In this manner the Normalists first began to suspect, and then became conscious of their fundamental opposition. Every possible position, available in this reaction against the hitherto prevalent conviction, has been since that time by turn developed into a special philosophical system. These systems, divergent, if compared with each other, were however in perfect agreement in their denial of the abnormal. After these philosophical systems had secured the assent of the leading men, the several sciences followed, and were immediately solicitous to introduce the new hypothesis of an infinite normal process as the starting-point of their special investigations in the domains of jurisprudence, medicine, natural science and history.

Then for a moment surely, public opinion was stupefied with sudden fright, but since the mass of the people lacked *personal* faith, this superficial reluctance was only of short duration. Within a quarter of a century the life-view of the Normalists had conquered in a literal sense the world in its leading center. And only he who adhered to the abnormalist view by virtue of his personal faith refused to join in the chorus of those who sang the praises of "modern thought," and at the first brunt, felt inclined to anathematize all science, retiring to the tent of mysticism. It is true, for a short time theologians tried to defend their cause apologetically, but this defense might be compared to a man who tries to adjust a crooked window-frame, while he is unconscious of the fact that the building itself is tottering on its foundations.

This is the reason why the abler theologians, especially in Germany, imagined that the best thing to do would be to avail themselves of one or the other of these philosophical systems as a prop to sustain Christianity. The first result of this compound of philosophy and theology was the so-called mediating theology, which gradually became poorer and poorer in its theological, richer and richer in its philosophical part, until at last modern theology lifted up its head and found its glory in the attempt to cleanse theology of its abnormal character in such a thorough manner that Christ was transformed into a man, born as we are born, who was not even entirely free of sin, and the Holy Scriptures into a collection of writings, for the most part pseudepigraphic and in every possible manner interpolated and filled with myths, legends and fables. The song of the Psalmist: "We see not our signs; they have set up their ensigns for signs," has been literally fulfilled by them. Christ and the Scriptures included, every sign of the abnormal was rooted out, and the sign of the normal process embraced as the only genuine criterion of truth. In this result, I repeat what I have already stated, there is nothing to surprise us. He, who subjectively looks upon his inner being and objectively upon the world around him as normal, *cannot* but speak as he does, *cannot* reach a different result, and would be *insincere* in his position as a scientific man, if he were to represent things in a different light. And therefore from a moral point of view, not thinking for a moment of such a man's responsibility in the judgment of God, nothing can be said against his personal stand-point, provided that, thinking as he does, he shows the courage to voluntarily leave the Christian church in all its denominations.

If the character of the keen and unavoidable conflict is thus and not otherwise, behold then the unconquerable position which Calvinism points out to us in the strain and struggle, resulting from this conflict. It does not keep itself busy with useless apologetics; it does not turn the great battle into a skirmish about one of the outworks, but immediately goes back to *human consciousness,* from which every man of science has to proceed as *his* consciousness. This consciousness, just on account of the abnormal character of things, is not the same in all. If the normal condition of things had not been broken, consciousness would emit the same sound from all; but as a matter of fact, this is not the case. In the one the *consciousness of sin* is very powerful and strong, in the other it is either feeble or entirely wanting. In the one the *certainty of faith* speaks with decision and clearness as a result of regeneration, the other does not even understand what it is. So also in the one the *Testimonium Spiritus Sancti* resounds loudly and in tones firm and strong, while the other declares that he has never yet heard its testimony. Now, these three, consciousness of sin, certainty of faith and the testimony of the Holy Spirit, are constituent elements in the consciousness of every Calvinist. They form its immediate contents. Without these three self-consciousness does not exist with him. This the Normalist disapproves, and, therefore, he tries to force *his* consciousness upon us, and claims that our consciousness has to be identical with his own. From his point of view nothing else could be expected. For if he conceded that there might be a real difference between his consciousness and ours, he would thereby have admitted a break in the normal condition of things. We, on the contrary, do not claim that *our* consciousness shall be found in *him*. It is true, Calvin maintains, that there is hidden in the heart of every man a "religious seed," — *semen religionis,* and that the "God-feeling,"—*sensus divinitatis,* confessed or unconfessed, in moments of intense mental strain, causes the soul to tremble, but it is no less true that it is just his system which teaches that human consciousness in a man who believes and in a man who disbelieves cannot agree, but that on the contrary disagreement is inevitable. He, who is not born again, cannot have a substantial knowledge of sin, and he, who is not converted, cannot possess certainty of faith; he who lacks the Testimonium Spiritus Sancti, cannot believe in the Holy Scriptures, and all this according to the thrilling saying of Christ himself: "Except a man be born again, he *cannot see* the kingdom of God"; and also according to the saying of the apostle: "The natural man *receiveth not* the things of the spirit of God." Calvin, however, does not excuse unbelievers on this account. The day will come when they will be convinced in their own conscience. But with regard to the *present* condition of things we, of course, have to acknowledge *two kinds of human consciousness*: that of the regenerate and the unregenerate; and these two cannot be identical. In the one is found what is lacking in the other. The one is unconscious of a break and clings accordingly to the *normal*; the other has an experience both of a break and of a change, and thus possesses in his consciousness the knowledge of the *abnormal*. If, therefore, it be true that man's own consciousness is his *primum-verum,* and hence must be also the starting-point for every scientist, then the logical conclusion is that it is an impossibility that both should agree, and that every endeavor to make them agree must be doomed to failure. Both, as honest men, will feel duty bound to erect such a scientific edifice for the whole cosmos, which is in harmony with the fundamental data, given in their own self-consciousness.

You perceive immediately how radical and fundamental this Calvinistic solution of the perplexing problem is; Science is not undervalued or pushed aside, but postulated for the cosmos as a whole and all its parts. The claim is maintained that your science has to form a complete whole. And the difference between the science of the Normalists and Abnormalists is not founded upon any differing result of investigation, but upon the undeniable difference which distinguishes the self-consciousness of the one from that of the other. *Free science* is the stronghold we defend against the attack of her tyrannical twin-sister. The Normalist tries to do us violence even in our own consciousness. He tells us that our self-consciousness must needs be uniform with his own, and that everything else we imagine we find in ours stands condemned as self-delusion. In other words, the Normalist wishes to wrest from us the very thing which, in our self-consciousness, is the highest and holiest gift for which a continual stream of gratitude wells up from our hearts to God. He calls a lie in our own souls that which is more precious and certain to us than our life. With royal pride our consciousness of faith, and the indignation of our heart, rise up against all this. We resign ourselves to the fate of being slighted and oppressed in the world, but we refuse to be dictated to by anyone in the sanctuary of our heart. We do not assail the liberty of the Normalist to build a well-construed science from the premises of his own consciousness, but our right and liberty to do the same thing we are determined to defend, if needs be, at any cost.

The parts are now exchanged. Not so very long ago the principal positions of Abnormalism were looked upon as axioms for all sciences in almost all universities, and the few Normalists, who at that time opposed the principle of their antagonists, found it difficult to find a chair. First they were persecuted, then outlawed, after that at the most tolerated. But at present they are the masters of the situation, control all influence, fill ninety per cent of all professorial chairs, and the result is that the Abnormalist, who has been forced out of the official house, is now obliged to look for a place where he may lay down his head. Formerly we showed them the door, and now this sinful assault upon their liberty is by God's righteous judgment avenged by their turning us out into the street, and so it becomes the question, if the courage, the perseverance, the energy, which enabled them to win their suit at last, will be found now in a still higher degree, with Christian scholars. May God grant it! You cannot, nay, you even may not think of it, deprive him, whose consciousness differs from yours, of freedom of thought, of speech and of the press. That they, from their standpoint pull down everything that is holy in your estimation, is unavoidable. Instead of seeking relief for your scientific conscience in downhearted complaints, or in mystic feeling, or in unconfessional work, the energy and the thoroughness of our antagonists must be felt by every Christian scholar as a sharp incentive himself also to go back to *his* own principles in his thinking, to renew all scientific investigation on the lines of these principles, and to glut the press with the burden of his cogent studies. If we console ourselves with the thought that we may without danger leave secular science in the hands of our opponents, if we only succeed in saving theology, ours will be the tactics of the ostrich. To confine yourself to the saving of your upper room, when the rest of the house is on fire, is foolish indeed. Calvin long ago knew better, when he asked for a *Philosophia Christiana,* and after all every faculty, and in these faculties every single science, is more or less connected with the antithesis of principles, and should consequently be permeated by it. As little may you seek your safety in shutting your eyes to the actual conditions of things, wherein so many Christians imagine they find a safe shield. Everything astronomers or geologists, physicists or chemists, zoologists or bacteriologists, historians or archeologists bring to light has to be recorded,—detached of course from the hypothesis they have slipped behind it and from the conclusions they have drawn from it,—but every fact has to be recorded by you, also, as a fact, and as a fact that is to be incorporated as well in your science as in theirs.

In order, however, to make this possible, university life has to be subjected again, just as in the days when Calvinism began its splendid career, to a radical change. Of late, university life all over the world presumed that science grew up only from one homogeneous human consciousness, and that nothing but learning and ability determined whether you might claim a professorial chair or not. No one thought, like William the Silent when he founded the Leyden University over against that of Louvain, of *two lines of universities,* opposed to one another on account of radical difference of principle. Since, however, the world-wide conflict between the Normalists and Abnormalists broke out in full force, the need of a division of university-life began again to be felt more generally on both sides. The first in the field were (I speak only of Europe) the unbelieving Normalists themselves, who founded the Université Libre of Brussels. Before this in the same Belgium the Roman Catholic university of Louvain, in virtue of old traditions, had been placed in opposition to the neutral-universities of Liege and Ghent. In Switzerland a university arose at Freiburg, renowned, although yet young, as an embodiment of the Roman Catholic principle. In Great Britain the same principle is followed in Dublin. In France, Roman Catholic faculties are pitted against the faculties of the State institutions. And also in the Netherlands, Amsterdam saw the birth of the Free University, for the general cultivation of the sciences on the foundation of the Calvinistic principle.

If now, according to the demands of Calvinism, Church and State withdraw, I do not say their liberal gifts but their high authority, from *university-life,* in order that the university may be allowed to take root and flourish in its own soil, then certainly the division, which is already begun, will be accomplished of itself and undisturbed, and in this domain also it will be seen that only a peaceful separation of the adherents of antithetic principles warrants progress,—honest progress,—and mutual understanding. We here call upon History as our witness. First, the emperors of Rome tried to realize the false idea of *one State,* but the division of their universal monarchy into a multitude of independent nations was needed to develop the hidden political powers of Europe. After the fall of the Roman Empire, Europe yielded to the enchantment of *one world-Church,* until the reformation dispelled this delusion, also, thus opening the way for a higher development of Christian life. Nowhere else is this as clearly seen as in the United States of America, where denominational multiformity gave a separate Church-embodiment to every differentiation of principle. In the idea of *one Science* only, the old curse of uniformity is yet maintained. But of this also it may be prophesied that the days of its artificial unity are numbered, that it will split up, and that in this domain also at least the Roman Catholic, the Calvinistic and the Evolutional principles will cause to spring up different spheres of scientific life, which will flourish in a multiformity of universities. We must have systems in science, coherence in instruction, unity in education. That is only really free, which, while it is strictly bound to its own principle, has the power to free itself from all unnatural bonds. The final result, therefore, will be, thanks to Calvinism, which has opened for us the way, that liberty of science will also triumph at last; first by guaranteeing full power to every leading life-system to reap a scientific harvest from its own principle;—and secondly, by refusing the scientific name to whatsoever investigator dare not unroll the colors of his own banner, and does not show emblazoned on his escutcheon in letters of gold the very principle for which he lives, and from which his conclusions derive their power.

FIFTH LECTURE

CALVINISM AND ART

IN this fifth lecture, which is the last but one, I speak of *Calvinism and Art*.*

It is not the prevailing tendency of the day that induces me to do this. Genuflection before an almost fanatical worship of art, such as our time fosters, should little harmonize with the high seriousness of life, for which Calvinism has pleaded, and which it has sealed, not with the pencil or chisel in the *studio,* but with its best blood at the stake and in the field of battle. Moreover the love of art which is so broadly on the increase in our times should not blind our eyes, but ought to be soberly and critically examined. It presents the fact, which is in every way explainable, that artistic refinement, thus far restricted to a few favored circles, now tends to gain ground among broader middle classes, occasionally even betraying its inclination to descend to the widest strata of lower society. It is the democratizing, if you like, of a life-utterance which hitherto recommended itself by its aristocratic allurements. And though the really inspired artist may complain that, with the majority, piano-playing is mere strumming, and painting little more than daubing, yet, the exuberant feeling of having a share in the privileges of art is so overwhelming, that the scorn of the artist is preferred to the abandonment of art-training in education. To have laid a production of your own, however poor, upon the altar of art becomes more and more the characteristic of an accomplished civilization. Finally, in all this the desire of enjoyment through ear and eye expresses itself, especially by means of music and of the

---

* Art has been defined as the embodiment of beautiful thought in sensuous form., as for example marble or speech. In *Calvinisme en Kunst,* Dr. Kuyper states: "as image-bearer of God, man possesses the possibility both to create something beautiful, and to delight in it. This "kunstvermogen" is in man no separate function of the soul but an unbroken (continuous) utterance of the image of God.

stage. And if it cannot be denied that many court these sensual pleasures in ways that are less noble and too often sinful, it is equally certain that in many instances this love of art leads men to seek enjoyment in nobler directions and lessens the appetite for lower sensuality. Especially in our great cities, stage-managers are able to provide such first rate entertainments, and the easy means of communication between the nations imparts such an international character to our best singers and players, that the finest artistic enjoyments are now brought for almost no price within the reach of an ever-widening class. Besides, it is but fair to concede that, threatened with atrophy by materialism and rationalism, the human heart naturally seeks an antidote against this withering process, in its artistic instinct. Unchecked, the dominating influences of money and of barren intellectualism would reduce the life of the emotions to freezing-point. And, unable to grasp the holier benefits of religion, the mysticism of the heart reacts in an art-intoxication. Hence, though I do not forget that the real genius of art seeks the heights of isolation rather than the plains below, and that our age, so poor in the production of real creative art, is deemed to warm itself at the splendid glow of the past; yea, though I admit that the homage of art by the profanum vulgus must necessarily lead to art-corruption, nevertheless, in my estimation, even the most injudicious aesthetical fanaticism stands far higher than the common race for wealth, or an unholy prostration before the shrines of Bacchus and Venus. In this cold, irreligious and practical age the warmth of this devotion to art has kept alive many higher aspirations of our soul, which otherwise might readily have died, as they did in the middle of the last century. Thus you see, I do not under-estimate the present aesthetical movement. But what in the light of History should be discountenanced is the mad endeavor to place it higher than, or even to make it of equal value with the religious movement of the 16th century; yet this is what I should be doing if I begged for Calvinism the favor of this new artistic movement. And therefore, when I plead the significance of Calvinism in the domain of art, I am not in the least induced to do so by this vulgarization of art, but rather keep my eyes fixed upon the Beautiful and the Sublime in its eternal significance, and upon art as one of the richest gifts of God to mankind.

Here, however, every student of history knows that I founder upon a deeply-rooted prejudice. Calvin, it is said, was personally devoid of the artistic instinct, and Calvinism, which in the Netherlands proved guilty of Iconoclasm, cannot but be incapable either of artistic development or of real, noteworthy art-production. A brief word therefore about this strong prejudice is here in order. Without putting too high an estimate upon his: "Wer nicht liebt Weib, Wein und Gesang," it is beyond dispute that Luther was more artistically disposed than Calvin; but what does it prove? Will you deny Hellenism its artistic laurels because, devoid of all sense of the beautiful, Socrates boasted of the beauty of his giant nose because it allowed his breath to pass more freely? Do the writings of John, Peter and Paul, the three pillars of the Christian Church, in a single word betray any special appreciation of artistic life? Yea, be it asked reverently, is there any instance in the Gospels of Christ ever pleading for art as such, or seeking its enjoyment? And when these questions, one by one, must be answered in the negative, have you therefore the right to deny the fact that Christianity as such has been of an almost invaluable significance to the development of art? And if not, why then would you accuse Calvinism on the mere ground that Calvin personally had little feeling for art? And when you speak of the Iconoclasm of the Beggars, should you forget that in the 8th century in the midst of the artistic and beautiful Grecian world the manly spirit of Leo Isaurus instigated a still more violent Iconoclasm, and should therefore the honor be denied to Byzantium of having produced the finest monuments? Do you ask for still further proof to the contrary? Well, more sharply even than Leo Isaurus in the 8th century or the Netherland's Beggars in the 16th century, did Mahomed in his Khorân militate against images of all kinds, but will this justify the charge that the Alhambra in Grenada and the Alcazar at Seville are no wonderfully beautiful products of architectural art?

We must not forget that the artistic instinct is a *universal* human phenomenon, but that in connection with national types, climates and countries, the development of that artistic instinct is most unequally divided among the nations. Who will look for a development of art in Iceland, and who on the other hand will not scent it, if I may so express myself, amidst the luxury of nature in the Levant? Is it then a matter of surprise that the South of

Europe was more favorable for the development of this artistic instinct than the North? And when History shows that Calvinism was most widely received by the people of the North, does it prove aught against Calvinism, that in nations living in a colder climate and of poorer natural surroundings, it was not able to quicken an artistic life such as flourished among the Southern nations? Because Calvinism preferred a worship of God in spirit and in truth, to sacerdotal wealth, it has been accused by Rome of being devoid of an appreciation of art, and because it disapproved of a woman debasing herself as an artist's model or casting away her honor in the ballet, its moral seriousness has clashed with the sensualism of those who deemed no sacrifice too sacred for the Goddess of Art. All this, however, concerns only the place which art has to occupy in the sphere of life, and the boundaries of its domain, but does not touch art itself. To view therefore from a higher platform the significance of Calvinism to art, follow me in the investigation of these three points: 1. why Calvinism was not allowed to develop *an art-style of its own*; 2. what flows from its principle for *the nature of art*; and 3. what it has actually done for its *advancement*.

All would be well, if only Calvinism had developed an architectural style of its own. Just as the Parthenon is boasted of at Athens, the Pantheon at Rome, the Saint Sophia at Byzantium, the Cathedral at Cologne, or the Saint Peter's at the Vatican, so also ought Calvinism to be able to exhibit an impressive structure, embodying all the fulness of its ideal. And that it did not do this is considered sufficient proof of its artistic poverty. Of course Calvinism is understood as having tried to ascend to the same artistic luxury, but is censured as having proved unable to accomplish it; its barren inflexibility being the obstacle that prevented every higher aesthetical development. And when the humanist boasts of the classic art of Old Hellas, the Greek Church of the Byzantine, and Rome of its Gothic Cathedral, then Calvinism is looked upon as standing perplexed by the painful charge of having lessened the fulness of human life. Now in opposition to this thoroughly unfair accusation, I maintain that for the very reason of its *higher* principle Calvinism was not allowed to develop such an architectural style of its own. I was bound in this connection to put architecture to the front, because both in classic and in so-called Christian art the absolute and all-embracing production of art was exhibited in architecture, all the other departments of art finally adapting themselves to the temple, church, mosque or pagoda. Scarcely a single art-style can be mentioned which did not arise from the center of divine worship and which did not seek the realization of its ideals in the sumptuous structure for that worship. This was the thriving of an impulse which in itself was noble. Art derived her richest motives from Religion. The religious passion was the gold-mine, which financially rendered her boldest conceptions possible. For the realization of her conceptions in this holy domain she found not only the narrow circle of art-lovers, but also the whole nation at her feet. Divine worship furnished the tie that united the separated arts. And what tells more still, by this connection with the Eternal, art received its inner unity and its ideal consecration. And this explains the fact that whatever the palace and the stage may have done for the development of art, it was always the sanctuary by which it was impressed with the stamp of a special character and to which it was indebted for a creative style. Art-style and the style of worship coincided. Now of course, if this wedding of art-inspired worship, with worship-inspired art be no intermediate stage, but the highest end to be obtained, then it must frankly be confessed that Calvinism cannot but plead guilty. If, however, it can be shown that this alliance of religion and art represents a *lower* stage of religious, and in general of human development, then it is plain that in this very want of a special architectural style, Calvinism finds an even higher recommendation. Being fully convinced that this is the case, I proceed to account for this conviction.

First then the aesthetic development of divine worship carried to those ideal heights of which the Parthenon and the Pantheon, the Saint Sophia and Saint Peter are the stone-embroidered witnesses, is only possible at that lower stage, in which the same form of religion is imposed upon a whole nation, both by prince and priest. In that case every difference of spiritual expression fuses into one mode of symbolical worship, and this union of the masses, under the leadership of the magistrate and the clergy, furnishes the possibility of defraying the immense expense of such colossal structures, and of ornamenting and decorating them. In the case, however, of a progressive development of the nations, when individual character-traits split the unity of the masses, Religion also rises to that higher plain where it graduates from the symbolical into the clearly-conscious life, and thereby necessitates both the division of worship into many forms, and the emancipation of matured religion from all sacerdotal and political guardianship. In the 16th century Europe was approaching, though slowly, this higher level of Spiritual development, and it was not Lutheranism with its subjection of the whole nation to the religion of the prince, but Calvinism with its profound conception of religious liberty, which initiated the transition. In every country where Calvinism has made its appearance, it has led to a multiformity of life-tendencies, it has broken the power of the State within the domain of religion, and to a great extent has made an end of sacerdotalism. As a result of this, it abandoned the symbolical form of worship, and refused, at the demand of art, to embody its religious spirit in monuments of splendor.

The objection that such a symbolic service had a place in Israel does not weaken my argument, it rather supports it. For does not the New Testament teach us that the ministry of shadows, naturally flourishing under the old dispensation, under the dispensation of fulfilled prophecy is "old and waxeth aged and is nigh unto vanishing away?" In Israel we find a state-religion, which is one and the same for the entire people. That religion is under sacerdotal leadership. And finally it makes its appearance in symbols, and is consequently embodied in the splendid temple of Solomon. But when this ministry of shadows has served the purposes of the Lord, Christ comes to prophesy the hour when God shall no longer be worshipped in the monumental temple at Jerusalem, but shall rather be worshipped in spirit and in truth. And in keeping with this prophecy you find no trace or shadow of art for worship in all the apostolic literature. Aaron's visible priesthood on earth gives place to the invisible High-priesthood after the order of Melchizedek in Heaven. The purely spiritual breaks through the nebula of the symbolical.

My second proof is that this agrees entirely with the higher relation between *Religion* and *Art*. Here I appeal to Hegel and Von

Hartmann who, both standing outside Calvinism, may be relied upon as being disinterested witnesses. Hegel says that art, which, at a lower stage of development, imparts to a still sensual religion its highest expression, finally helps it by these very means to cast off the fetters of sensuality; for though it must be granted that at a lower level it is only the aesthetical worship that liberates the spirit, nevertheless, he concludes, "beautiful art is not its highest emancipation," for that is only found in the realm of the invisible and spiritual. And Von Hartmann even more emphatically declares that: Originally Divine worship appeared inseparably united to art, because, at the lower stage, Religion is still inclined to lose itself in the aesthetic form. At that period, all the arts, he says, engage in the service of the cult, not merely music, painting, sculpture and architecture, but also the dance, mimicry and the drama. The more, on the other hand, Religion develops into spiritual maturity, the more it will extricate itself from art's bandages, because art always remains incapable of expressing the very essence of Religion. And the final result of this historic process of separation, he concludes, must be that Religion, when fully matured, will rather entirely abstain from the stimulant by which aesthetic pseudo-emotion intoxicated it, in order to concentrate itself wholly and exclusively upon the quickening of those emotions which are *purely religious.*"

And both Hegel and Von Hartmann are correct in this fundamental thought. Religion and Art have each a life-sphere of their own; these may at first be scarcely distinguishable from each other and therefore closely intertwined, but, with a richer development, these two spheres necessarily separate. Looking at two babies in a cradle you can scarcely tell which is boy or girl, but when, having reached the years of maturity, they stand before you, as man and woman, you see them both with forms, and traits, and modes of expression peculiarly their own. And so, arrived at their highest development, both Religion and Art demand an independent existence, and the two stems which at first were intertwined and seemed to belong to the same plant, now appear to spring from a root of their own. This is the process from Aaron to Christ, from Bezaleel and Aholiab to the Apostles. And, by virtue of that same process, Calvinism occupies a higher standpoint in the 16th century than Romanism could reach. Consequently Calvinism was neither able, nor even permitted, to develop an art-style of its own from its religious principle. To have done this would have been to slide back to a lower level of religious life. On the contrary, its nobler effort must be to release religion and divine worship more and more from its sensual form and to encourage its vigorous spirituality. This it was enabled to do because of the powerful pulse-beat by which at that time the religious life coursed through the arteries of mankind. And the fact that in these days our Calvinistic churches are deemed cold and *unheimish*, and a reintroduction of the symbolical in our places of worship is longed for, we owe to the sad reality that the pulsebeat of the religious life in our times is so much fainter than it was in the days of our martyrs. But so far from borrowing from this the right of redescending to a lower level of religion, this faintness of the religious life ought to inspire the prayer for a mightier in-working of the Holy Spirit. Second childhood, in your old age, is a painful, retrograde movement. The man who fears God, and whose faculties remain clear and unimpaired, does not on the brink of age return to the playthings of his infancy.

One more objection might maintain itself after this demonstration, and that too I want to face. The question may be asked whether a really independent life-tendency should not create its own art-style, even if it developed itself as absolutely secular. Let the real meaning of the objection be well understood. It does not suggest that Calvinism if truly possessed of an æsthetic significance should have given a certain direction to the practice of art, for the fact that Calvinism has truly done this will presently show itself. The point of this objection hits deeper, and puts the question whether in the first place a secular art-style is conceivable; and in the second place, whether the creation of such a purely secular and dominating art-style could have been demanded of Calvinism. The answer I make to the first is: that in the history of art no record of the rise of such an all-embracing art-style independent of Religion, is to be found. Mark you, I do not here speak of a school of a single art, but of an art-style which puts a concentric impress upon all the arts together. To a certain degree it could be asserted of Roman art and of that of the Renaissance that, although devoid of a leading religious impulse, they nevertheless reached an all-sided revelation in art-forms. Speaking of architecture, the dome in Roman and Byzantine art is not an expression of a religious thought but of political energy. The dome symbolizes world-power, and, though it may be in a different sense, of the Renaissance also it must be confessed that it did not take its rise in religion, but in the circles of civil and social life. Now the Renaissance will be considered more fully in the third part of this lecture, but with respect to the Roman art-style I here answer, first, that a style, which borrowed almost all its motives from Greek art can scarcely boast of an independent character; and secondly, that, in Rome, the State-idea had become so identified with the Religious idea, that when, in the period of the emperors, art reached its height of prosperity while sacrifices were burned to Divus Augustus, it is unhistorical to consider State and Religion any longer as being at that time separate spheres.

But, apart from this historic outcome, it may be questioned, whether such an all-embracing art-style ever *could* have originated outside of Religion. The rise of such a style demands a central motive in the mental and emotional life of a people, which shall dominate the whole existence from within, and which consequently carries its effect from this spiritual center to its outermost circumference. Not of course as though a national world of art ever could be the product of intellectual thought. Intellectual art is no art, and the effort put forth by Hegel to draw out from thoughts, militated against the very nature of art. Our intellectual, ethical, religious and æsthetic life each commands a sphere of its own. These spheres run parallel and do not allow the derivation of one from the other. It is the central emotion, the central impulse, and the central animation, in the mystical root of our being, which seeks to reveal itself to the outer world in this fourfold ramification. Art also is no side-shoot on a principal branch, but an independent branch that grows from the trunk of our life itself, even though it is far more nearly allied to Religion than to our thinking or to our ethical being. If, however, it be asked how there can arise a unity of conception embracing these four domains, it constantly appears that in the finite this unity is only found at that point where it springs from the fountain of the Infinite. There is no unity in your thinking save by a well-ordered philosophical system, and there is no system of philosophy which does not ascend to the issues of the Infinite. In the same way there is no unity in your moral existence save by the union of your inner existence with the moral world-order, and there is no moral world-order conceivable but for the impression of an Infinite power that has ordained order in this moral world. Thus also no unity in the revelation of art is conceivable, except by the art-inspiration of an Eternal Beautiful, which flows from the fountain of the Infinite. Hence no characteristic all-embracing art-style can arise except as a consequence of the peculiar impulse from the Infinite that operates in our inmost being. And since this is the very privilege of Religion, over intellect, morality and art, that she alone effects the communion with the Infinite, in our self-consciousness, the call for a secular, all-embracing art-style, independent of any religious principle, is simply absurd.

Understand that art is no fringe that is attached to the garment, and no amusement that is added to life, but a most serious power in our present existence, and therefore its principal variations must maintain, in their artistic expression, a close relation with the principal variations of our entire life; and since, without exception, these principal variations of our entire human existence are dominated by our relation to God, would it not be both a *degradation* and *an underestimation* of art, if you were to imagine the ramifications, into which the art-trunk divides itself, to be independent of the deepest root which all human life has in God? Consequently no art-style has sprung from the Rationalism of the 18th century, nor from the principle of 1789, and however grievous it may be to our 19th century, all her efforts to create a new art-style of her own have ended in perfect failure, and then only do her artistic productions possess a real charm when she allows herself to be inspired by the wonders of the past.

Thus by itself the possibility must be denied that a proper art-style can originate independently of religion; but even if this were otherwise, it would still be illogical, and this was my second argument, to demand such a secular tendency of Calvinism. For how can you desire that a life-movement, which found the origin of its power in the arraignment of all men and of all human life before the face of God, should have sought the impulse, the passion and the inspiration for its life *outside of God* in so exceedingly important a domain as that of the mighty arts? There remains, therefore, no shadow of a reality in the scornful reproach that the non-creation of an architectural style of its own is a conclusive proof of Calvinism's artistic poverty. Only under the auspices of its religious principle could Calvinism have created a general art-style, and just because it had reached a so much higher stage of religious development, its very principle forbade it the symbolical expression of its religion in visible and sensual forms.

Hence the question must be differently stated. And this brings us to our second point. The question is not whether Calvinism produced what, with its higher view-point, it was no longer allowed to create, *viz.,* a general art-style of its own, but *what interpretation of the nature of art flows from its principle.* In other words, is there in the life- and world-view of Calvinism a place for art, and if so, what place? Is its principle opposed to art, or, if judged by the standards of the Calvinistic principle, would a world without *art* lose one of its ideal spheres? I do not speak now of the abuse, but simply of the use of art. In every domain, life is bound to respect the dimensions of this domain. Encroachment on the domain of others is always unlawful; and our human life will only then attain its nobler harmony when all its functions coöperate in just proportion to our general development. The logic of the mind may not scorn the feelings of the heart, nor should the love of the beautiful silence the voice of conscience. However holy Religion may be, it must keep within its own bounds, lest, in crossing its lines, it degenerate into superstition, insanity or fanaticism. And, in the same way, the too exuberant passion for art which laughs at the whispering of conscience, must end in an unlovely discord quite different from what the Greeks exalted in their kalokagathos. The fact, for instance, that Calvinism arrayed itself against all unholy play with woman's honor, and stigmatized every form of immoral artistic enjoyment as a degradation, lies therefore outside our scope. All this properly denounces the abuse, while it carries no weight whatever with the question of the lawful use. And that the lawful use of art was not opposed, but encouraged and even recommended, by Calvin himself, his own words readily prove. When the Scripture mentions the first appearance of art, in the tents of Jubal, who invented the harp and organ, Calvin emphatically reminds us that this passage treats of "excellent gifts of the Holy Spirit." He declares that in the artistic instinct God had enriched Jubal and his posterity with rare endowments. And he frankly states that these inventive powers of art prove most evident testimonies of the Divine bounty. More emphatically still, he declares, in his commentaries on Exodus, that "all the arts come from God and are to be respected as Divine inventions." According to Calvin, these precious things of the natural life we owe originally to the Holy Ghost. In all Liberal Arts, in the most as well as in the least important, the praise and glory of God are to be enhanced. The arts, says he, have been given us for our comfort, in this our depressed estate of life. They react against the corruption of life and nature by the curse. When his colleague, Prof. Cop, at Geneva, took up arms against art, Calvin purposely instituted measures, by which, as he writes, to restore this foolish man to sounder sense and reason. The blind prejudice against Sculpture, on the ground of the Second Commandment, Calvin declares unworthy of refutation. He exults in Music as a marvelous power to move hearts and to ennoble tendencies and morals. Among the excellent favors of God for our recreation and enjoyment, it occupies in his mind the highest rank. And even when art condescends to become the instrument of mere entertainment to the masses, he asserts that this sort of pleasure should not be denied them. In view of all this we may say that Calvin esteemed art, in all its ramifications, as a gift of God, or, more especially, as a gift of the Holy Ghost; that he fully grasped the profound effects worked by art upon the life of the emotions; that he appreciated the end for which art has been given, *viz.*, that by it we might glorify God, and ennoble human life, and drink at the fountain of higher pleasures, yea even of common sport; and finally, that so far from considering art as a mere imitation of nature, he attributed to it the noble vocation of disclosing to man a higher reality than was offered to us by this sinful and corrupted world.

Now if this implied nothing beyond the personal interpretation of Calvin, his testimony would of course have no conclusive value for Calvinism in general. But when we observe that Calvin himself was not artistically developed, and that therefore he must have derived this brief system of Aesthetics* from his principles, he may be credited with having expounded the Calvinistic consideration of art as such. To go direct to the heart of the question, we begin with Calvin's last saying, *viz.*, that art reveals to us a higher reality than is offered by this sinful world. You are familiar with the question, already mentioned, whether art should imitate nature or should transcend it. In Greece grapes were painted with such accuracy that birds were deceived by their appearance and tried to eat them. And this imitation of nature seemed the highest ideal to the Socratic school. Herein lies the truth, all too often forgotten by idealists, that the forms and relations exhibited by nature are and ever must remain the fundamental forms and relations of all actual reality, and an art which does not watch the forms and motions of nature nor listen to its sounds, but arbitrarily likes to hover over it, deteriorates into a wild play of fantasy. But on the other hand, all idealistic interpretation of art should be justified in opposition to the purely empirical, as often as the empirical confines its task to mere imitation. For then the same mistake is committed in art so often committed by scientists when they confine their scientific task to the mere observation, computation and accurate report of facts. For even as science has to ascend from the phenomena to the investigation of their inherent order, to the end that man, enriched by the knowledge of this order, may propagate nobler species of animals, flowers and fruits, than nature, herself, could produce, so also it is the vocation of art, not merely to observe everything visible and audible, to apprehend it, and reproduce it artistically, but much more to discover in those natural forms the order of the beautiful, and, enriched by this higher knowledge, to produce a beautiful world that transcends the beautiful of nature. And this is what Calvin asserted: *viz.*, that the arts exhibit gifts which God has placed at our disposal, now that, as the sad consequence of sin, the real beautiful has fled from us. Your decision here depends entirely upon your interpretation of the world. If you are considering the world as the realization of

---

* Esthetics may be defined as the science of beauty and taste; the branch of knowledge that pertains to the fine arts and art criticism. There is no generally accepted Esthetics. There are three schools: the sensualistic (Hogarth); the empirical, (Helmholtz); and the idealistic, owing its origin to Kant.

the absolute good, then there is none higher, and art can have no
other vocation than to copy nature. If, as the pantheist teaches,
the world proceeds, by slow processes, from the incomplete to perfection, then art becomes the prophecy of a further phase of life
to come. But if you confess that the world once *was* beautiful, but
by the curse has become *undone,* and by a final catastrophe is to
pass to its full state of glory, excelling even the beautiful of paradise, then art has the mystical task of reminding us in its productions of the beautiful that was lost and of anticipating its perfect
coming luster. Now this last-mentioned instance is the Calvinistic
confession. It realized, more clearly than Rome, the hideous, cor-
rupting influences of sin; this led to a higher estimation of the nature of paradise in the beauty of original righteousness; and guided
by this enchanting remembrance, Calvinism prophesied a redemption of outward nature also, to be realized in the reign of celestial
glory. From this standpoint, Calvinism honored art as a gift of the
Holy Ghost and as a consolation in our present life, enabling us
to discover in and behind this sinful life a richer and more glorious
background. Standing by the ruins of this once so wonderfully
beautiful creation, art points out to the Calvinist both the still visible lines of the original plan, and what is even more, the splendid
restoration by which the Supreme Artist and Master-Builder will
one day renew and enhance even the beauty of His original
creation.

If thus, on this principal point, Calvin's personal interpretation
agrees entirely with the Calvinistic confession, the same applies to
the next point in question. If the Sovereignty of God is and remains, for Calvinism, its unchangeable point of departure, then art
cannot originate from the Evil One; for Satan is destitute of every
creative power. All he can do is to abuse the good gifts of God.
Neither can art originate with man, for, being a creature himself,
man cannot but employ the powers and gifts put by God at his disposal. If God is and remains Sovereign, then art can work no enchantment except in keeping with the ordinances which God ordained for the beautiful, when He, as the Supreme Artist, called
this world into existence. And further, if God is and remains
Sovereign, then he also imparts these artistic gifts to whom He
will, first even to Cain's, and not to Abel's posterity; not as if art

were Cainitic, but in order that he who has sinned away the highest gifts, should at least, as Calvin so beautifully says, in the lesser gifts of art have some testimony of the Divine bounty. That artistic ability, that art-capacity, as such, can have room in human nature, we owe to our creation after the image of God. In the real world, God is Creator of everything; the power of really producing new things is His alone, and therefore He always continues to be the creative artist. As God, He alone is the original One, we are only the bearers of His Image. Our capacity to create after Him and after what He created, can only consist in the *unreal* creations of art. So we, in our fashion, may imitate God's handiwork. We create a kind of cosmos, in our Architectural monument; to embellish nature's forms, in Sculpture; to reproduce life, animated by lines and tints, in our Painting; to transfuse the mystical spheres in our Music and in our Poetry. And all this because the beautiful is not the product of our own fantasy, nor of our subjective perception, but has an objective existence, being itself the expression of a Divine perfection. After the Creation, God saw that all things were good. Imagine that every human eye were closed and every human ear stopped up, even then the beautiful remains, and God sees it and hears it, for, not only "His Eternal Power," but also His "Divinity," from the very creation, has been perceived in His creature, both spiritually and somatically. An artist may notice this in himself. If he realizes how his own art capacity depends upon his having an eye for art, he must necessarily come to the conclusion that the original eye for art is in God Himself, Whose art capacity is all-producing, and after Whose image the artist among men was made. We know this from the creation around us, from the firmament that overarches us, from the abounding luxury of nature, from the wealth of forms in man and animal, from the rushing sound of the stream and from the song of the nightingale; for how could all this beauty exist, except created by One Who preconceived the beautiful in His own Being, and produced it from His own Divine perfection? Thus you see that the Sovereignty of God, and our creation after His Likeness, necessarily lead to that high interpretation of the origin, the nature and the vocation of art, as adopted by Calvin, and still approved by our own artistic instinct. The world of sounds, the world of forms, the world of tints, and the world of poetic ideas, can have no other source than God; and it is our privilege as bearers of His image, to have a perception of this beautiful world, artistically to reproduce, and humanly to enjoy it.

And thus I come to my third and last point. We found that the want of an art-style of its own, far from being an objection to Calvinism, on the contrary indicates the higher stage of its development. After that, we considered how exalted an interpretation of the nature of art flows from the Calvinistic principle. And now let us see how nobly Calvinism has encouraged the progress of the arts both in principle and in practice.

And here, in the first place, I draw your attention to the important fact that it was Calvinism which, by releasing art from the guardianship of the Church, first recognized its majority. I do not deny that the Renaissance had the same tendency, but, with the Renaissance, this was marred by a too one-sided preference for the Paganistic, and a passion for ideas more Heathen than Christian; while Calvin, on the other hand, kept firmly to the Christian ideas, and more sharply even than any other Reformed opposed every Paganistic influence. To deal justly, however, with the older Christian Church a somewhat fuller explanation is here in place. The Christian Religion made its appearance in the Greek and Roman world, which, though thoroughly demoralized, still recommended itself by its high civilization and its artistic splendor. Therefore, in order to oppose principle to principle, Christianity was bound, at the outset, to react against the then-dominating over-estimation of art, and thereby to break the dangerous influence which Paganism was exercising, in its last convulsion, by the enchantment of its beautiful world. As long, therefore, as the struggle with Paganism remained a struggle for life or death, the relation of Christianity to art could not but be an hostile one. This first period was followed almost immediately by the influx into the highly civilized Roman Empire of the still almost barbaric Germanic tribes, after whose speedy baptism the center of power gradually removed from Italy to beyond the Northern Alps, thus giving to the Church, as early as the 8th century, an almost exclusive ascendancy over the whole of Europe. Thanks to this constellation, the Church for several centuries became the guardian of high-er human life, and so nobly did she acquit herself of this exalted task that no religious hatred or party prejudice dares question any longer the glorious result she then achieved. In the literal sense of the word, all human development of that period depended en-tirely upon the Church. No science and no art could prosper un-less shielded by ecclesiastical protection. And hence originated that specifically Christian art, which, in its first passion, tried to em-body the maximum of spiritual essence in the minimum of form and tint and tone. It was no art copied from nature, but art in-voked from out the spheres of heaven, which fettered music in the Gregorian chains, the pencil and chisel of which longed after acos-mic creations, and which only in the building of the cathedrals at-tained the really Sublime and reaped imperishable fame. All edu-cational guardianship, meanwhile, leads to its own dissolution. A right-minded guardian intends to render his guardianship superf-luous as soon as possible, and he who tries to prolong his control, even after his ward has reached maturity, creates an unnatural re-lation and makes his guardianship itself an incentive to resistance. When therefore the first education of Northern Europe was com-pleted, and the church still persisted in swaying her absolute scep-tre across the entire domain of life, four great movements were started from as many different sides, viz., the *Renaissance* in the domain of art, the *Republicanism* of Italy in politics, *Humanism* in science, and centrally, in Religion, the *Reformation*.

No doubt these four movements received their impulse from very different, and in some cases conflicting principles, but they all agreed on this one point, viz., that they tried to escape from ecclesiastical tutelage, and to create a life of their own in accord-ance with their own principle. Hence it is not at all surprising that, in the 16th century, these four powers repeatedly acted in concert. It was the one human life that, weary of any further guardianship, hastened in every way after a freer development, and therefore, when the old guardian tried by main force to hold back the declaration of maturity, it was but natural that those four pow-ers should encourage one another fiercely to resist, nor to desist before freedom was obtained. Without this quadruple alliance not only would the tutelage of the Church have persevered over all Europe, but—the rebellion once crushed—its rule would have become even more grievous and intolerable than beforehand. Thanks to this coöperation, the bold undertaking was crowned with enduring success, and the combatants, by their combined energy, earned the everlasting glory of having brought art and science, as well as politics and religion, to the full enjoyment of maturity.

Will it be fair on this ground to assert that Calvinism has freed Religion, and not Art, and that the honors of the emancipation of art belong exclusively to the Renaissance? I readily grant that the Renaissance has a right to claim its share of the victory, especially in so far as it stimulated art herself to vindicate her liberty by her wonderful productions. Aesthetic genius, if I may so call it, had been implanted by God Himself in the Greek, and only by hailing again, amid loud rejoicings, the fundamental laws of art, which Greek genius had discovered, could art justify her claim to an independent existence. This by itself, however, could not have achieved the desired liberation. For the church of those days did not in the least oppose classical art as such. On the contrary, she welcomed the Renaissance, and Christian art did not hesitate a moment to enrich herself with the best the Renaissance had to offer. In the so-called *Cinquecento,* or high-Renaissance, Bramante and Da Vinci, Michael Angelo and Raphael, stored the Romish Cathedrals with treasures of art, quite unique and inimitable, never to be surpassed. Thus the old tie continued to unite Church and Art, and this of itself established a permanent patronage. The real liberation of art required much more patent energies. From principle, the Church was to be forced back to her spiritual realm. Art, having hitherto confined herself to the holy spheres, had now to make her appearance in the social world. And in the Church, Religion had to put aside her symbolical robes, in order that, after having ascended to the higher spiritual level, her life-giving breath might animate the whole world. Just as Von Hartmann truly observes: "It is pure spiritual Religion which with one hand deprives the artist of his specifically religious art, but which, with the other, offers him, in exchange, a whole world, to be religiously animated." Now Luther certainly *desired* such a pure, spiritual Religion, but Calvinism was the first to *grasp* it. First under the stirring impulses of Calvinism, our fathers broke with the *splendor ecclesiae,* i.e., with her outward glitter, and so also with her vast possessions, by which art was financially held in bondage. And although Humanism rebelled against this oppressive and unnatural state of things, it could never hope to effect a radical change if left to its own resources. Only think of Erasmus. Triumph in the struggle of that time was not reserved for the man who carried on the strife for Religious liberty by mere criticism, but only for him, who, standing on an higher stage of religious development, overcame the symbolical religion as such. And, therefore, we may boldly assert that it was Calvinism which prompted the spirited impulse by which the victory was won, and, by its indefatigable perseverance, has put an end to the unjustified tutelage of the church over all human life, art included.

Meanwhile I readily grant that this outcome would have been purely accidental, if Calvinism had not, at the same time, led to a deeper interpretation of human life and so of human art. When, under Victor Emmanuel, with the help of Garibaldi,* Italy was made free, the day of liberty also dawned for the Waldenses, in Middle and Southern Italy, but neither the *Re galantuomo,* nor Garibaldi, had even thought of the Waldensians. Thus it were possible that in its struggle for human liberty Calvinism also cut the tie that thus far held art a captive, but without having in the least intended to do this, by virtue of its principle. And therefore I must still illustrate the second factor, which alone decides the case. I have already, more than once, called your attention to the important significance of the Calvinistic doctrine of "common grace," and of course in this lecture on art I must refer to it again. That which is to be ecclesiastical must bear the stamp of faith, therefore genuine *Christian* art can only go out from believers. Calvinism, on the contrary, has taught us that all liberal arts are gifts which God imparts promiscuously to believers and to unbelievers, yea, that, as history shows, these gifts have flourished even in a larger measure outside the holy circle. "These radiations of Divine Light," he wrote, "shone more brilliantly among unbelieving people than among God's saints." And this of course quite reverses the proposed order of things. If you limit the higher enjoyment of art to regeneration, then this gift is exclusively the portion of believers,

---

* Garibaldi, Italian patriot and liberator, 1807-1882.

and must bear an ecclesiastical character. In that case it is the outcome of *particular grace*. But if, at the hand of experience and history, you become persuaded that the highest art-instincts are *natural* gifts, and hence belong to those excellent graces which, in spite of sin, by virtue of *common grace,* have continued to shine in human nature, it plainly follows that art can inspire both believers *and* unbelievers, and that God remains Sovereign to impart it, in His good pleasure, alike to Heathen and to Christian nations. This applies not only to art, but to all the natural utterances of human life, and is illustrated by the comparison in early times between Israel and the other nations. As far as holy things are concerned, Israel is chosen, and is not only blessed above all nations, but stands among all nations, isolated. In the question of Religion, Israel has not only a larger share, but Israel *alone* has the truth, and all the other nations, even the Greeks and the Romans, are bent beneath the yoke of falsehood. Christ is not partly of Israel and partly of the nations; He is of Israel alone. Salvation is of the Jews. But just in proportion as Israel shines forth from within the domain of Religion, so is it equally backward when you compare the development of its art, science, politics, commerce and trade to that of the surrounding nations. The building of the Temple required the coming of Hiram from a heathen country to Jerusalem; and Solomon, in whom, after all, was found the Wisdom of God, not only knows that Israel stands behind in architecture and needs help from without, but by his action he publicly shows that he, as the king of the Jews, is in no way ashamed of Hiram's coming, which he realizes as a natural ordinance of God.

So Calvinism, on the ground both of the Scriptures and of history, has arrived at the confession, that, wherever the Sanctuary discloses itself, all unbelieving nations stand outside, but that nevertheless, in their secular history, they are called by God to a special vocation, and form by their very existence, an indispensable link in the long chain of phenomena. Every utterance of human life requires a special disposition in blood and in descent, and proper adaptations of lot and incident as well as of natural environment and climatic effects are to contribute to its development. In Israel all this was adapted to the holy heritage which it was to receive in the Divine Revelation. But if Israel was chosen for the sake of Religion, this in no way prevented a parallel election of the Greeks for the domain of philosophy and for the revelations of art, nor of the Romans for the classical development within the domain of Law and of State. The life of art also has both its provisional development, and its later unfoldings, but in order to insure a more vigorous growth, it wanted first of all clear self-consciousness in its centrum that, once for all, the unchangeable foundations of its ideal existence might be brought to light. Such a phenomenon as art arrives at this self-revelation once only, and that revelation, once granted to the Greek, remains classical, tonegiving and for ever dominant. And although a further art-development may seek newer forms and richer material, the nature of the original find remains the same. Thus Calvinism was not only able, but bound, to confess that, by the grace of God, the Greeks were the primordial nation of art; that owing to this classical Greek development, art conquered its right of independent existence; and that although it certainly ought to radiate also in the sphere of Religion, it should in no wise be engrafted in a dependent sense upon the ecclesiastical tree. Therefore, being a return of art to her rediscovered fundamental lines, the Renaissance did not present itself to Calvinism as a sinful effort, but as a divinely ordered movement. And as such Calvinism encouraged the Renaissance not by pure accident, but with clear consciousness and definite purpose, in accordance with its deepest principle.

Hence there is no question that, simply as an involuntary result of its opposition to the Hierarchy of Rome, Calvinism should at the same time have encouraged the emancipation of art. On the contrary, it demanded this liberation and was bound to effect it, within its own circle, as a consequence of its world- and life-view. The world after the fall is no lost planet, only destined now to afford the Church a place in which to continue her combats; and humanity is no aimless mass of people which only serves the purpose of giving birth to the elect. On the contrary, the world now, as well as in the beginning, is the theater for the mighty works of God, and humanity remains a creation of His hand, which, apart from salvation, completes under this present dispensation, here on earth, a mighty process, and in its historical development is to glorify the name of Almighty God. To this end He has ordained for this humanity all sorts of life-utterances, and among these, art occupies a quite independent place. Art reveals ordinances of creation which neither science, nor politics, nor religious life, nor even revelation can bring to light. She is a plant that grows and blossoms upon her own root, and without denying that this plant may have required the help of a temporary support, and that in early times the Church lent this prop in a very excellent way, yet the Calvinistic principle demanded that this plant of earth should at length acquire strength to stand alone and vigorously to extend its branches in every direction. And thus Calvinism confessed that, inasmuch as the Greeks had first discovered the laws by which the growth of the art-plant is governed, they therefore remain entitled to bind every further growth and every new impulse of art to their first, their classical development, not for the sake of stopping short with Greece, or of adopting her Paganistic form without criticism. Art, like Science, cannot afford to tarry at her origin, but must ever develop herself more richly, at the same time purging herself of whatsoever had been falsely intermingled with the earlier plant. Only, the law of her growth and life, when once discovered, must remain the fundamental law of art for ever; a law, not imposed upon her from without, but sprung from her own nature. And so, by loosening every unnatural tie, and cleaving to every tie that is natural, art must find the inward strength required for the maintenance of her liberty. Calvin therefore does not estrange art, science, and religion, from one another; on the contrary, what he desires is that all human life shall be permeated by these three vital powers together. There must be a *Science* which will not rest until it has thought out the entire cosmos; a *Religion* which cannot sit still until she has permeated every sphere of human life; and so also there must be an *Art* which, despising no single department of life adopts, into her splendid world, the whole of human life, religion included.

Let this suggestion of the wide extension of the domain of art introduce my last point, viz., that Calvinism has also *actually and in a concrete sense advanced the development of the arts*. It scarcely needs a reminder that, in the realm of art, Calvinism was not able to play the rôle of a sorcerer, and could only work with natural data. That the Italian has a more tuneful voice than the Scot, and that the German is carried away by a more passionate impulse of song than the Netherlander, are simple data with which art had to reckon, under Roman supremacy, as well as under that of Calvinism. An undeniable fact, which explains why it is neither logical nor honest to reproach Calvinism for that which is merely due to the differences of national character. The truth is equally plain that, in the Northern countries of Europe, Calvinism was not able to produce, as by magic, marble, porphyry or free-stone, from the ground, and that therefore the arts of sculpture and architecture, which require rich, natural stone, were more readily developed in those countries where quarries abound, than in a country such as the Netherlands, where the ground consists of clay and mire. Poetry, music, and painting, therefore, can alone be considered here as the three free arts that are most independent of all natural data. This does not imply that the Flemish and Dutch city-hall fails to hold a position of honor all its own among the creations of architecture. Louvain and Middleburg, Antwerp and Amsterdam still bear witness to what Dutch art wrought in stone. And he who has seen the statues in Antwerp and at the tomb of William the Silent, carved by Quellinus and by De Keyzers, does not question the ability of our artists of the chisel. But this is subject to the objection that the style of our City Hall was found long before Calvinism made its appearance in the Netherlands, and that, even in its later development, it exhibits no single feature that can remind one of Calvinism. By virtue of its principle Calvinism built no cathedrals, no palaces and no amphitheatres, and was unable to populate the vacant niches of these gigantic buildings with sculptured ornaments.

Indeed, the merits of Calvinism, with respect to art, are to be found elsewhere. Not in the objective, but exclusively in the more subjective arts which, not depending upon the patronage of wealth and not in want of the marble quarry, have their spontaneous rise in the human mind. Of poetry I can make no further mention in this connection. To that purpose I should have to disclose to you the treasures of our own Dutch Literature, for the narrow bounds within which our Netherland language is confined have excluded our poetry from the world at large. This privilege of making their poetry a world phenomenon is only reserved for those larger nations, whose language, being spoken by millions and millions, becomes a vehicle for international intercourse. But if the province of *language* for smaller nations is limited, the *eye* is international, and music heard by the *ear* is understood in every heart. In order, therefore, that we may trace the influence of Calvinism upon the development and the welfare of art, we must limit ourselves, in the international sense, to the two subjective and independent arts, those of *painting* and *music*.

Now of both these arts it is to be stated that, before the days of Calvinism, they soared high above the common life of the Nations, and that only under the Calvinistic influence did they descend to the so much richer life of the people. As regards painting, just recall the productions of Dutch art by brush and etching-needle in the 16th and 17th centuries. Rembrandt's name alone is here sufficient to summon a whole world of art-treasures before your mind's eye. The museums of every country and continent still vie with each other, to the utmost, in their effort to obtain some specimen of his work. Even your brokers have respect for an art-school whose returns represent so vast a capital. And even in our days the masters all over the world are still borrowing their most effectual motives and their best art-tendencies from what, at that time, demanded the world's admiration as an entirely new school of painting. Of course this does not say that all these painters were personally staunch Calvinists. In the earlier art-school, which flourished under the influence of Rome, the "bon Catholiques" were also very rare. Such influences do not operate personally, but put their impress upon surroundings and society, upon the world of perceptions, of representations and of thought; and as a result of these various impressions an art-school makes its appearance. And, taken in this sense, the antithesis between the past and the present in the school of Dutch art is unmistakable. Before this period, no account was taken of the people; *they* only were considered worthy of notice who were superior to the common man, *viz.,* the high world of the Church and of the priests, of knights and princes. But, since then, the people had come of age, and under the auspices of Calvinism, the art of painting, prophetic of a democratic life of later times, was the first to proclaim the people's maturity. The family ceased to be an annex to the Church, and asserted its standing in its independent significance. By the light of common grace it was seen that the non-churchly life was also possessed of high importance and of an all-sided art-motive. Having been overshadowed for many centuries by class-distinctions, the common life of man came out of its hiding-place like a new world, in all its sober reality. It was the broad emancipation of our ordinary earthly life, and the instinct for liberty, which thereby captured the heart of the nations and inspired them with delight in the enjoyment of treasures so long blindly neglected. Even Taine has sounded the praises of the blessing, which went forth from the Calvinistic love of liberty to the realm of art, and Carrière, who himself was equally far from sympathizing with Calvinism, loudly proclaims that Calvinism alone was able to plough the field on which free art could flourish.

It has frequently been remarked, moreover, that the idea of election by free grace has contributed not a little toward interesting art in the hidden importance of what was seemingly small and insignificant. If a common man, to whom the world pays no special attention, is valued and even chosen by God as one of His elect, this must lead the artist also to find a motive for his artistic studies in what is common and of every-day occurrence, to pay attention to the emotions and the issues of the human heart in it, to grasp with his artistic instinct their ideal impulse, and, lastly, by his pencil to interpret for the world at large the precious discovery he has made. Even foolish and drastic extravagances became the motive for art-productions, merely as revolutions, of the human heart and as manifestations of human life. Man was also to be shown the image of his folly, that he might depart from evil. Thus far the artist had only traced upon his canvas the idealized figures of prophets and apostles, of saints and priests; now, however, when he saw how God had chosen the porter and the wage-earner for Himself, he found interest not only in the head, the figure and the entire personality of the man of the people, but began to reproduce the human expression of every rank and station. And if thus far the eyes of all had been fixed constantly and solely upon the sufferings of the "Man of Sorrows," some now began to understand that there was a mystical suffering also in the general woe of man, revealing hitherto unmeasured depths of the human heart, and thereby enabling us to fathom much better the still deeper depths of the mysterious agonies of Golgotha. Ecclesiastical power no longer restrained the artist, and princely gold no longer chained him in its fetters. If artist, he also was man, mingling freely among the people, and discovering in and behind their human life, something quite different from what palace and castle had hitherto afforded him, something, too, which proved to be much more valuable than the keenest eye had ever surmised. As Taine so significantly says: To Rembrandt, human life hid its face behind many sombre hues, but even in that chiaroscuro* his grasp upon that life was profoundly real and significant. As the result therefore of the declaration of the people's maturity and of the love of liberty which Calvinism awakened in the hearts of the nations, the common but rich human life disclosed to art an entirely new world, and, by opening the eye for the small and the insignificant, and by opening the heart for the sorrows of mankind, from the rich content of this newly discovered world, the Dutch school of art has produced upon the canvas those wondrous art-productions which still immortalize its fame, and which have shown the way to all the nations for new conquests.

Finally, as to the significance Calvinism had for Music, we face one of its excellencies which, though less widely known, is notwithstanding highly important—as Mr. Douen taught us ten years ago, in his two big volumes on Marot. Music and painting here run parallel. Even as in the ecclesiastical-aristocratic period it was only the high and the holy that interested the masters of the pencil, so in music the plain chant of Gregory was dominant, which abandoned rhythm, despised harmony, and which according to a professional critic, by its provisionally conservative character barred the way to the further artistic development of music. Far below the level of this stately chant flowed the freer song of the people, too often, alas, inspired by the worship of Venus, which at the times of the so-called "donkey-festivals," much to the chagrin of ecclesiastical officials, penetrated even the walls of the churches, and there occasioned those repulsive scenes which the Council of Trent first succeeded in putting under the ban. The Church alone

---

* Chiaroscuro from the Latin "clarus": clear, and oscuro: obscure. It indicates a blending of light and shades in pictures.

was privileged to make music, while that which the people produced was scorned, as being beneath the dignity of the art. Even in the oratory itself, while the people were allowed to listen to the holy music, they were forbidden to join in the song. Thus, as an art, music was almost entirely deprived of its independent standing. Only in so far as it could serve the church was it permitted to flourish artistically. Whatever it undertook on its own responsibility had no higher call than the popular use. And as in every department of life, Protestantism in general, but Calvinism more consistently, bridled the tutelage of the church, so also was music emancipated by it, and the way opened to its so splendid modern development. The men who first arranged the music of the Psalm for the Calvinistic singing were the brave heroes who cut the strands that bound us to the Cantus firmus, and selected their melodies from the free world of music. To be sure, by doing this, they adopted the people's melodies, but as Douen rightly remarks, only in order that they might return these melodies to the people purified and baptized in Christian seriousness. Music also would flourish, henceforth, not within the narrow limitations of particular grace, but in the wide and fertile fields of common grace. The choir was abandoned; in the sanctuary the people themselves would sing, and therefore Bourgeois* and the Calvinistic virtuosi who followed him were bound to make their selections from the popular melodies, but with this end in view, *viz.*, that now the people would no longer sing in the saloon or in the street, but in the sanctuary, and thus, in their melodies, cause the seriousness of the heart to triumph over the heat of the lower passions.

If this is the general merit of Calvinism, or rather the change which it effected in the domain of music, by forcing the idea of the laity to give room to that of the general priesthood of believers, historic accuracy requires a still more concrete elucidation. If Bourgeois was the great master whose works still assure him a front rank among the most notable composers of Protestant Europe, it is also worthy of note that this Bourgeois lived and la-

---

* Loys Bourgeois, born about 1510 at Paris, in 1541 followed Calvin to Geneva where he became "chartre" of the church. He was one of the first "psalmbewerkers." But since he desired to introduce still more "meerstemmige" psalms, he got into conflict with Calvin and his consistory, and in 1557 returned to Paris. He published his "vierstemmige" Psalter in Lyons (1547) and Paris (1554). Also wrote: *"Le droict chemin de musique,"* 1550.

bored in Geneva, under the very eyes of Calvin and even partly under his direction. It was this same Bourgeois who had the courage to adopt rhythm and to exchange the eight Gregorian modes for the two of major and minor from the popular music; to sanctify its art in consecrated hymn, and so to put the impress of honor upon that musical arrangement of tunes, from which all modern music had its rise. In the same way Bourgeois adopted the harmony or the song of several parts. He was the man who wedded melody to verse by what is called *expression*. The solfeggio, *i.e.*, the singing by note, the reduction of the number of chords, the clearer distinction of the several gamuts, etc., by which the knowledge of music was so much simplified, is all owing to the perseverance of this Calvinistic Composer. And when Goudimel,* his Calvinistic colleague, once at Rome the teacher of the great Palestrina, listening to the singing of the people in the church, discovered that the higher voices of the children outstripped the tenor, which had thus far held the lead, he for the first time gave the leading part to the soprano; a change of far-reaching influence which has ever since been maintained.

Pardon me if for a moment I detained you with these particulars, but the merits of Protestantism, and more particularly of Calvinism, in music are of too high an order to suffer longer depreciation without protest. I fully acknowledge that Calvinism exercised over some arts only an indirect influence, by the declaration of their maturity, and by affording them liberty to flourish in their own independence, but on music, the influence of Calvinism was a very positive one, due to its spiritual worship of God, which provided no room for the more material arts, but assigned a new rôle to song and to music by the creation of melodies and songs for the people. Whatever the old school did to join itself to the newer development of music, the modern music remained unnatural to the cantus firmus, because it sprang from a quite different root. Calvinism on the other hand not only joined itself to it, but under the leadership of Bourgeois and Goudimel gave it its first im-

---

* Claude Goudimel, born Besancon, France, 1505 or 1510. About 1540 he opened a School of Music. That Palestrina at one time was one of his pupils has been denied. He embraced the Reformed religion and settled at Lyons where he was murdered during the night of St. Bartholomew, 1572. He furnished music for the Psalms (1562) and published tunes still in use.

pulse, so that even Roman Catholic writers are constrained to acknowledge that our beautiful development of music in the last and present centuries for the most part owed its rise to the heretical church-hymns.

That in a later period Calvinism lost almost all influence in this domain, cannot be denied. For a long time Anabaptism overwhelmed us with its dualistic prejudices, and an unhealthy spiritualism prevailed. But when on that account, with entire disregard of our great musical past, Calvinism is accused by Rome of æsthetic dullness, it is well to call to mind that the great Goudimel was murdered by Romish fanaticism in the massacre of St. Bartholomew. This fact is suggestive; for we naturally ask with Douen: Has that man any right to complain about the stillness of the forest, who with his own hand has caught and killed the nightingale?

CALVINISM AND THE FUTURE

THE chief purpose of my lecturing in this country was to eradicate the wrong idea that Calvinism represented an exclusively dogmatical and ecclesiastical movement.

Calvinism *did* not stop at a church-order, but expanded in a *life-system*, and did not exhaust its energy in a dogmatical construction, but created a *life-* and *world-view*, and such a one as was, and still is, able to fit itself to the needs of every stage of human development, in every department of life. It raised our Christian religion to its highest spiritual splendor; it created a church order, which became the preformation of state confederation; it proved to be the guardian angel of science; it emancipated art; it propagated a political scheme, which gave birth to constitutional government, both in Europe and America; it fostered agriculture and industry, commerce and navigation; it put a thorough Christian stamp upon home-life and family-ties; it promoted through its high moral standard purity in our social circles; and to this manifold effect it placed beneath Church and State, beneath society and home-circle a fundamental philosophic conception strictly derived from its dominating principle, and therefore all its own.

This, of itself, excludes every idea of imitative repristination, and what the descendants of the old Dutch Calvinists as well as of the Pilgrim fathers have to do, is not to copy the past, as if Calvinism were a petrifaction, but to go back to the living root of the Calvinist plant, to clean and to water it, and so to cause it to bud and to blossom once more, now fully in accordance with our actual life in these modern times, and with the demands of the times to come.

This explains the subject of my final lecture. *A new Calvinistic development needed by the wants of the future.*

The prospect of this future does not present itself to us, as every student of sociology will acknowledge, in bright colors. I would not go so far as to assert that we are on the eve of universal social bankruptcy, but that the signs of the times are ominous admits of no denial. To be sure, in the control of nature and her forces, immense gains are being registered year by year, and the boldest imagination is unable to foretell to what heights of power in this respect the race may attain in the next half century. As a result of this, the comforts of life are increasing. World-intercourse and communication are constantly becoming more rapid and widespread. Asia and Africa, until recently dormant, gradually feel themselves drawn into the larger circle of stirring life. Aided by sport, the principles of hygiene exert a growing influence. Consequently, we are physically stronger than the preceding generation. We live longer. And in combating the defects and infirmities that threaten and afflict our bodily life, surgical science makes us marvel at her achievements. In brief, the material, tangible side of life holds out the fairest of promises for the future.

And yet discontent makes itself heard, and the thinking mind cannot suppress its misgivings; for, however high one may value the material things, they do not fill out the round of our existence as men. Our personal life as men and citizens subsist not in the comforts that surround us, nor in the body, which serves us as a link with the outward world, but in the spirit that internally actuates us; and in this inner consciousness we are becoming more and more painfully aware how the hypertrophy of our external life results in a serious atrophy of the spiritual. Not as if the faculties of thought and reflection, the arts of poetry and letters, were in abeyance. On the contrary, empirical science is more brilliant in her attainments than ever, universal knowledge spreads in constantly widening circles, and civilization, in Japan, for instance, is almost dazzled by her too rapid conquests. But even the intellect does not constitute the mind. Personality is seated more deeply in the hidden recesses of our inner being, where character is formed, whence the flame of enthusiasm is kindled, where the moral foundations are laid, where love's blossoms bud, whence spring consecration and heroism, and where in the sense for the Infinite, our time-bound existence reaches out unto the very gates of eternity. It is in regard to this seat of personality that we hear on all sides the complaint of empoverishment, degeneracy, and petrifaction. The prevalence of this state of *malaise* explains the rise of a spirit like Arthur Schopenhauer's; and the wide acceptance of his pessimistic doctrine reveals to what a deplorable extent this fatal Sirocco has scorched already the fields of life. It is true, Tolstoi's efforts show force of character, but even his religious and social theory is a protest along the whole line against the spiritual degeneracy of our race. Friedrich Wilhelm Nietzsche* may give us offence by his sacrilegious mockery, still what else is his demand for the *"Uebermensch"* (over-man), but the cry of despair wrung from the heart of humanity by the bitter consciousness that it is spiritually pining away? What is Social Democracy also but one gigantic protest against the insufficiency of the existing order of things? Even Anarchism and Nihilism but too plainly demonstrate that there are thousands upon ten thousands who would rather demolish and annihilate everything, than continue to bear the burden of present conditions. The German author of the *"Decadenz der Völker"* descries nothing in the future but decay and social ruin. Even the sober-minded Lord Salisbury recently spoke of peoples and states for whose unceremonious burial preparations were already being made. How often has not the parallel been drawn between our time and the golden age of the Roman empire, when the external brilliancy of life likewise dazzled the eye, notwithstanding that the social diagnosis could yield no other verdict than "rotten to the very core." And, although on the American continent, in a younger world, a relatively healthier tone of life prevails than in senescent Europe, yet this will not for a moment mislead the thinking mind. It is impossible for you to shut yourselves off hermetically from the old world, as you form no humanity apart, but are a member of the great body of the race. And the poison having once entered the system at a single point, in due time must necessarily pervade the whole organism.

Now the serious question with which we are confronted is whether we can expect that by natural evolution a higher phase of social life will develop out of the present spiritual decline. The an-

---

* F. W. Nietzsche, 1844-1900. German philosopher; died insane. Author of *Thus Spake Zarathustra*.

swer history supplies to this question is far from encouraging. In India, in Babylon, in Egypt, in Persia, in China and elsewhere, like periods of vigorous growth have been succeeded by times of spiritual decadence; and yet in not one of these lands has the downward course finally resolved itself in a movement towards higher things. All these nations to this day have persevered in their spiritual stagnation. In the Roman empire alone has the dark night of boundless demoralization been broken by the dawn of a higher life. But this light did not arise through evolution; it shone from the Cross of Calvary. The Christ of God appeared, and by His Gospel alone was the society of that time saved from certain destruction. And again, when towards the close of the middle ages Europe was threatened with social bankruptcy, a second resurrection from the dead and a manifestation of new vital power were witnessed, now among the peoples of the Reformation, but this time also not by way of evolution, but again through the same Gospel for which the hearts were thirsting, and whose truth was freely proclaimed as never before. What antecedents, then, does history furnish to lead us to expect in the present instance an evolution of life from death, whilst the symptoms of decomposition already suggest the bitterness of the grave? Mohammed, it is true, in the seventh century succeeded in creating a stir among the dead bones throughout the entire Levant by throwing himself upon the nations as a second Messiah, greater even than the Christ. And assuredly if the coming of another Christ, surpassing in glory the Christ of Bethlehem, were possible, then the cure for moral corruption were found. Hence some, indeed, have been anxiously looking for the coming of some glorious "Universal Spirit," who might again instil his vitalizing power into the heart-blood of the nations. But why dwell longer on such idle fancies? Nothing *can* possibly surpass the God-given Christ, and what we are to look for, instead of a second Messiah, is the second coming of the same Christ of Calvary, this time with His fan in His hand for judgment, not to open up for our sin-cursed life a new evolution, but to receive at its goal and solemnly to conclude the history of the world. Either this second coming, therefore, is near at hand, and what we are witnessing are the death-throes of humanity; or a rejuvenation is still in store for us; but if so, that rejuvenation can come only through the old and yet ever new Gospel which, at the beginning of our era, and again at the time of the Reformation, has saved the threatened life of our race.

The most alarming feature, however, of the present situation is the lamentable absence of that receptivity in our diseased organism, which is indispensable to the effecting of a cure. In the Greco-Roman world such receptivity did exist; the hearts opened spontaneously to receive the truth. To an even stronger degree this receptivity existed in the age of the Reformation, when large masses cried for the gospel. Then, as now, the body suffered from anemia, and blood-poisoning even had set in, but there was no aversion to the only effectual antidote. Now it is precisely this that distinguishes our modern decadence from the two preceding ones, that with the masses the receptivity for the Gospel is on the decrease, whilst with the scientists the positive aversion to it is on the increase. The invitation to bow the knee before Christ, as God, is met so often with a shrug of the shoulders, if not with the sarcastic rejoiner: "Fit for children and old women, not for us men!" The modern philosophy, which gains the day, considers itself in ever-increasing measure as having *outgrown* Christianity.

Therefore, first of all, the question must be answered what has brought us to this pass, a question deriving its paramount importance from the fact that only a correct diagnosis can lead to effective treatment. Now, historically, the cause of the evil is found in nothing else than in the spiritual degeneration which marked the close of the preceding century. The responsibility for this degeneration undoubtedly rests in part with the Christian churches themselves, not excepting those of the Reformation. Worn out by their struggle with Rome, these last churches had fallen asleep, had allowed leaf and flower to wither on their branches, and had apparently become forgetful of their duties in reference to humanity at large, and the whole sphere of human life. It is not necessary to enter upon this more fully. It may be taken for granted that towards the end of that century the general tone of life had become vapid and common-place, ignoble and base at heart. The eagerly-devoured literature of that period furnishes the proof. By way of reaction against this, the proposal was then made by deistic and atheistic philosophers, first in England, but afterwards chiefly in France on the part of the Encyclopedists, to place the whole of life on a new basis, turn upside down the existing order of affairs, and arrange a new world on the assumption that human nature continues in its uncorrupted state. This conception was an heroic one, and awakened response; it struck some of the noblest chords of the human heart. But in the great Revolution of 1789 it was put into execution in its most dangerous form; for in this mighty revolution, in this upheaval not only of political conditions, but even more of convictions, ideas, and usages of life, two elements should be sharply distinguished. In one respect it was an imitation of Calvinism, whilst in another respect it was in direct opposition to its principles. The great Revolution, it should not be forgotten, broke out in a Roman Catholic country, where first in the night of St. Bartholomew, and subsequently by the revocation of the edict of Nantes, the Huguenots had been slaughtered and banished. After this violent suppression of Protestantism in France, and other Roman Catholic countries, the ancient despotism had regained its ascendency, and to these nations all the fruits of the Reformation had been lost. This, by way of caricature of Calvinism, invited and compelled the attempt to strike for freedom by external violence, and to establish a pseudo-democratic state of affairs, which was to preclude for ever a return to despotism. Thus the French Revolution, by meeting violence with violence, crime with crime, strove after the same social liberty which Calvinism had proclaimed among the nations, but which had been attempted by Calvinism in the course of a purely spiritual movement. By this the French Revolution in a sense executed a judgment of God, the result of which affords, even to Calvinists, cause for rejoicing. The shades of De Coligny were avenged in the September murders of Mazas.

But this is only one side of the medal. Its reverse discloses a purpose directly *opposed* to the sound Calvinistic idea of liberty. Calvinism, by virtue of its profoundly serious conception of life, had strengthened and consecrated the social and ethical ties; the French Revolution loosened and entirely unfastened them, detaching life not merely from the Church, but also from God's ordinances, even from God Himself. Man as such, each individual henceforth, was to be his own lord and master, guided by his own free will and good pleasure. The train of life was to rush forward even more rapidly than heretofore, but no longer bound to follow the track of the divine commandments. What else could result than wreckage and ruin? Enquire of the France of today what fruit the fundamental idea of her grand Revolution has yielded to the nation after its first century of free sway so rich in horrors, and the answer comes in a most pitiful tale of national decadence and social demoralization.

Humbled by the enemy from beyond the Rhine, internally rent by partisan fury, dishonored by the Panama cabal, and more still by the Dreyfus case, disgraced by its pornography, the victim of economic retrogression, stationary, nay, even decreasing in population, France, as has been well said by Dr. Garnier, a medical authority on the subject, has been led by egotism to degrade marriage, by lust to destroy family-life and presents today, in wide circles, the disgusting spectacle of men and women lost in unnatural sexual sin. I am aware that there are still thousands upon thousands of families in France living without reproach, who dearly grieve at the moral ruin of their country, but then these are the very circles which have resisted the false pretenses of the Revolution; and, on the other hand, the almost bestialized circles are those that have succumbed to the first onset of Voltairianism.

From France this spirit of dissolution, this passion of wild emancipation, has spread among the other nations, especially through the medium of an infamously obscene literature, and infected their lives. Then nobler minds, particularly in Germany, perceiving what depth of wickedness had been reached in France, made the bold attempt of realizing this enticing and reducing idea of "emancipation from God" in a higher form while yet retaining its essence. Philosophers of the first rank, in a stately procession, each for himself constructed a cosmology endeavoring to restore a firm foundation to social and ethical relations, either by putting them on the basis of natural law, or by giving them an ideal substratum evolved from their own speculation. For a moment this attempt seemed to have a fair chance of success; for, instead of atheistically banishing God from their system, these philosophers sought refuge in Pantheism, and thus made it feasible to found the social structure, not as the French, on a state of nature or on the atomistic will of the individual, but on the processes of history and the collective will of the race, unconsciously tending towards the highest goal. And, indeed, for more than half a century this philosophy has imparted a certain stability to life; not that any real stability was inherent in the system themselves, but because the established order of law and strong political institutions in Germany lent the indirect support of tradition to the walls of an edifice which otherwise would have immediately collapsed. Even so, however, it could not prevent that in Germany also, the moral principles became more and more problematic, moral foundations more and more insecure, no other right than that of actual law received recognition; and, however much German and French development might differ between themselves, both agreed in their aversion to, and rejection of, traditional Christianity. Voltaire's *"Ecrasez l'infâme"* is already left far behind by Nietzsche's blasphemous utterances on the Christ, and Nietzsche is the author whose works are being most eagerly devoured by the young *modern* Germany of our day.

After this manner, then, we in Europe at least, have arrived at what is called *modern life,* involving a radical breach with the Christian traditions of the Europe of the past. The spirit of this *modern life* is most clearly marked by the fact that it seeks the origin of man not in creation after the image of God, but in evolution from the animal. Two fundamental ideas are clearly implied in this: (1) that the point of departure is no longer the ideal or the divine, but the material and the low; (2) that the sovereignty of God, which ought to be supreme, is denied, and man yields himself to the mystical current of an endless process, a *regressus* and *processus in infinitum.* Out of the root of these two fertile ideas a double type of life is now being evolved. On the one hand the interesting, rich, and highly organized life of University circles, attainable by the more refined minds only; and at the side of this, or rather far beneath it, a materialistic life of the masses, craving after pleasure, but, in their own way, also taking their point of departure in matter, and likewise, but after their own cynical fashion, emancipating themselves from all fixed ordinances. Especially in our ever-expanding large cities this second type of life is gaining the upper hand, overriding the voice of the country districts, and is giving a shape to public opinion, which avows its ungodly character more openly in each successive generation. Money, pleasure, and social power, these alone are the objects of pursuit; and people are constantly growing less fastidious regarding the means employed to secure them. Thus the voice of conscience becomes less and less audible, and duller the lustre of the eye which on the eve of the French Revolution still reflected some gleam of the ideal. The fire of all higher enthusiasm has been quenched, only the dead embers remain. In the midst of the weariness of life, what can restrain the disappointed from taking refuge in suicide? Deprived of the wholesome influence of rest, the brain is over-stimulated and over-exerted till the asylums are no longer adequate for housing the insane. Whether property be not synonymous with theft, becomes a more and more seriously mooted question. That life ought to be freer and marriage less binding, is being accepted more and more on an established proposition. The cause of monogamy is no longer worth fighting for, since polygamy and polyandry are being systematically glorified in all products of the realistic school of art and literature. In harmony with this, religion is, of course, declared superfluous because it renders life gloomy. But art, art above all, is in demand, not for the sake of its ideal worth, but because it pleases and intoxicates the senses. Thus people live in time and for temporal things, and shut their ears to the tolling of the bells of eternity. The irrepressible tendency is to make the whole view of life concrete, concentrated, practical. And out of this modernized private life there emerges a type of social and political life characterized by a decadence of parliamentarism, by an ever stronger desire for a dictator, by a sharp conflict between pauperism and capitalism, whilst heavy armaments on land and on sea, even at the price of financial ruin, become the ideal of these powerful states whose craving for territorial expansion threatens the very existence of the weaker nations. Gradually the conflict between the strong and the weak has grown to be the controlling feature of life, arising from Darwinism itself, whose central idea of a *struggle for life* has for its mainspring this very antithesis. Since Bismarck introduced it into higher politics, the maxim of the right of the stronger has found almost universal acceptance. The scholars and experts of our day demand with increasing boldness that the common man shall bow to their authority. And the end can only be that once more the sound principles of democracy will be banished, to make room this time not for a new aristocracy of nobler birth and higher ideals, but for the coarse and overbearing *kratistocracy* of a brutal money power. Nietzsche is by no means exceptional, but proclaims as its herald the future of our modern life. And while the Christ, in divine compassion, showed heart-winning sympathy with the weak, modern life in this respect also takes the precisely opposite ground that the weak must be supplanted by the strong. Such, they tell us, *was* the process of selection to which we, ourselves, owe our origin, and such is the process which, in us and after us, must work itself out to its ultimate consequences.

---

*Meanwhile, as observed above, it should not be forgotten that there flows in modern life a side-current, of nobler origin. A host of high-minded men arose, who, shrinking from the uneasy chill of the moral atmosphere, and taking alarm at the brutality of the prevailing egotism, endeavored to put new warmth in life partly by means of altruism, partly by means of a mystical cult of the feelings, partly even by means of the name Christianity. Though in accord with the school of the French Revolution in their breach with Christian tradition and in their refusal to recognize any point of departure besides that of empiricism and rationalism, these men nevertheless, by accepting, as Kant does, a crass dualism, tried to escape from the fatal consequences of their principle. It is precisely from this dualism that they drew the inspiration for the many noble ideas elaborated in their theories, embodied in their poetry, conjured up before our imagination in touching novels, commended to our consciences in ethical treatises, and, let us never forget, realized not infrequently in the serious pursuit of life. With them conscience, side by side with the intellect, had maintained its authority, and that human conscience is so richly endowed, (geïnstrumenteerd) by God. To the vigorous initiative of these men we owe the numerous sociological investigations and practical measures, which have allayed and alleviated so much suffering, and by an ideal altruism have put to shame the selfishness

---

* The following paragraph has been revised after the Dutch original.

in many a heart. Having a personal predisposition for mysticism, some of them claimed the right to emancipate the inner life of the soul from all restraints of criticism. To lose one's self in the Infinite, and to feel the stream of the Infinite pulsate through the deepest recesses of the inner life, meant to them desirable piety. Others again—especially theologians,—to a less extent divorced from Christianity by reason of their antecedents, office, or scholarly occupation, falling in with this altruism and mysticism, set themselves the task of so metamorphosing the Christ that He might continue to glitter from the throne of humanity, as the highest ideal of the modernized human heart. Each and all inspired by sincerity and inspiring by their ideal intent, these endeavors may be traced from Schleiermacher down to Ritschl.* He, therefore, who would look down upon such men, would only dishonor himself. Much rather we ought to thank them for what they endeavored to save, also those women of noble aspirations, who by their character-novels, written in a similar Christian spirit, have counteracted so much that was base, and have fostered so many precious germs. Even Spiritism, fraught with error though it be, has often received its impulse from the alluring hope that the contact with the eternal world, destroyed by criticism, could thus be reëstablished through the medium of visions. Unfortunately, however boldly conceived this ethical dualism might be, and whatever bold metamorphoses this mysticism might indulge in, there always lurked behind it the naturalistic, rationalistic system of thought which the intellect had devised. They extolled the normal character of their cosmology over against the abnormalism of our belief; and the Christian religion, being abnormalistic in principle and mode of manifestation, inevitably lost ground to such an extent that some of our best men did not shrink from professing that they preferred not only Spiritism, but Mohammedanism, and Schopenhauer or even Buddhism to the old evangelical faith. It is true that the entire phalanx of theologians from Schleiermacher to Pfleiderer continued to pay high honors to the name of Christ. but it is equally undeniable that this remained possible only by subjecting Christ and the Christian confession to ever bolder metamorphoses. A painful fact, but one

---

* Albrecht Ritschl, 1822-1889. German theologian.

which becomes absolutely evident, if you compare the creed now current in these circles with the confession for which our Martyrs died.

Even confining ourselves to the Apostles' Creed, which for almost two thousand years substantially has been the common standard of all Christians, we find that the belief in God as the "Creator of heaven and earth" has been abolished; for creation has been supplanted by evolution. Abolished also has been the belief in God the Son, as born of the Virgin Mary, through the conception from the Holy Ghost. Abolished further, with many, the belief in His resurrection and ascension and return to judgment. Abolished, finally, even the belief of the church in the resurrection of the dead, or at least in the resurrection of the body. The name of the Christian religion is still being retained, but in essence it has become a quite different religion in its principle, even of a diametrically opposite character. And when incessantly the charge is brought against us, that in point of fact the traditional Christ of the Church involves a complete metamorphosis of the genuine Jesus, whilst the modern interpretation has lifted the veil off the true character of the historical Jesus of Nazareth, we can but answer that, after all, historically, not this modern conception of Jesus of Nazareth, but the Church's confession of the Christ is the one that has conquered the world; and that century after century, the best and most pious of our race have paid homage to the Christ of tradition and rejoiced in Him as their Savior in the shadow of death.

Though desiring to be second to none, therefore, in sincere appreciation of what is noble in such attempts, I am fully settled in my conviction that no help is to be expected from that quarter. A theology which virtually destroys the authority of the Holy Scriptures as a sacred book; which sees in sin nothing but a lack of development; recognizes Christ for no more than a religious genius of central significance; views redemption as a mere reversal of our subjective mode of thinking; and indulges in a mysticism dualistically opposed to the world of the intellect,—such a theology is like a dam giving way before the first assault of the inrushing tide. It is a theology without hold upon the masses, a quasi-religion utterly powerless to restore our sadly tottering moral life to even a temporary footing.

May more perhaps be expected from the marvelous energy displayed in the latter half of this century by Rome? Let us not too hastily dismiss this question. Though the history of the Reformation has established a fundamental antithesis between Rome and ourselves, it would nevertheless be narrow-minded and short-sighted to underestimate the real power which even now is manifest in Rome's warfare against Atheism and Pantheism. Only ignorance of the exhaustive studies of Romish philosophy and of Rome's successful efforts in social life, could account for such a superficial judgment. Calvin in his day already acknowledged that, as against a spirit from the Great Deep, he considered Romish believers his allies. A so-called orthodox Protestant need only mark in his confession and catechism such doctrines of religion and morals as are not subject to controversy between Rome and ourselves, to perceive immediately that what we have in common with Rome concerns precisely those fundamentals of our Christian creed now most fiercely assaulted by the modern spirit. Undoubtedly on the points of the ecclesiastical hierarchy, of man's nature before and after the Fall, of justification, of the mass, of the invocation of saints and angels, of the worship of images, of purgatory, and many others, we are as unflinchingly opposed to Rome as our fathers were. But does not current literature show that these are not now the points on which the struggle of the age is concentrated? Are not the lines of battle drawn as follows: Theism over against Pantheism; sin over against imperfection; the divine Christ of God over against Jesus the mere man; the cross a sacrifice of reconciliation over against the cross as a symbol of martyrdom; the Bible as given by inspiration of God over against a purely human product; the ten commandments as ordained by God over against a mere archæological document; the ordinances of God absolutely established over against an ever-changing law and morality spun out of man's subjective consciousness? Now, in this conflict Rome is not an antagonist, but stands on our side, inasmuch as she also recognizes and maintains the Trinity, the Deity of Christ, the Cross as an atoning sacrifice, the Scriptures as the Word of God, and the

Ten Commandments as a divinely-imposed rule of life. Therefore, let me ask if Romish theologians take up the sword to do valiant and skilful battle against the same tendency that we ourselves mean to fight to the death, is it not the part of wisdom to accept the valuable help of their elucidation? Calvin at least was accustomed to appeal to Thomas of Aquino. And I for my part am not ashamed to confess that on many points my views have been clarified through my study of the Romish theologians.

This, however, does not in the least involve that our hope for the future may be placed in Rome's endeavor, and that we, idle ourselves, may await Rome's victory. A rapid survey of the situation will suffice to convince us of the contrary. To begin with your own continent, can South America for a moment stand a comparison with the North? Now in South and Central America the Roman Catholic Church is supreme. It has exclusive control in this territory, Protestantism not even counting as a factor. Here, then, is an immense field in which the social and political power, which Rome can bring to bear upon the regeneration of our race, can freely exert itself, a field, moreover, in which Rome is not a recent arrival, but which she has occupied for almost three centuries. The youthful development of the social organism of these countries has stood under her influence; she has remained in control also of their intellectual and spiritual life since their liberation from Spain and Portugal. Moreover, the population of these States is derived from such European countries as have always been under the undisputed sway of Rome. The test, therefore, is as complete and fair as possible. But in vain do we look in those American Romish States for a life which elevates, develops energy, and exerts a wholesome influence outside. Financially they are weak, comparatively unprogressive in their economic conditions; in their political life they present the sad spectacle of endless internal strife; and, if one were inclined to form an ideal picture of the future of the world, he might almost do so by imagining the very opposite of what is the actual situation in South America. Nor can it be pleaded in excuse of Rome that this is due to exceptional circumstances, for in the first place this political backwardness is met with not only in Chili, but likewise in Peru, Brazil as well as in the Venezuelan Republic; while, crossing from the New to the Old

World, we reach, in spite of ourselves, the same conclusion. In Europe, also, the credit of all Protestant states is high, that of the Southern countries which are Roman Catholic, is at a painful discount. Economic and administrative affairs in Spain and Portugal, and not less than in Italy, offer cause for continual complaint. The outward power and outside influence of these states is visibly declining. And, what is more discouraging still, infidelity and a revolutionary spirit have made such inroads in these countries, that half of the population, though still nominally Romish, has in reality broken with all true religion. This may be seen in France, which is almost entirely Roman Catholic, and yet has voted time and again with overwhelming majorities against the advocates of religion. In fact we may say that, in order to appreciate the noble, energetic traits of the Romanists, one must observe them, not in their own countries, where they are on the decline, but in the centre of Protestant North Germany, in Protestant Holland, and England, and in your own Protestant United States. In regions where, deprived of a controlling influence, they adjust themselves to the polity of others and concentrate their strength as an opposition party, under such leaders as Manning and Wiseman, Von Ketteler and Windthorst, they compel our admiration by the enthusiastic championship of their cause.

But even apart from this *testimonium paupertatis* furnished by Rome herself through the mismanagement in Southern Europe and South America, where she has full sway, in the contest of the nations also her power and influence are visibly waning. The balance of power in Europe is now gradually passing into the hands of Russia, Germany, and England, every one of them non-Romish States, and on your own continent the Protestant North holds the supremacy. Since 1866 Austria has been continually retrogressing, and at the death of the present Emperor will be seriously threatened with dissolution. Italy has attempted to live beyond its resources: it strove to be a great, colonial, naval power, and the result is that it has brought itself to the verge of economic ruin. The battle of Addua dealt the deathblow to more than her colonial aspirations. Spain and Portugal have absolutely lost all influence on the social, intellectual, and political development of Europe. And France, which only fifty years ago, made all Europe tremble at the unsheathing of her sword, is now herself anxiously scanning the Sibylline books of her future. Even from a statistical point of view, the power of Rome is all the while decreasing. Economic and moral depression has in more than one Romish country brought about a considerable decrease of the birthrate. Whilst in Russia, Germany, England, and the United States population is growing, it has in some Romish countries become almost stationary. Even now statistics give only the smaller half of Christendom to the Roman Catholic Church, and it is safe to predict that within the next half century its share will be less than forty per cent. However highly, therefore, I may be inclined to value the inherent power of Roman Catholic unity and scholarship for the defense of much we also count sacred, and though I do not see how we could repulse the attack of Modernism save by combined exertion, nevertheless there is not the slightest prospect that the political supremacy will ever again pass into Rome's hands. And, even if this were to happen contrary to expectations, who could possibly rejoice as in the realization of his ideal, if he beheld the conditions now prevailing in Southern Europe and South America, reproduced elsewhere?

We may, in fact, even put it more strongly: it would be a step backwards in the course of history. Rome's world and life-view represents an older and hence lower stage of development in the history of mankind. Protestantism succeeded it, and hence occupies a spiritually higher standpoint. He who will not go backwards, but reaches after higher things, must therefore either stand by the world-view once developed by Protestantism, or, on the other hand, for this, too, is conceivable, point out a still higher standpoint. Now this is what the latter modern philosophy does indeed presume to do, acknowledging Luther as a great man for his time, but hailing in Kant and Darwin the apostles of a much richer gospel. But this need not detain us. For our own age, however great in invention, in the display of powers of mind and energy, has not advanced us a single step in the establishment of principles, has in no wise given us a higher view of life, and has yielded us neither greater stability nor greater soundness in our religious and ethical, that is, truly human existence. The solid faith of the Reformation it has bartered for shifting hypothesis; and in so far as it ventured upon a systematized and strictly logical life-view it did not reach forward, but backward, to that heathen wisdom of pre-Christian times, of which Paul testified that God has put it to shame by the foolishness of the Cross. Let no one therefore say: Ye who, because history does not go backward, protest against a return to Rome, ye yourselves have no right to make a stand on Protestantism; for after Protestantism came Modernism. The pertinence of such an objection must be denied, as long as my contention be not disproved, that the material advance of our century has nothing in common with advancement in the matter of ethical principles, and that what Modernism offers us is not modern, but rather very antique; not posterior, but anterior to Protestantism, reaching back to the Stoa and to Epicurus.

Only along the lines of Protestantism, therefore, can a successful advance be attempted, and on those lines indeed salvation is sought at present, by two different tendencies, both of which must lead to bitter disappointment. The one of these is *practical,* the other *mystical* in character. Without hope of defence against modern criticism and still less against criticism of dogma, the former, the practical tendency, holds that Christians can do no better than fall back upon all manner of Christian works. Its devotees are at a loss what attitude to assume towards the Scriptures; they have become themselves estranged from dogma; but what is to prevent such hesitating believers from sacrificing their person and their gold to the cause of philanthropy, evangelism, and missions! This even offers a threefold advantage: it unites Christians of all shades of opinion, alleviates much misery, and has a conciliatory attraction for the non-Christian world. And, of course, this propagandism through action must be gratefully and sympathetically hailed. In the century that has passed, Christian activity was indeed far too limited; and a Christianity that does not prove its worth in practice, degenerates into dry scholasticism and idle talk. It would be a mistake, however, to suppose that Christianity can be confined within the limits of such practical manifestation. Our Savior made whole the sick and fed the hungry, but the paramount thing in His ministry was, after all, that in strict allegiance to the Scriptures of the old Covenant, He openly proclaimed His own Divinity and Mediatorship, the expiation of sins through His blood, and His coming to judgment. No central dogma, in fact, has ever been confessed by the Church of Christ which was not the intellectual definition of what Christ proclaimed about His own mission to the world, and about the world to which He was sent. He healed the sick body, but He even more truly bound up our spiritual wounds. He rescued us from Paganism and Judaism, and translated us into a wholly new world of convictions of which He Himself, as the God-ordained Messiah, constituted the center. Besides, as far as our dispute with Rome is concerned, we should not lose sight of the fact that in Christian works and devotion Rome still outstrips us. Nay, let us acknowledge without reserve that even the unbelieving world is beginning to rival us, and that in deeds of philanthropy, she tries more and more to overtake us. In missions, to be sure, unbelief does not follow in our footsteps; but pray how can we continue to prosecute missions, unless we have a well-defined Gospel to preach? Or is it possible to imagine anything more monstrous than so-called liberal missionaries preaching only humanity and colorless piety, and met by the pagan sages with the answer that they themselves in their cultured circles have never taught or believed anything else than just this modern humanism?

Does perhaps the other tendency, the *mystical* one, possess stronger powers of defence? What *thinker* or student of history would affirm this? No doubt mysticism eradiates a fervor that warms the heart; and woe betide the giant of dogma and the hero of action, who are strangers to its depths and tenderness. God created hand, head, and heart; the hand for the deed, the head for the world, the heart for mysticism. King in deed, prophet in profession, and priest in heart, shall man in this threefold office stand before God, and a Christianity that neglects the mystic element grows frigid and congeals. We are, therefore, to be accounted fortunate whenever a mystic atmosphere envelops us, making us breathe the balmy air of spring. Through it life is made truer, deeper, and richer. But it would be a sad mistake to suppose that mysticism, taken by itself, can bring about a reversal in the spirit of the age. Not Bernard of Clairvaux but Thomas of Aquino, not Thomas à Kempis but Luther, have ruled the spirits of men. Mysticism is, in its very nature, seclusive, and strives rather to avoid contact with the outside world. Its very strength lies in the indifferentiated life of the soul, and on this account it cannot take a positive stand. It flows along a subterranean bed and does not show sharply demarcated lines above the ground. What is worse, history proves that all one-sided mysticism has always become morbid, and has ultimately degenerated into a mysticism of the flesh, astounding the world with its moral infamy.

Accordingly, although I rejoice in the revival of both the practical and mystical tendencies, both will result in loss instead of gain, if they are expected to compensate for the abandonment of the Truth of Salvation. Mysticism is sweet, and Christian works are precious, but the seed of the Church, both at the birth of Christianity and in the age of the Reformation, has been the blood of martyrs; and our sainted martyrs shed their blood not for mysticism and not for philanthropic projects, but for the sake of convictions such as concerned the acceptance of truth and the rejection of error. To live with consciousness is man's well-nigh divine prerogative, and only from the clear, unobscured vision of consciousness proceeds the mighty *word* that can make the times reverse their current, and cause a revolution in the spirit of the world. It is self-deception, therefore, and only self-deception, when these practical and mystical Christians believe they can do without a Christian life and world-view of their own. No one can do without that. Everyone who thinks he can abandon the Christian truths, and do away with the Catechism of Reformation, lends ear unawares to the hypotheses of the modern world-view and, without knowing how far he has drifted already, swears by the Catechism of Rousseau and Darwin.

Therefore, let us not stop half-way. As truly as every plant has a root, so truly does a principle hide under every manifestation of life. These principles are interconnected, and have their common root in a fundamental principle; and from the latter is developed logically and systematically the whole complex of ruling ideas and conceptions that go to make up our life and world-view. With such a coherent world and life-view, firmly resting on its principle and self-consistent in its splendid structure, Modernism now confronts Christianity; and against this deadly danger, ye, Christians, cannot successfully defend your sanctuary, but by placing, in opposition to all this, *a life- and world-view of your own, founded as firmly on the base of your own principle, wrought out with the same clearness and glittering in an equally logical consistency.* Now this is not obtained by either Christian works or mysticism, but only by going back, our hearts full of mystical warmth and our personal faith manifesting itself in abundant fruit, to that turning-point in history, and in the development of humanity which was reached in the Reformation. *And this is equivalent to* a return to Calvinism. There is no choice here. Socinianism died an inglorious death; Anabaptism perished in wild revolutionary orgies. Luther never worked out his fundamental thought. And Protestantism, taken in a general sense, without further differentiation, is either a purely negative conception without content, or a chameleon-like name which the deniers of the God-Man like to adopt as their shield. Only of Calvinism can it be said that it has consistently and logically followed out the lines of the Reformation, has established not only Churches but also States, has set its stamp upon social and public life, and has thus, in the full sense of the word, created for the whole life of man a world of thought entirely its own.

I feel convinced that, after what I have said in my first lectures, no one will accuse me of underrating Lutheranism; yet the present Emperor of Germany has no less than three times furnished an example of the evil after-effects of Luther's apparently slight mistakes. Luther was misled into recognizing the Sovereign of the land as the head of the Established Church, and what have we, as a result of this, been called upon to witness from German's eccentric Emperor? First of all, that Stöcker, the champion of Christian democracy, was dismissed from his court, merely because this bold defender of the freedom of the churches had so much as expressed the wish that the Emperor should abdicate his chief episcopate. Next, that at the sailing of the German squadron for China, Prince Henry of Russia was instructed to carry to the far Orient not the "Christian" but the *"imperial* gospel." More recently that he called upon his loyal subjects to be faithful in the performance of their duties, urging as a motive that after death they were to appear before God . . . and His Christ? . . . No; but . . . before God . . . *and the great Emperor*. And finally, on the banquet of Porta Wesphalia, that Germany had to continue its labors undisturbedly under the blessing of peace, as enjoined, he concluded, *by the outstretched hand of the great Emperor, who here stands above us*. Ever bolder encroachment, it will be noticed, of Cæsarism upon the essence of the Christian religion. These, as you see, are far from mere trifles; rather, they touch principles of world-wide application, for which our forefathers in the age of the Reformation fought their great battles. To repristination I am as averse as any man; but in order to place for the defence of Christianity, principle over against principle, the world-view over against world-view, there lies at hand, for him who is a Protestant in bone and marrow, only *the Calvinistic principle* as the sole trustworthy foundation on which to build.

What, then, are we to understand by this return to Calvinism? Do I mean that all believing Protestants should subscribe, the sooner the better, to the Reformed symbols, and thus all ecclesiastical multiformity be swallowed up in the unity of the Reformed church-organization? I am far from cherishing so crude, so ignorant, so unhistorical a desire. As a matter of course, there is inherent in every conviction, in every confession, a motive for absolute and unconditional propagandism, and the word of Paul to Agrippa: "I would to God that with little or with much, not only you, but also all that hear me this day, might become such as I am," must remain the heartfelt wish not only of every good Calvinist, but of every one who may glory in a firm immovable conviction. But so ideal a desire of the human heart can never be realized in this our dispensation. First of all, not one Reformed standard, not even the purest, is infallible as was the word of Paul. Then, again, the Calvinistic confession is so deeply religious, so highly spiritual that, excepting always periods of profound religious commotion, it will never be realized by the large masses, but will impress with a sense of its inevitability only a relatively small circle. Furthermore, our inborn one-sidedness will always necessarily lead to the manifestation of the Church of Christ in many forms. And, last not least, absorption on a large scale by one Church of the members of another can only take place at critical moments in history. In the ordinary run of things eighty per cent of the Christian population die in the Church in which they were born and baptized. Besides, such an identification of my program with the absorption of one Church by another would be at variance with the whole tendency of my argument. Not ecclesiastically, confined to a narrow circle, but as a phenomenon of universal significance, have I commended to you the Calvinism of history. Therefore, what I ask may in the main be reduced to the following four points: (1) that Calvinism shall no longer be ignored where it still exists, but be strengthened where its influence continues; (2) that Calvinism shall again be made a subject of study in order that the outside world may come to know it; (3) that its principles shall again be developed in accordance with the needs of our time, and consistently applied to the various domains of life; and (4) that the Churches which still lay claim to confessing it, shall cease being ashamed of their own confession.

First, then, Calvinism should no longer be ignored where it still exists, but rather be strengthened where its historical influences are still manifest. A pointing out in detail, with even some degree of completeness, of the traces that Calvinism has everywhere left behind in social and political, in scientific and æsthetic life, would in itself demand a broader study than could be thought of in the rapid course of a lecture. Allow me, therefore, addressing an American audience, to point out a single feature in your own political life. I have already observed in my third lecture how in the preamble of more than one of your Constitutions, while taking a decidedly democratic view, nevertheless not the atheistic standpoint of the French Revolution, but the Calvinistic confession of the supreme sovereignty of God, has been made the foundation, at times even in terms, as I have pointed out, corresponding literally with the words of Calvin. Not a trace is to be found among you of that cynic anti-clericalism which has become identified with the very essence of the revolutionary democracy in France and elsewhere. And when your President proclaims a national day of thanksgiving, or when the houses of Congress assembled in Washington are opened with prayer, it is ever new evidence that through American democracy there runs even yet a vein which, having sprung from the Pilgrim Fathers, still exerts its power at the present day. Even your common school system, inasmuch as it is blessed with the reading of Scripture and opening prayer, points, though with decreasing distinctness, to like Calvinistic origin. Similarly in the rise of your university education, springing for the larger part from individual initiative; in the decentralized and autonomous character of your local governments; in your strict and yet not nomistic Sabbath-observance; in the esteem in which woman is held among you, without falling into the Parisian deification of her sex; in your sense for domesticity; in the closeness of your family ties; in your championship of free speech, and in your unlimited regard for freedom of conscience; in all this your Christian democracy is in direct opposition to the democracy of the French Revolution; and historically also it is demonstrable that you owe this to Calvinism and to Calvinism alone. But, lo and behold, while you are thus enjoying the fruits of Calvinism, and while even outside of your borders the constitutional system of government as an outcome of Calvinistic warfare, upholds the national honor, it is whispered abroad that all these are to be accounted blessings of Humanism, and scarcely any one still thinks of honoring in them the after-effects of Calvinism, the latter being believed to lead a lingering life only in a few dogmatically petrified circles. What I demand then, and demand with an historic right, is that this ungrateful ignoring of Calvinism shall come to an end; that the influence it has exerted shall again receive attention where it still remains stamped upon the actual life of today; and that, where men of a wholly different spirit would unobservedly divert the current of life into French revolutionary or German-pantheistic channels, you on this side of the water, and we on our side, should oppose with might and main such falsification of the historic principles of our life.

That we may be enabled to do so, I contend in the second place, for an historical study of the principles of Calvinism. No love without knowledge; and Calvinism has lost its place in the hearts of the people. It is being advocated only from a theological point of view, and even then very one-sidedly, and merely as a side is-

sue. The cause of this I have pointed out in a previous lecture.
Since Calvinism arose, not from an abstract system, but from life
itself, it never was in the century of its prime presented as a sys-
tematic whole. The tree blossomed and yielded its fruit, but without any one having made a botanic study of its nature and growth.
Calvinism, in its rise, rather acted than argued. But now this
study may no longer be delayed. Both the biography and biology
of Calvinism must now be thoroughly investigated and thought
out, or, with our lack of self-knowledge, we shall be side-tracked
into a world of ideas that is more at discord than in consonance
with the life of our Christian democracy, and cut loose from the
root on which we once blossomed so vigorously.

Only through such study will there become possible what I
named in the third place: the development of the principles of Calvinism in accordance with the needs of our modern consciousness,
and their application to every department of life. I do not exclude
theology from this; for theology, too, exercises its influence upon
life in all its ramifications; and it is, therefore, sad to see how even
the theology of the Reformed Churches has in so many a country
come under the sway of wholly foreign systems. But, at all events,
theology is only one of the many sciences that demand Calvinistic
treatment. Philosophy, psychology, æsthetics, jurisprudence, the
social sciences, literature, and even the medical and natural sciences, each and all of these, when philosophically conceived, go
back to principles, and of necessity even the question must be put
with much more penetrating seriousness than hitherto, whether the
ontological and anthropological principles that reign supreme in the
present method of these sciences are in agreement with the principles of Calvinism, or are at variance with their very essence.

Finally, I would add to these three demands—historically justified as it seems to me—still a fourth, that those Churches which
lay claim to professing the Reformed faith, shall cease being
ashamed of this confession. You have heard how broad my conception and how wide my views are, even in the matter of ecclesiastical life. In free development only do I see the salvation of this
Church-life. I exalt multiformity and hail in it a higher stage of
development. Even for the Church that has the purest confession,
I would not dispense with the aid of other Churches in order that

its inevitable one-sidedness may thus be complemented. But what has always filled me with indignation was to behold a Church or to meet the office-bearer of a Church, with the flag furled or hidden under the garb of office, instead of being thrown out boldly to display its glorious colors in the breeze. What one confesses to be the truth, one must also dare to practice in word, deed, and whole manner of life. A Church Calvinistic in origin and still recognizable by its Calvinistic confession, which lacks the courage, nay rather which no longer feels the impulse to defend that confession boldly and bravely against all the world, such a Church dishonors not Calvinism but itself. Albeit the Church reformed in bone and marrow may be small and few in numbers, as Churches they will always prove indispensable for Calvinism; and here also the smallness of the seed need not disturb us, if only that seed be sound and whole, instinct with generative and irrepressible life.

And thus my final lecture is rapidly drawing to its end. But before I close, I feel nevertheless that one question continues to press for an answer, which accordingly I shall not refuse to face, the question, namely, at what I am aiming in the end: at the abandonment or at the maintenance of the doctrine of election. Thereunto allow me to contrast with this word *Election* another word that differs from it in a single letter. Our generation turns a deaf ear to *Election,* but grows madly enthusiastic over *Selection.* How, then, may we formulate the tremendous problem that lies hidden behind these two words, and in what particular do the solutions of this problem, as represented by these two, almost identical formulas, differ? The problem concerns the fundamental question: *Whence are the differences?* Why is not all alike? Whence is it that one thing exists in one state, another in another? There is no life without differentiation, and no differentiation without inequality. The perception of difference the very source of our human consciousness, the causative principles of all that exists and grows and develops, in short the mainspring of all life and thought. I am therefore justified in asserting that in the end every other problem may be reduced to this one problem: Whence are those differences? Whence is the dissimilarity, the heterogeneity of existence, of genesis, and consciousness? To put it concretely, if you were a plant you would rather be a rose than mushroom; if insect, butter-fly rather than spider; if bird, eagle rather than owl; if a higher vertebrate, lion rather than hyena; and again, being man, richer than poor, talented rather than dull-minded, of the Aryan race rather than Hottentot or Kaffir. Between all these there is differ-entiation, wide differentiation. Everywhere then *differences,* dif-ferences between the one being and the other; and that, too, such differences as involve in almost every instance, *preference.* When the hawk rends and tears the dove, whence is it that these two creatures are thus opposed to, and different from each other? This is the one supreme question in the vegetable and animal kingdom, among men, in all social life, and it is by means of the theory of *Selection* that our present age attempts to solve this problem of problems. Even in the single cell it posits differences, weaker and stronger elements. The stronger overcomes the weaker, and the gain is stored up in a higher potency of being. Or, should the weaker still maintain its subsistence, the difference will be mani-fest in the further course of the struggle itself.

Now the blade of grass is not conscious of this, and the spider goes on entrapping the fly, the tiger killing the stag, and in those cases the weaker being does not account to itself for its misery. But we men are clearly conscious of these differences, and by us therefore the question cannot be evaded, whether the theory of Selection be a solution calculated to reconcile the weaker, the less richly endowed creature, with its existence. It will be acknowleded that in itself this theory can but incite to a more furious struggle, with a *lasciate ogni speranza, voi che'ntrate* for the weaker being. Against the ordinance of faith that the weaker shall succumb to the stronger, according to the system of election, no struggle can avail. The reconciliation, not springing from the facts, would therefore have to spring from the *idea.* But what is here the idea? Is it not this, that, where these differences have once become es-tablished, and highly differentiated beings appear, this is either the result of chance, or else the necessary consequence of blind natu-ral forces? Now, are we to believe that suffering humanity will ever become reconciled to its suffering by *such* a solution? Nev-ertheless I welcome the progress of this theory of Selection; and

I admire the penetration and power of thought of the men who commend it to us. Not forsooth, on account of what it urges upon us as a truth; but because it has mustered courage to attack once more the most fundamental of all problems, and thus in point of profundity reaches the same depth of thought, to which Calvin boldly descended.

For this is precisely the high significance of the doctrine of *Election* that, in this dogma, as long as three centuries ago, Calvinism dared to face this same all-dominating problem, solving it, however, not in the sense of a blind selection stirring in unconscious cells, but honoring the sovereign choice of Him Who created all things visible and invisible. The determination of the existence of all things to be created, of what is to be camellia or buttercup, nightingale or crow, hart or swine, and, equally among men, the determination of our own persons, whether one is to be born as girl or boy, rich or poor, dull or clever, white or colored, or even as Abel or Cain, is the most tremendous predestination conceivable in heaven or on earth; and still we see it taking place before our eyes every day, and we ourselves are subject to it in our entire personality; our entire existence, our very nature, our position in life being entirely dependent on it. This all-embracing predestination, the Calvinist places, not in the hand of man, and still less in the hand of a blind natural force, but in the hand of Almighty God, Sovereign Creator and Possessor of heaven and earth; and it is in the figure of the potter and the clay that Scripture has from the time of the Prophets expounded to us this all-dominating election. Election in creation, election in providence, and so election also to eternal life; election in the realm of *grace* as well as in the realm of *nature*. Now, when we compare these two systems of *Selection* and *Election,* does not history show that the doctrine of Election has century upon century, restored peace and reconciliation to the hearts of the believing sufferer; and that all Christians hold election as we do, in honor, both in *creation* and in *providence*; and that Calvinism deviates from the other Christian confessions in this respect only, that, seeking unity and placing the glory of God above all things, it dares to extend the mystery of Election to spiritual life, and to the hope for the life to come?

This then is what Calvinistic dogmatic narrowness amounts to. Or rather, for the times are too serious for irony or jest, let every Christian, who cannot yet abandon his objections, at least put this all-important question to himself: Do I know of another solution of this fundamental world-problem enabling me better to defend my Christian faith, in this hour of sharpest conflict, against renewed Paganism collecting its forces and gaining day by day? Do not forget that the fundamental contrast has always been, is still, and will be until the end: *Christianity* and *Paganism*, the idols or the living God. So far there is a deeply felt truth in the drastic picture drawn by the German Emperor, representing Buddhism as the coming enemy. A closely drawn curtain hides the future; but Christ has prophesied to us on Patmos the approach of a last and bloody conflict, and even now Japan's gigantic development in less than forty years has filled Europe with fear for what calamity might be in store for us from the cunning "yellow race" forming so large a proportion of the human family. And did not Gordon testify that his Chinese soldiers, with whom he defeated the Taipings, if only well drilled and officered, made the most splendid soldiers he ever commanded? The Asiatic question is in fact of most serious import. The problem of the world took its rise in Asia, and in Asia it will find its final solution; and, both in technical and material development, the issue has shown that heathen nations, as soon as they awake, and arise from their lethargy, rival us almost instantly.

Of course, this danger would be far less menacing in case Christendom, in both the Old and the New World, stood united around the Cross, shouting songs of praise to their King, and ready as in the days of the crusades to advance to the final conflict. But how when *pagan* thought, *pagan* aspiration, *pagan* ideals are gaining ground even among us and penetrating to the very heart of the rising generation? Have not the Armenians, just because the conception of Christian solidarity has become so sadly weakened, been basely and cravenly abandoned to the fate of assassination? Has not the Greek been crushed by the Turk, while Gladstone, the Christian statesman, politically a Calvinist to the very core, who had the courage to brand the Sultan "Great Assassin," has departed from among us? Accordingly radical determination must be insisted upon. Half-measures cannot guarantee the desired result. Superficiality will not brace us for the conflict. Principle must again bear witness against principle, world-view against world-view, spirit against spirit. And here, let him who knows better speak, but I for one know of no stronger and no firmer bulwark than Calvinism, provided it be taken in its sound and vigorous formation.

And if you retort, half mockingly, am I really naïve enough to expect from certain Calvinistic studies a reversal in the Christian world-view, then be the following my answer: The quickening of life comes not from men: it is the prerogative of God, and it is due to His sovereign will alone, whether or not the tide of religious life rise high in one century, and run to a low ebb in the next. In the moral world, too, we have at one time spring, when all is budding and rustling with life, and again, the cold of winter, when every vital stream congeals, and all religious energy is petrified.

Now the period in which we are living at present, is surely at a low ebb religiously.

Unless God send forth His Spirit, there will be no turn, and fearfully rapid will be the descent of the waters. But you remember the Aeolian Harp, which men were wont to place outside their casement, that the breeze might wake its music into life. Until the wind blew, the harp remained silent, while, again, even though the wind arose, if the harp did not lie in readiness, a rustling of the breeze might be heard, but not a single note of ethereal music delighted the ear. Now, let Calvinism be nothing but such an Aeolian Harp,—absolutely powerless, as it is, without the quickening Spirit of God—still we feel it our God-given duty to keep our harp, its strings tuned aright, ready in the window of God's Holy Zion, awaiting the breath of the Spirit.

THE END